The Societal Unconscious

Research on the Education and Learning of Adults

VOLUME 8

The titles published in this series are listed at *brill.com/esre*

The Societal Unconscious

Psychosocial Perspectives on Adult Learning

Edited by

Henning Salling Olesen

BRILL
SENSE

LEIDEN | BOSTON

Cover illustration: Photograph by Clane Gessell

All chapters in this book have undergone peer review.

The Library of Congress Cataloging-in-Publication Data is available online at http://catalog.loc.gov

ISSN 2542-9345
ISBN 978-90-04-42025-0 (paperback)
ISBN 978-90-04-42026-7 (hardback)
ISBN 978-90-04-42027-4 (e-book)

This book is printed on acid-free paper and produced in a sustainable manner.

CONTENTS

FOREWORD

The idea for this book emerged out of a number of conversations and suggestions raised when Kirsten Weber, much too early, passed away in November 2015. Several people – researchers, colleagues and friends in the international community of adult education research – expressed their wish to undertake some kind of homage, an arrangement or a publication to honor her work. It seemed to us, at that time, that the right way of paying tribute to her would be to give continuity to her intellectual and practical efforts to develop the quality and political relevance of critical research into the learning of adults – and particularly to promote her particular inspirations from the Frankfurt School integration of critical theory and psychoanalytic social science.

She used those ideas as a leverage and a background to bring depth into empirical research on adult learning, not least the learning of working class women and those professions that are mostly inhabited by women. By doing so, she was also participating in the shaping of research on adult education and learning as an academic field in its own right.

So, after many informal discussions with several people in ESREA and with colleagues inside and outside the Adult Education field, we shared the idea to organize a symposium during the ESREA Triennial Conference that was underway. The symposium was held in Maynooth September 2016, and included papers and presentations from Regina Becker-Schmidt, Lynn Froggett, Thomas Leithäuser, Karsten Mellon, Linden West and Henning Salling Olesen. The papers have been elaborated afterwards and form the backbone of this volume.

As mentioned, it seemed quite obvious that the symposium as well as the book should focus on the perspectives of psychodynamic and critical social theory for adult learning and education, which was Kirsten Weber's lifelong engagement. She had a background in the tradition of (Danish and European) reform pedagogy and in the critical theory of the Frankfurt School, but most of her career was devoted to the emerging field of adult education research. She took a role as a committed inmate – and acted also as a critical liaison with the broader academic arena of critical gender and social research, that is not confined to Education or any other particular discipline. In the last quarter of the former century, adult education research was growing with deep roots in educational policies and practices. Critical thinking was very directly engaged with educational practices, based in community work or, more broadly, liberal individualism, and opposing instrumentalism in the system of education and training. Much academic activity was committed, at that time, to progressive developmental projects which soon had to fight their way under increasingly neo-liberal regimes – leaving little space for theoretical work or for deep critical questioning.

Kirsten Weber was engaged in developing theoretical concepts and methods that could connect theory and practice – not in the sense of applied instrumental knowledge – but rather concepts to engage critical interaction with agents of the field – adult learners, teachers in professional further education, moderators and leaders in trade unions political education, and also policy makers – enabling a reflection of societal conditions and contradictions, and stimulating processes of self-critical awareness among professionals and institutions. From her unflagging interaction, over the years, with practitioners in different contexts of adult education, she developed a reflective pedagogy that illuminated the framework factors which shape education, of any kind, extending the field of professional orientation from the classroom into the entire lifeworld of the students, their biographies, their everyday life, and their motives and aspirations for the future. In a very broad sense, it meant engaging in political solidarity with and understanding of the agents in the field of practice, both learners and professionals, insisting at the same time on the need for a critical position based in thorough theoretical reflection.

This effort is totally in line with the struggles and passions that many of us, researchers in adult education and learning, bring to ESREA and to our communities and webs of affiliation. Kirsten Weber's particular contribution to the field was to sustain the challenge of recognizing the unconscious dimensions of subjective processes which need to be included in a critical social science about learning and education. She reminded us that the unconscious is not only an individual and intimate dimension, but it is pervasive, and effective, all around as well as inside us, as pinpointed by the title of this book, *The Societal Unconscious*.

As said, the best way to honor an academic is to discuss her ideas, keep them alive, transform them, and use them to make, hopefully, a better society.

Laura Formenti
University of Milano Bicocca, Italy
Chair of the European Society for Research on the Education of Adults – ESREA

THE EUROPEAN SOCIETY FOR RESEARCH ON THE EDUCATION OF ADULTS (ESREA)

ESREA is a European scientific society. It was established in 1991 to provide a European-wide forum for all researchers engaged in research on adult education and learning and to promote and disseminate theoretical and empirical research in the field. Since 1991 the landscape of adult education and learning has changed to include more diverse learning contexts at formal and informal levels. At the same time, there has been a policy push by the European Union, OECD, UNESCO and national governments to promote a policy of lifelong learning. ESREA provides an important space for these changes and (re)definition of adult education and learning in relation to research, theory, policy and practice to be reflected upon and discussed. This takes place at the triennial conference, network conferences and through the publication of books and a journal.

ESREA RESEARCH NETWORKS

The major priority of ESREA is the encouragement of co-operation between active researchers in the form of thematic research networks which encourage interdisciplinary research drawing on a broad range of the social sciences. These research networks hold annual/biennial seminars and conferences for the exchange of research results and to encourage publications.

The current active ESREA networks are:

- Access, Learning Careers and Identities
- Active Democratic Citizenship and Adult Learning
- Adult Educators, Trainers and their and Professional Development
- Between Global and Local: Adult Learning and Development
- Education and Learning of Older Adults
- Gender and Adult Learning
- History of Adult Education and Training in Europe
- Interrogating Transformative Processes in Learning: An International Exchange
- Life-history and Biographical Research
- Migration, Ethnicity, Racism and Xenophobia
- Policy Studies in Adult Education
- Working Life and Learning

ESREA TRIENNIAL EUROPEAN RESEARCH CONFERENCE

In order to encourage the widest possible forum for the exchange of ongoing research activities ESREA holds a triennial European Research Conference. The conferences have been held in Strobl (1995), Bruxelles (1998), Lisbon (2001), Wroclaw (2004), Seville (2007), Linköping (2010), Berlin (2013) and Maynooth (2016).

ESREA JOURNAL

ESREA publishes a scientific open access journal entitled *The European Journal for Research on the Education and Learning of Adults* (RELA). All issues of the journal can be read at www.rela.ep.liu.se. You can also find more information about call for papers and submission procedures on this website.

ESREA BOOKS

ESREA's research networks and conferences have led to the publication of over forty books. A full list, giving details of the various publishers, and the books' availability, is on the ESREA website. ESREA's current book series is published in co-operation with Brill Sense.

Further information on ESREA is available at www.esrea.org

Emilio Lucio-Villegas
Barbara Merrill
Marcella Milana
Henning Salling Olesen

ACKNOWLEDGEMENTS

The editor is grateful to Paul Farmer, who assisted with the language revision of several chapters.

Clane Gissel, New York, took the cover photograph and generously allowed us to process the light and resolution for the book's illustration. Kathrin Heim assisted with this graphic work. Søren Weber assisted with the design of the book and provided the photo of Kirsten Weber. Ritta Juel Bitsch and Kim Fomsgård have, with patience and care, prepared the manuscript for printing.

NOTES ON CONTRIBUTORS

Regina Becker-Schmidt is professor emerita at the Institute of Sociology and Social Psychology, University of Hanover. Her research focuses on the critical theory of society, a psychoanalytically oriented social psychology and gender studies. She studied sociology, philosophy, economics and social psychology at the Goethe University Frankfurt and at the Sorbonne in Paris. From 1964 she worked at the Institute for Social Research in Frankfurt am Main. From 1973 until her retirement in 2002 she was professor at the University of Hanover.

Sissel Merete Finholt-Pedersen is a theologian from The Norwegian School of Theology, Religion and Society and holds a minor in Psychology from the University of Oslo. She defended her Ph.D. at the doctoral school of People and Technology, Roskilde University in 2018.

Laura Formenti is professor at the Milano-Bicocca University. She has a Degree in Psychology and a Ph.D. in Education. She is the Chair of the European Society for Research on the Education of Adults and the Italian Universities' Network for Lifelong Learning.

Lynn Froggett is one of the founders and now chair of the Association for psychosocial Studies. She was conferred a Doctorate Honoris Causa at the University of Roskilde in 2016.

Åse Høgsbro Lading is an associate professor emerita and part-time lecturer at the Department of Psychology and Educational Studies, Roskilde University. Her research uses psychosocial perspectives to explore organizational and personal relations in the context of modernization in private and public spheres.

Thomas Leithäuser is professor emeritus at University of Bremen. His research has been mainly focused on the social psychology of everyday life, combining theoretical orientations from psychoanalysis and Marxist social theory. After his retirement he has been an affiliated professor at Roskilde University.

Karsten Mellon is Associate Professor at University College Absalon, Denmark. He holds a Ph.D. from the doctoral school of People and Technology Roskilde University (2018). Mellon's research interests are in life history, education and leadership.

Sissel Finholt-Pedersen defended her Ph.D. at the doctoral school of People and Technology, Roskilde University in 2018. She is a theologian from The Norwegian

School of Theology, Religion and Society and holds a minor in Psychology from the University of Oslo.

Peter Henrik Raae is Associate Professor Emeritus at University of southern Denmark, Odense. His main research areas are school development in the perspective of public modernization, focusing pedagogical leadership and management. He is a member of the International Research Group for Psychosocietal Analyses.

Henning Salling Olesen is professor in Adult and Continuing Research at University of Roskilde, and the founding director for the Graduate School of Lifelong Learning 1996–2007. He was chair for ESREA 1998–2013, and is co-editor of the *European Journal for Research in the Education and Learning of Adults* (RELA). He is advisory professor at East China Normal University, Shanghai, and was conferred an honorary doctorate by the University of Tampere in 2014.

Kirsten Weber was a professor at Roskilde University at the Department of Psychology and Educational Studies. She retired due to illness in 2013 and passed away in 2015.

Linden West is a Professor of Education and a psychoanalytic psychotherapist. He holds a Ph.D. and uses interdisciplinary psychosocial perspectives in his work. His recent book, written with Laura Formenti, is titled *Transforming Perspectives in Lifelong Learning and Adult Education.*

KIRSTEN WEBER IN MEMORIAM

Kirsten Weber was born in 1951. She was the child of a bank clerk making his way up and a daughter of solid local middle class business. It was a family rebellion when she joined the student movement from 1968 and feminist groups in the early 1970's, and took her time with studies and political activism until graduation as a magister of Theory of Education, a very traditional discipline at Copenhagen University, in 1983. She went on as a college teacher in a college of preschool and social pedagogy and was a prominent figure in that field, as a college teacher and an active speaker and expert of social pedagogy until she was in 1989 hired into research by Roskilde University.

As a researcher she first engaged in a major research in collaboration with the trade union movement about the training and education of shop stewards and trade union elected representatives. She particularly engaged with the trade unions of female workers in human service and industry and unskilled workers, and while research was meant to evaluate and improve the highly organized training programs (at the time) of Danish unions her theoretical research framework was focussing on the entire social situation and experience of those workers, and the conditions for social learning in a broader sense, drawing on insights from political and gender movements. Later, as a tenure scholar at Roskilde University, she continued this type of empirical research but increasingly engaged in the academic development of the field, continuing a critical dispute with the discipline of education. Drawing on work of the Frankfurt School critical theory and Thomas Leithäuser she reiterated the development of a research methodology based on thematic group discussions and interpretation, and with this background she joined the Life History project at Roskilde University and was a leading colleague in the formation of a doctoral program of lifelong learning research. She engaged strongly in international research collaboration, among others in the ESREA networks "Biography and Life History Research" and "Adult Education and Labour Market".

In the context of the life history project, which revolved around the developing of methodology for understanding the soci(et)al nature of subjectivity and learning, the idea arose to seek to further explore the psychodynamic inspiration into social science in collaboration with people from outside education and learning research. Kirsten Weber took a leading role in bringing together some of the most important international scholars that had influenced our research, including in the first place Thomas Leithäuser, Christina Morgenroth, Wendy Hollway and Tony Jefferson. In particular she coined the strategy to connect German and British intellectual traditions, being aware of the differences between the forms of influence of psychodynamic thinking in these countries. In the annual workshop which became the International Research Group for Psychosocietal Analysis this exploration was mediated in collaborative interpretation of empirical material. The research group which has later been known by its nickname "Squid" – referring to one of the pleasures of meeting in the Inter University Center in Dubrovnik – has been meeting once a year ever since 2001, spending a week with interpretation workshops and discussion of themes in which the psychodynamic approach to social research has seemed productive.

Kirsten Weber however continued to work on the "inner" arena of adult education and learning research, not least as a supervisor for numerous PhD students at Roskilde. At the time she died she had for a couple of years been hindered from international networking by health problems – which eventually forced her to give up her professional work in 2013.

She is still remembered as a dynamic and lively companion among scholarly colleagues abroad and even more in the professional community in Denmark.

HENNING SALLING OLESEN

INTRODUCTION

The Scholarly Landscape

This book is primarily addressed to the community of researchers and practitioners dealing with adult learning. Its starting point is that research into adult education and adult learning cannot (today, and even less in the foreseeable future) be seen as an isolated sub-discipline within pedagogy, with a well-defined object and a connection to specific institutions or a particular professional practice. Learning processes do not only, and probably not even primarily, take place in the more or less professional and intentionally structured activities that have learning as their purpose. On the contrary, learning is a human process necessity that logically precedes these, and a potential dimension of all life activities. The concept of lifelong learning, which sometimes appears to be a commandment in a "politics of necessity", can also be perceived more sympathetically as a reminder of a socio-psychological reality: we learn as we live. In addition to the recognition of a wider social context which is more realistic than most educational intentions and ideas comes the realization that learning processes are embedded in an experience process that has both conscious and unconscious aspects. The concern of this book is to justify and further develop approaches of critical research to adult learning processes – and constraints on learning – in this broader context.

By thus transcending the idealistic thinking that has characterized pedagogy and much of the tradition of liberal enlightenment and education, this approach aligns itself with material and practice-theoretical learning research. The particular feature of the psychosocial approach presented here is that within a holistic societal theoretical framework, it recognizes a psychodynamic reality which is unconscious. As such it is unavailable for observation and can only be recognized indirectly through its influence on consciousness and agency, but it is nevertheless a life process and not a speculative assumption or construction. The inspiration for this thinking comes from the psychoanalytic theory of the unconscious. We can understand the psychodynamics of learning in the light of life-historical interaction and relational experiences that are continually incorporated and changed intrapsychically and interpsychically, interfering with our social practice. The recognition and access to this psychodynamics is based on interpretations of its manifestations, from dream interpretation and psychoanalytic therapy to cultural analysis: in this way, it is part of a hermeneutic tradition. A critical hermeneutic interpretation not only aims to understand subjective meanings, motives and aims, but equally to understand the societal background of subjectivity and to see and appreciate the subjective contributions to societal relations, i.e. the dialectical relationship with a historical dimension.

In the understanding of the dialectic between the societal totality and the constitution of the individual psyche as a subject, the concept of the unconscious plays a central role: what it consists of, its importance for adult learning and consciousness, and how we can explore it at different levels. In the concept of the unconscious, there is no reference to a particular "substance" or to specific "places". The concept refers to a multilevel dynamics that play a role in individual and communal mental life as well as in the forms of consciousness, culture and knowledge that are part of our social everyday life. "The *societal* unconscious" in the title of the book emphasizes the connection between what is usually seen as an individual phenomenon with a domain of meanings and insights that are excluded from *societal* articulation and attention, following the Frankfurt School's social theory. The individual becomes a subject through relationships to the world and the ways in which it is encountered and encouraged in relations to others and the world at large, and how these experiences are internalized and create grounds for ways of living with oneself and others. When the originally entirely dependent encounters societal conditions which are in conflict with its wishes and needs it develops unconscious psychic defences against certain motives or realizations. The individual psychic unconscious is seen as a trace of such psychosocial forms of exchange and societal contradictions. Although they are exiled from or appear distorted on the social surface they have not disappeared and therefore remain a source of permanent tension in the development of the individual and society. In this book a psychosocial approach is proposed as a framework in which one can explore these psychosocially dynamic processes on different levels.

The individual chapters in this book are therefore largely concerned with how we can interpret the relationship between the visible/conscious and invisible dimensions in specific everyday life contexts. They examine a number of the areas where this relationship appears. Although a common feature is that these dynamics are social, and are transformed and materialized at all levels of social interaction, the contributions reflect both subject-related differences in their focus of interest and the discussion of theoretical issues and disagreements. The editorial thinking has not been to present contributions within one unified theory and methodology, but to illustrate how a broadening of the scope of learning research and attending to the psychodynamics of the social could enable a new understanding of learning, while at the same time showing how a learning perspective may help to discover emerging subjective dynamics in the research of social realms not concerned with learning in the first place.

Learning in school must be understood in a context of everyday life. This is true in spite of the fact that school-based, institutional forms of adult and continuing education in addition to child and youth education supplement or replace learning processes in the community and workplace contexts of everyday life. Firstly, because there is much truth in the old saying "If you want to understand what is going on in a classroom then look at life outside, too". Secondly, because learning is one of the most important subjective dimensions of social life. In fact, the question of what and when people learn from their everyday life as a whole, and especially why they often cannot integrate certain experiences in their conscious ways of dealing with life, might in fact be the most important challenge for researchers and practitioners: understanding how learning takes place through social (interaction) experiences, and in particular why these experiences are often not turned into insights. If research into adult learning is to avoid the dead end of uncritical professionalization, its field must be adult life in the broad sense and, in particular, its subjective dimensions: "subjectivity in society".

This broadening of the horizon can be traced both in practice and research in adult education. Political systems still perceive education (non-formal education and instruction, training) as the way to promote lifelong learning, and therefore also seek to professionalize and industrialize adult and continuing education as a sector (Jütte & Lattke, 2014; Jütte, Nicoll, & Sallling Olesen, 2011). But adult education research has in recent decades moved from the ambition to define itself as a discipline, "andragogy", partly based on knowledge of the particular features of adult learning processes (Knowles, 1980, 1984), and with a focus on improving the efficiency of teaching adults, towards a broader horizon involving important social conditions for adults in general (gender relations, labour market, ageing).

Accordingly, adult education research has in recent years been inspired and informed by interdisciplinary developments in social and cultural empirical research and theorizing which form important, though hardly dominant, streams in critical social sciences. Most importantly, with a turn to qualitative methodologies, this enables a focus on subjectivity and the cultural dimensions of the social. With regard to adult education research, these social science paradigms and traditions have inspired methodological developments which shift the perspective away from just teaching and instruction in more or less organized education over to empirical research into learners' everyday lives and life experiences and the wider cultural and social environments (Salling Olesen, 2006). These developments can be clearly traced in the development of work in the ESREA research networks, in RELA, and in books published in the ESREA book series (e.g. Merrill, Galimberti, Nizinska, & González-Monteagudo, 2018; Ostrouch-Kaminska & Vieira, 2015; West, Alheit, Andersen, & Merrill, 2007). The books cover a variety of topics, e.g. ethnographic awareness of cultural difference and relativity, gender studies emphasizing critiques of generalized (and gendered) concepts of the individual, historical contextualization of learners and educational activities, learning in social and cultural collectives, the study of workplace organizations and the influence of technological developments, among many others. Concepts and ideas of cultural and social circumstances have been deconstructed and the more or less hidden power relations have been exposed, which has given way to a reinterpretation and new discussion of the values and political engagements which are always involved in knowing and learning.

These developments of new empirical interests are productive alternatives to a more speculative and/or normative concern with the mission of teaching and education. The centrality of the life world perspective and the experience of the learner seems to be a useful starting point for understanding the complexity of learning processes. It has enabled a differentiated understanding of learning processes as interaction between individual life histories and specific environments. Not least, it has provided a basis for understanding learning in working life as more than a one-sided embellishment of and adaptation to technologies and work organizations. It has provided raw material for an ideological-critical perspective, pointing out that educational ideas have often been blind to gender, class and ethnicity, but more specifically, also to the unconscious aspects of living and learning. But in this way, it has also necessitated and begun a theoretical exploration of who "the many learners" can be: women, and even working class women in a particular labour market situation, or young men of different ethnic background (than white Caucasian), or young women in a society characterized by sexualized gender stereotypes, and many more – all learners are different.

Qualitative research is most often in its core an effort to understand and visualize living people's own motives and experiences as independent and legitimate dynamics. What people learn and want to take with them can often be far from what is expected by society around them. From a political perspective the qualitative approach to understanding people's learning processes (and educational participation) is a logical and political opposition to the demands of capitalist modernization that people just learn to be employable and economically profitable. In this frame of thought, the subject of social life and learning remains with the many, as we know it from the roots of adult education in social movements and subcultural collectives. And what might be important: it usually involves the hope that "they will find something good for themselves" rather than a particular formulated notion of a goal and expected learning outcomes.

Recognizing and studying empirically the life experiences and life situations that shape the individual, one also moves into a more complex and differentiated understanding of individual subjects than merely seeing them as sovereign, rational, and independent free-willed practitioners. Theoretically, one is thus also on the way to challenge or transcend the universal notion of the individual subject which is the basic concept of Bildung and emancipation in a humanistic tradition, yet often paradoxically linked with the idea that the educator, the teacher and the school assume final responsibility for the subject's general education and learning. Despite these tendencies, research into adult education and adult learning processes has so far remarkably sidestepped from questioning the notion of the free individual subject. In relation to children, there has been a discussion of the contradictions of socialization and of connections between societal conditions and the shaping of subjectivity; however, this is only to a limited extent true of research on adult learning processes. One might see the emphasis on the idea of a free, rational and autonomous subject, both in relation to individual learners and learning processes, and in relation to professional agency, as a respectful identification with the adult student – in critical opposition to instrumental learning psychology, social engineering and particular adult teaching and instruction strategies. However, societal conditions are preferably understood as external obstacles or favourable conditions for the unfolding of individual and communal subjective aspirations, which is the basic form of emancipation and autonomy. This tendentious dichotomization of the psychological and the societal, subjects versus society, theoretically imposes some limitations on the understanding of the dialectical relationship between individual learning and historical development processes. This book addresses this challenge with its introduction to psychosocial theory and methodological inspirations, and especially the theory of unconscious dimensions of subjectivity and the attempts to understand these as socially and relationally produced and socially active mechanisms.

Admittedly, it is not the only bid for a discussion of the relationship between society and subjectivity that has been offered to us from general social science, nor the one which has won the most followers. Other critical approaches have addressed these issues (Fejes & Salling Olesen, 2010). Some of them are relatively uncritical in the sense that they account for experiences and figures of thought in immediate everyday practice. Others raise the issue of the human subject, transforming it into a more complex, socially and historically produced and fluent reality which must be studied in context. In particular, it may be pertinent to mention various versions of discourse analytic approaches from the Anglophone world, Francophone practice theories, and cultural-history activity theory originating from Russian cultural psychology. I will not become involved in a purely theoretical discussion of differences and similarities, strengths and weaknesses, but prefer to see a psychosocial approach as an innovative contribution in relation to a historical situation which challenges all our figures of thought and requires new thinking.

The perspective of the long historical development lines in adult education and education policy has often had the nature of one-sided stories of progress or decay that have set the framework for policy and implementation, to the detriment of the understanding of the complexity of the societal struggles and nuances of individual learning processes. Both adult education and associated research have been and are linked to an enlightenment and education effort that has been normatively and practically opposed to authoritarian powers and traditional cultural and social repression. In the developed capitalist world, which must be considered to include the whole of Europe, despite great differences, free and conducive social spaces and the Bildung of enlightened people (through education!) are closely connected and mutually reinforcing. This has made the normative ideas of the free individual and autonomous practices self-legitimizing. The abstract nature of this normative identification has provided ample room for other perceptions of the subject in social life, which in different ways also accompany modernization.

First of all, an individualized "economic man", which reduces people's subjective drive to the pursuit of self-interest, or "greed". In the first two decades of the new millennium, the discourse about adult learning and education has been replaced by "lifelong learning" and a consensual policy of necessity, driven by international elites of bureaucrats, business managers and policy makers with an outlook on global competition. This societal shift on the political level only became recognized while it was being implemented in more or less neoliberal policy and discourse. "Learning" has been seen as an instrumental, ultimately economically motivated process of assimilative transfer of knowledge and skills necessary for employability and economic efficiency, and discussions of education have also been re-focused on "educational outcomes" and "competences". The implicit subject-construction has been the one of global capitalism, the individual without home and values. As true as this concept of a human subject is a reduction, there is even greater demand for opposing ideas based in identity-political essentialisms such as nationalism and ethnocentrism. This is where we stand – with ecological disaster, increasing inequality, Brexit, xenophobia and illiberal regimes. In such an environment where traditional ideas of emancipation seem to fail politically the challenge for critical research is to explore dynamics and material resources within and beyond education which envision endogenous social change (Nicoll & Olesen, 2013). And there seems to be good reasons to adopt a critical and deconstructive view of the traditional concepts of subjectivity and liberation.

However, we must not limit the view to the centres of the capitalist world. In other parts of the world, the establishment of basic material and political prerequisites for individual freedom and democratic participation is far from being realized, and literacy and education still have a key role (UNESCO, 2016). But this does not mean that they will be following the same path as the western capitalist world. For learning research, first of all, it can be assumed that forms of subjectivity are different in other societal and cultural environments. In a globalizing world, we must seek to discover the particular forms of modernization processes which result from the inevitable interference between capitalist globalization and local culture and experience, and we must include empirical methods suited to capture not only the already formulated subjective goals but also those which are emergent. It also raises theoretical questions as to which notions of autonomy and subjectivity are relevant in the modernization processes underway in postcolonial environments in Africa and Asia, in China and in Latin America, reflected in the whole discussion of the "Southern theory" and alternative epistemologies (Connell, 2007; de Sousa Santos, 2014).

This book continues a development of qualitative research from the 1990s and 2000s focusing on how material societal relationships and historical change are developing at the level of everyday life, in the form of human efforts and actions that are at the same time expressing conscious experiences and goals and being influenced by unconscious drivers (not drives!) originating in the social experiences of life histories.

PART 2: LEARNING, EXPERIENCE AND THE UNCONSCIOUS: THE PSYCHOANALYTIC INSPIRATION

Psychosocial approaches seek to uncover the inner connection between psyche and society by integrating a critical view of society's totality, founded in Marxist theory, with an interactive and cultural understanding of psychodynamics based on psychoanalysis. Both are controversial and the connection between them in particular. Especially psychodynamic thinking has had limited influence on research into education and learning. An obvious way of understanding the immunity against this theorem is the tendency to identify, in a humanistic or social way, with the autonomous adult learner. Psychoanalytic theory may seem to challenge something that for adult educators is a central value: respect for the learner subject's integrity. Psychodynamic understandings are also partly based on very complicated and extensive theory traditions – there is considerable confusion between psychoanalytic (individual) therapy and psychodynamic cultural analysis – and theories cannot immediately be implemented in practical agency strategies.

The first part of the book will seek to bring these theoretical assumptions down to earth through three complementary contributions. Kirsten Weber's doctoral thesis was one of the first attempts to integrate critical social sciences and psychoanalysis through application in empirical adult education research. Her study demonstrates a fundamental redefinition of the adult educational field based on a concept of experience from a German tradition, directly from Oskar Negt and indirectly from Theodor Adorno and a broader Hegelian tradition of thinking. It is an empirical study of a specific adult educational field, namely the learning processes of adult working women in practice-oriented trade union training programmes (Weber, 1995). Women's life context has of course changed a lot since then, trade unions alike, but the study presents a new model for understanding adult learning. The chapter that is included in translation here deals with the setting of a framework for the analysis, the female life context and experience, through non-pedagogical concepts derived from Marxism, psychoanalysis and gender theory.

Why was this groundbreaking? The concept of experience actually has a long presence in progressive pedagogy (Dewey, 1971; Negt, 1964; Negt & Kluge, 2016), and since the 1980s, various forms of experience-based teaching have played a certain role in adult education practice. This is usually an expression of the sympathetic endeavour to take the participants and their experience seriously and it stresses the dependence on social and cultural processes of learning. Often, the concept has been linked to an educational practice where teaching is part of activity in social environments or movements. However, there is also a contradiction here: the concept of experience was used as a critique of institutions, arguing that students' experience and subjective processing of it should define the resources and goals of the pedagogy. On the other hand, when conceived as another recipe in the steady turnover of "faiths" in pedagogy, it will in practice usually imply a tendency to operationalize the experiences of the participants as an opportunity, a starting point or a motivational amplifier in an institutional teaching whose goals and content are, however, determined by other considerations (curriculum, teacher intentions, employability). The experience must therefore be operationalized and made manageable and usable. In this operationalization, the learner becomes objectified, either as the bearer of singular individualized experiences, or perceived as a member of a stereotyped group with allegedly shared experience. This is a critical point of general pedagogical relevance, but it may be particularly important in relation to adult learning. Even when adults participate in institutional education and training, it is usually a subordinate part of their overall life, and they meet teachers and content with a weighty and immediate experience base. If particular elements are colonized and detached from the subjective life history as a means of didactic operationalization, the learning is bound to fail or have a limited result. "The challenge is not to include adult students' experiences in teaching but to find out how adult education can succeed to become a moment in students' experience building" (Salling Olesen, 1989).

The tension between a practical orientation in adult education and the respect for the subjective and holistic nature of individual and collective learning processes is a permanent challenge. The concept of Bildung has in a certain historical context been an attempt to reconcile the interest in knowledge transfer with an emancipatory idea by establishing a canon of Bildung in the form of a curriculum assumed to be the key to personal development and social liberation. In adult education this has not worked very well – not only because the emancipatory idea was historically overtaken, but also because it is based on an idealistic and normative conception of the subject instead of a critical-analytical interest in the learning processes that actually (may) take place in subjects of different generations, class, gender and life experience. The requirement for adult education research must be the establishment of knowledge and concepts that can at one and the same time produce practically relevant insights into the life context of adult people and a criticism of the ideological routines of thinking that relate to (professional) pedagogical practice.

Kirsten Weber's work is an early attempt to solve this dilemma in progressive adult education that is just as relevant today. By analysing the participants' subjective experiences based on gender and class, drawing on the Frankfurt School and psychoanalytic social psychology, and on women's research and trade union analysis, she established an external framework for understanding the educational work of Danish trade unions. The concept of experience establishes an axis of reflection from the individual's perceptible everyday lifeworld, through collective learning processes to the overall cultural production on a societal level (knowledge, class culture, political ideas) (Negt, 1999; Negt & Kluge, 1972, 2016; Salling Olesen, 1985, 2007). It emphasizes the foundation of experience in the real (material) life situation, and thus the individual and collective importance of learning processes is subject to objective societal dynamics. It enables the examination of temporally inconsistent structures: on the one hand, through individual fields of conflict and psychodynamics, and on the other hand, the structuration through contradictions in the different levels of the societal environment, which is both the content of learning processes and its conditions.

Kirsten Weber's study is a continuation of a critique of institutional education that draws on the European reform pedagogy tradition and the student movement of the previous century. In the specific research case, she examines a borderland of institutional education: on the one hand, it is a highly intentional organization with goals, frameworks and social control. On the other hand, it is a political education that relates to the proud traditions of community education, and ideally identifies the union organization with the working women as the potential collective subjects. Here, there is also an inherent contradiction: it sets a framework for political learning processes based on the participant workers' own experience, but these were often blocked in the organizational politics. These contradictions are revealed in the study, not through ideological criticism of the labour movement or the instrumental self-understanding of the education, but through analysis of observations and interviews with the participants, i.e. female union representatives.

The analysis of the representatives of the working women aimed to understand how their lives looked to themselves. The intention was not to classify or stereotype, nor to explain why they thought this or that, but to try to understand a subjective experience process in which the education had meant more or less, and all the time with an awareness of what might not yet be conscious but emergent in their experience. Weber used inspirations from a depth-hermeneutic methodology that was developed in cultural research and adapted to everyday life research (Leithäuser, Salje, Volmerg, Volmerg, & Wutka, 1977; Volmerg, Senghaas-Knobloch, & Leithäuser, 1986), and later developed by the Roskilde research group into psychosocial interpretation practice (Salling Olesen, 2012) The analysis draws on theoretical concepts derived from Marxist social theory and psychodynamic gender theory, here applied to adult education and learning. However, it is a hermeneutic study based on the Frankfurt School's epistemology, which is most clearly formulated by Theodor Adorno: the principle of non-identity, i.e. that social reality is always historical and that theoretical concepts are not identical to but are always in a dialectical relationship with the specific subject of cognition (Adorno, 2001).

This analysis thus draws on a number of theoretical and methodological foundations developed outside the field, and the two other contributions in this part are written without the pedagogical perspective, but by the researchers who were the direct inspirations for Kirsten Weber's approach. They deal in a different way with the constitution of subjectivity in a broader societal context.

Regina Becker-Schmidt, who has written one of these chapters, stands as an exponent of a Marxist feminism in the Frankfurt School tradition. She has not only produced ground breaking research into female industrial workers' life experience and subjective involvement in their work, but has also theoretically formulated the gender-theoretical concept of dual socialization – "die doppelte Vergeselschaftung" (Becker-Schmidt & Knapp, 1987), which places the gender relationship as an integral part of the capitalist social structure – a capitalism-critical conceptualization of what has been referred to in sociological gender research as intersectionality – which points critically to the tendency to neglect the gender relationship in the Frankfurt School's class analysis and thus also to the political thinking that was associated with class experience. Her chapter in this book was originally written in connection with the women's university that she organized in connection with EXPO in Hanover in 2000, and which brought together women from all over the world in a discussion of gender theory and women's situation (Becker-Schmidt, 2002). The chapter, based on this concept of dual socialization, points out that women are stretched daily between different life contexts and are forced to bridge the gap between working life and family life. In the emotional contradictions that follow are both the need and the resources for emancipation and empowerment. Biographical studies of women's lives are key, because women's emancipation must be their own work and must grow out of concrete and personal everyday experience.

This is the analysis and gender political programme that Kirsten Weber unfolds in the analysis of the union women's ambivalent experience in formulating their own needs in a male-dominated trade union movement. The method for her critical hermeneutical analysis of the women's experiences drew partly on the development by Thomas Leithäuser and his colleagues of a depth-hermeneutic approach to everyday experiences. It was inspired by phenomenological societal analysis, i.e. studying society at the level of the lifeworld, and in particular by Alfred Lorenzer's ambitious integration of psychoanalysis and Marxism into his materialistic socialization theory and later into the development of a depth-hermeneutical cultural analysis. Leithäuser and his colleagues in Bremen transferred these approaches to a number of major empirical analyses of working life and other aspects of everyday life and of the dynamics of consciousness processes, without any thought for learning processes or adult education. Kirsten Weber's analysis draws on all these factors. Today there is a clearer picture of how the psychoanalytically inspired cultural analysis that Lorenzer developed was transposed to another subject field and another community level through the analyses of Leithäuser and colleagues, and how this forms a stepping stone for further transposition into the learning process analysis, where, via the synergy with Becker-Schmidt's concepts of ambivalence, it becomes sensitive to the complexity of the female worker representatives' learning processes.

As mentioned before, psychoanalytic concepts have often been misunderstood or simply rejected because of limited insights into what these theories have to offer. With this in mind, I asked Thomas Leithäuser to contribute to this book with a clarification of the status of psychoanalytic inspiration, and account for the important anchoring in Lorenzer's interactive socialization theory, which provides some crucial preconditions for the productiveness of the analysis in learning theory. Hence the third chapter in Part 1 is written by Leithäuser about psychoanalysis as a social science. This chapter very briefly plays out the fundamental difference between psychoanalysis as a therapeutic practice and as a cultural analysis applying psychodynamic concepts and also interpretative methodology inspired by psychoanalysis. Leithäuser has himself integrated his own original speciality, developmental psychology, with the social study of everyday working life and consciousness building. He explains some of the basic notions which may make it easier to read the following texts for the reader with little or no knowledge of psychodynamic thinking, and prevent some possible misunderstandings of the role of psychodynamic concepts and methodology.

When we understand learning processes in the context of experience, it presumes an understanding of a dialectical relationship between a subject and the outside world. The psychosocial understanding of this subject intuitively connects it to the individual in the first place: the individual becomes a subject by building experience through relationships to the world. The experiences from this interaction have conscious as well as unconscious dimensions which can be traced in individual psychodynamics. However, it is a point that we talk about "subjectivity" rather than "the subject". Since the individual is being constituted as a subject in a dialectical relationship with the outside world, subjectivity cannot be confined to the individual organism alone. We can, therefore, trace the importance of psychodynamics, and of unconscious processes, at all levels of the societal structure. Learning cannot be understood without its embedding in social relations and a cultural context even including the societal organizing forces that we can preliminarily call global capitalism. Therefore, we must understand learning processes in mutual dialectic relationships with social and cultural processes that immediately manifest themselves at other levels of societal structure.

Most of the following chapters are demonstrations of psychosocial analysis in different realms. Each chapter presents a holistic approach to specific social phenomena, going far beyond the scope of adult education and learning, and demonstrate in particular the potentials of a psychodynamic approach to the social. The idea is thus to coin the epistemological principle of the non-identical specificity of concrete phenomena in different realms. I have subdivided the empirical material into three tiers of exploration, Parts 2–4. Part 2 relates to the understanding of individual learning and learning careers in the context of life histories. Part 3 deals with the subjective dimensions of groups and institutions. Part 4 includes two chapters which deal with the psychodynamic dimensions of historical and political processes. Finally, Part 5 contains a chapter summarizing the methodological basis of a psychosocial approach.

This composition does not represent an attempt to split the contributions in a simple division of labour, each responding to a partition of an epistemic object. On the contrary, it is intended to emphasize that psychodynamics and the relevance of the concept of the unconscious are not related solely to individual psychic phenomena. Further, societal and historical relations, without being any kind of deterministic structures, penetrate every level of the social, including emotions and consciousness within individuals, social relations between individuals and institutional practices.

PART 2: UNDERSTANDING INDIVIDUAL LEARNING AND LEARNING CAREERS IN LIFE HISTORY

The chapters in this part of the book deal with development of empirical research into the micro processes of learning and the dynamics of individual learner careers. Learning is seen as rooted in the experience of everyday life, from early life in connection with material survival in childhood as a matter of adaptation and innovative changes, cultivated in social and cultural development, sometimes in the arts, sometimes in social organization and politically articulated. We should therefore understand individual adult learning by focusing on the lifeworld of learner subjects. We should attend to all those areas of life where we individually and collectively meet challenges and may learn (or resist the implications of what we learn). One example is the learning related to working life. Working life challenges are also opportunities for learning. What is learned depends on the life affordances (Billett, 2001) but also on the potential learner subjects, the employees. This means that although we realize that learning is situated and depends on participation in social practices in the workplace (Lave & Wenger, 1991), we need to analyse it as an experience process of the workers. This does not mean to re-introduce an individual learner subject. With the concept of experience gained from Negt and Adorno, it means interpreting societal as well as psychosocial aspects of workers' experience. The response to problematizing the concept of the free, rational individual learner subject is to explore the diversity and the complexity of learning on the basis of the specific learners.

I will elaborate a little on the conceptual "genealogy" because it may help to understand how strategic responses to challenges of adult education developed into psychosocial research into learning and subjectivity in a much broader sense. Until the millennium, research was still mainly committed to promotion of adult and continuing education. Adult education was basically seen as a general good. The challenge seemed to be to develop an interdisciplinary approach to understanding adults' participation (and non-participation) in adult education (Kondrup, 2013). Integrating a subjective dimension in the sociological study of structural patterns would enable the understanding of participation or the lack of it, and the life history analysis was a response to this challenge (Rubenson & Salling Olesen, 2007; Salling Olesen, 1989; Becker-Schmidt, this volume). A biography or life history approach offered simple and tested data production with immediate plausibility. Furthermore, it would not only provide insight into aspects of motivation and participation in education and training, but also into the subjective significance of content in learning processes. In this way, it opened a more differentiated and critical perspective on the relevance of education and alternative directions of learning from the perspective of the learner. A biographical approach was therefore adopted, in the first place using well established practical methodological experiences in empirical biographical research, drawing on inspiration from educational biographical research in Europe (Alheit, 1994a, 1994b; Alheit & Dausien, 2002) as well as sociological biographical methodology (Rosenthal, 1995). Moving from an explanatory type of social research, this enabled a theoretical investigation into the driving forces in *educational* activity and the effects of education in the context of learners' life histories. Methodologically, the tool was a hermeneutic procedure applied to interview transcripts, but soon the awareness of the relation between the narrator, the character being told (the persona), and the living person whose life was being told required a historical/empirical differentiation in the complex relationship between individuals and their past and present environment. This again posed new questions about the theorizing of the learner subjectivity. The narrators were interpreting their own lives through their life experiences, their present situation and their more or less reflective ideas about their possible future, and the researchers interpreted their interpretation. This led to more systematically engaging with the psychodynamic problematizing of the individual subject as well as the researcher subject, and to take inspiration from psychodynamic interpretation methodology, including the concept of the societally unconscious. A combination of a lifeworld perspective on the social and a psychodynamic theory of subjectivity is seen as a key to overcome the obvious weakness in the assumption of the free, rational and enlightened individual subject without letting go of the focus on the subjective aspects of experience and learning. Later followed many and varied empirical studies of people who on their own initiative or encouraged by their institution related to learning and education in the light of crises and upheavals, especially in their work and career (Dybbroe, 2002, 2012; Larsen, Salling Olesen, & Tsanaka, 1998; Salling Olesen, 1994, 1996; Salling Olesen & Weber, 2002; Weber, 1995, 2007, 2010).

However, at this time around the millennium the shift in the political environment took place with the arrival of the new lifelong learning policy and discourse. The political perspective on adult education became more ambiguous. The critical research focus on the learner assumed a new direction – in the first place the critique of the neoliberal policies and the potentially individualizing economic drivers – and more fundamentally the societal nature of subjectivity and conditions of autonomy under the societal pressure for individual submission to economic rationales. This was no theoretical news for a psychosocietal concept of subjectivity, on the contrary. But the awareness of the contestable and ambiguous nature of learning and education accentuated a more radical perspective for learning research: escaping the submissive individualization in neoliberalist learning policy goes through experience based learning (Negt, 1964) and developing "sociological imagination"(Mills, 1959). It became essential to emphasize that the life history framework, although interpreting individuals and micro dynamics, is actually studying subjectivity as a societal dynamic. For example, studying working class women in the context of class and general societal gender relations, with the concept of "double socialization" (Becker-Schmidt) explores the ambivalences of individual life experience in the light of *societal* contradictions and historical conflicts of wage labour and gender relations. Especially in light of the work of Thomas Leithäuser, Regina Becker-Schmidt and other German researchers linked to a psychodynamic theory and analysis of subjectivity, new concepts were introduced, problematizing the idea of an individual subject and its self-interpretation central to (auto)biographical narratives (Salling Olesen, 2011). This genealogy, moving from biography to a psychosocial life history framework in the perspective of a historical shift in the political environment where the concern for adult education and training was superimposed by the agenda of lifelong learning, is also visible in the three chapters in this part which all discuss psychosocial interpretations, but in thematically layered variation.

The first chapter "Aggression, Recognition and Qualification" is from the early phase of the life history approach in education, working with data from just before the millennium. It presents psychosocial interpretations of strong emotions in two educational processes. The subtitle "On the social psychology of adult education and learning in everyday life" draws the connection between the emotional engagement in the educational setting and learning related to work and to the participants' wider identifications. The first case is based on interviews with participants in a retraining programme in which long-term unemployed men in a region in industrial decline were trained to work as skilled social educators in a psychiatric ward. There are glimpses of unusually aggressive reactions from participants who used to be male breadwinners but have to shift to a female work domain in order to find any job. This also involves dealing with professionals who are women and a female organization culture. They are learning new skills but they also have to go through a challenging identity process. The other case is based on interviews with participants in a professional continuing education programme for social educators with little professional education background, working in youth leisure clubs as pedagogical social workers. Emotions are evoked by some students with social problems in their own life, who are regarded by other students as unsuitable for the programme. At first sight, these reactions seem rational in terms of the risk to their (shared) professional status, but they are also remarkably strong, coming from students in a professional social work programme who should be prepared to accept social problems. This emotional charge may be interpreted as an unconscious articulation of a more general feeling of lack of recognition of their work. The empirical material in both cases consists of relatively deep interpretations of interviews which directly refer to the educational setting, but also involving reference to the work domains for which the learning was preparing the participants. The analyses are selective in the sense that they highlight the emotional involvement of the students in apparently trivial situations and provide psychodynamic interpretations which link these emotions to the participants' work identity process, thus illustrating the methodological points from the book that was translated in excerpt in this volume, Part 1 (Weber, 1995).

The next two contributions are products of PhD projects that were designed with significant inspiration from later developments, where the life-historical approaches are more elaborated. They are based on biographical data that are analysed psychodynamically in the context of profession theory. Karsten Mellon's chapter refers to a project on students in professional education with untraditional (non-academic) backgrounds. On the basis of life-historical interviews, the study analyses the students' perception of their past life, the decision to seek a new education and career, and their experience of how past life experiences have been rejected, used or transformed in the programmes they are attending, with a study environment primarily aimed at other types of students. The chapter presents a single case of a woman who, on her way to becoming a teacher, reflects on her childhood, her past work experience and, not least, her mother's employment as a milk lady in a school. In the analysis, both elements of the told life story, i.e. the narrator's representation of the relationships in her family and her strong identification with the mother's literally nurturing role in a school, are interpreted in the light of the narrator's current identity process, which is naturally oriented towards her coming profession and the immediate educational experience.

The second PhD project that forms the background for Sissel Finholt-Pedersen's chapter was about the relation of theology students to their coming profession as ministers. The material included three interviews with each of 12 theology students at various stages of their study programme. The interviewees all talked in detail about their life historical background to their choice of education, their present relation to Christianity and a possible priestly ministry, and their education and short experiences of practice. The students consistently express doubts and ambivalences as to the priestly ministry, and in particular its preaching dimension. These subjective expressions were partly interpreted in the light of individual life-historical differences, especially gender relationships. The immediate impression is of a discussion of and personal positioning as to the priesthood, to which several have strong familial ties, but their words may also be interpreted as a partly unconscious projective handling of personal ambivalences. The personal beliefs and attitudes towards preaching play a major role, but also a discussion of the future content of the profession and professional roles other than being a minister. The Norwegian religious struggle between an academic theology historically rooted in a Danish-influenced bureaucracy elite and a more confessional folk religion, also involving the two educational institutions represented in the sample, is traced in the students' different professional imaginations. In the chapter, interpretations from two cases are presented in more detail, a man and a woman, also pointing to gender aspects.

The two chapters show how a psychosocial life-historical analysis can shed new light on a type of learning that has primarily been explored sociologically, or more narrowly (and affirmatively) within the perspective of the individual profession. It is a common point that professions on the one hand are societally structured and historically changing frameworks, and on the other hand the subject of the students' identification and imaginations. Together, the two analyses illustrate how personal life stories form part of the identity formation and subjective experience formation and learning that take place through the education and the first practical experience with the profession, and together provide an individually specific and professionally differentiated identity.

The common feature of the three chapters in this part is to focus on the importance of emotional dynamics in education and learning processes, but also to understand that these emotional dynamics are the result of social experiences (socialization) and are effective as subjective impulses in a social context which in these cases is mediated by work and professions. The nature of hermeneutic interpretations of interview texts and interaction protocols underlines the complexity of these contexts, and demonstrates the theoretical point that these can only be recognized as individual exemplary subjective expressions.

PART 3: UNDERSTANDING INTERACTION AND LEARNING IN ORGANIZATIONS AND INSTITUTIONS

In a psychosocial approach, the relationship between the historical structure of society as a whole and the constitution of the individual psyche as a subject is understood as a dialectical interaction in which unconscious exchange and tension relationships play an important role. The understanding of this dialectical interaction between society and psyche is not the same as an insight into how this interaction occurs and how it develops. Sometimes it has meant that theoretical, political and more existential thinking have been captured in a relatively simplistic idea of a correspondence between psychic defence mechanisms and forms of societal repression, either optimistically as a direct correspondence between "awareness raising" and societal liberation or dystopic beliefs that what is societally displaced returns destructively. Such thinking is not very productive for strategic agency, nor does it provide a good understanding of everyday practice. As initially emphasized, it is in the concrete social phenomena and relationships of everyday life that the psychodynamic and the social are intertwined, not as complementary perspectives or theories but as interwoven materiality. In this context, the intermediate level of society constituted by groups, institutions and organizations plays an interesting role precisely because it is an intermediate level in social formation, which allows for particular insight into the complexity and the many forms and levels of communication that connect the entire societal and psychodynamic levels, with dynamics that go both ways: How does the societal imprint of the psychodynamics actually take place, materially? And how does the impact of psychodynamics on social consciousness and agency affect society as a whole, the historical changes?

One might expect this intermediate level to be theorized and investigated as just such a link between subjective agency in the microsocial environment, the lifeworld, and fundamental historical changes and ruptures at the macro-social level; one might also expect the fact that everyday life in institutions and organizations presumes and consists of tacit social practices to be reflected theoretically. This is not really the case. Although the relationship between social and psychological factors and between individual agency and social structures is present everywhere, most research focuses on explicit and conscious dimensions, maybe because they are oriented towards practice in situations that are taken for granted.

Subjective dimensions of historical changes in social formation are most often conceptualized as by collective or institutional actors or factors. In critical research, institutions have been widely regarded as "imprints" of capitalist power relations. Group processes were only marginally dealt with in Marxist social theory. In institutional theory, organizations and institutions are ontologically independent entities that contribute independently to societal dynamics. However, their inner interaction and basis in individual subjects is theoretically unclear and seems to rest on a rather questionable premise of independent individual subjects. In management and organization theory, one can also see a historical trend from technical-functional concepts over informal social to cultural understandings of the organization. This development probably reflects a real historical change that attaches increasing importance to social interaction and the organizational members' consciousness, and includes something that can be seen as subjective agency, cf the concept of sense making (Weick, 2009). In a more traditional industrial setting, the concept of the "workers' collective" (Lysgård, 1961) referred to the collective subjective agency.

Although both cultural and industrial sociological analyses see organizations as a result of the members' actions and consciousness, a theorization of the subjective dynamics and their background in the actors' experiences is lacking. This is, however, found in psychoanalytic social psychology, which in particular concentrates on understanding how the social psychology of groups shapes organizations. Here, it is a question of involving psychodynamic subjectivity theory for analysis of (and intervention in) group processes at the micro level in local organizations. On the other hand, the societal aspect of the organization is primarily understood as a functional framework, with e.g. the concept of the organization's "main task" which in the Tavistock tradition denotes the organization's societal legitimacy and ultimate condition of existence. Most dialectically, however, Menzies Lyth's analysis of how institutions' organizational structure can be seen as psychic defences against subjectively unbearable aspects of work in a hospital (Lyth, 1988). Such unconscious defences do not really work, because they do not integrate the problem. By extrapolation, it can on the other hand be assumed that real relief from those unbearable aspects might, conversely, induce or enable institutional changes.

Within this landscape, I believe that a psychosocial empirical approach could provide critique and constructive advance. The combination of socialization theory, the Frankfurt-based theory of non-identity and depth-hermeneutic interpretation offers some tools for contextualizing everyday life phenomena in interpretations that include a psychodynamic as well as a historical dimension. In the Dubrovnik group, we have systematically worked with empirical materials from our own research in various fields, especially education and learning processes, based on the assumption that material dialectics can be studied through empirical analysis at the everyday life level. Part 3 of the book contains three contributions on schools and museums as organizational processes. Two of the contributions in Part 4, both Danish, but primarily rooted in the British social psychological research tradition, try to move further down the Tavistock path by analysing the relationship between societal changes and social psychological dynamics in the rather special workplace of the school.

Åse Lading has studied the collegial relationships in a group of teachers at a general high school (grammar school) in connection with an organizational reform that requires increased collegial cooperation in the form of teacher teams. The reform is welcomed by some members of the teaching staff while others see their professional identity and associated collegial relationships threatened. The subsequent conflict puts the teachers' traditional mutual tolerance under severe pressure. Based on a Bion-inspired organizational psychological approach, an interpretation of the "opponents" of the reform is presented as forming a "fight/flight" basic assumption group. They defensively take flight from the conflict by staying silent in the public space and thereby withdrawing from influencing organizational development. A few years later, when Åse Lading returns to the same school, the dynamics in the group of teachers have changed considerably. Old contradictions seem superimposed by a new common work identity which is centred on positive values such as collegial stability and reliability. The changes are seen in the context of a marked intensification of the teachers' work demands and possibly also the impact of the financial crisis on society as a whole, which make the teachers feel more dependent on each other. However, it is also noted that teachers show little interest in taking part and speaking up for themselves in the democratic fora of the organization. The analysis raises the question of whether this silence on controversial themes is inherited within the organization, i.e. as unconscious traces of a previous defensive way of handling conflicts which do not have unambiguous solutions.

Peter Henrik Raae writes in the next chapter about school management in primary schools during a period when a new management structure that strengthened the role of the school leaders in relation to the teaching staff and also tightened the requirements for accountability in relation to the authorities and the outside world, which were in the process of being developed. His analytical framework also draws on the British social psychology tradition. But instead of seeking to understand the significance of the personality of the leader for the organization, the focus is on the interdependence between leader and organization in which the leader's subjective situation is equally determined by the social circumstances, both by the political mandate and by all the employees. In an interview with a school leader who immediately seems to have this demanding situation under full control, the analysis uncovers an underlying defensive dimension of the leader's heroic position which actually turns out to be counterproductive to the development of the organization. The manager's defensive behaviour can be identified as "manic defence" (Klein, 1975). But instead of just being analysed as an individual defence, the heroic leadership position is seen as part of the social situation; the unconscious defence mechanism seems to coincide with a coping strategy that is politically required as part of a societal change of the school framework.

In terms of methodology, another interesting aspect appears: a collusion between interviewee and researcher that arises in the interview, where the researcher shows emotional solidarity with the school leader's need for help in a difficult situation. This observation was elaborated on in the collective interpretation of the Dubrovnik group, moving from considerable confusion about the organizational context to a substantial understanding of the collusion as a response to the school leader's need for help. This point is developed in the chapter as a more general transfer/counter-transfer relation which can be seen as a general methodological dimension of the interaction between the societal environment and the interpretation of the psychodynamic relations in the field (Salling Olesen & Leithäuser, 2018).

The third contribution deals with the institutional level in a way that points to the dialectical relationship between learning within the institution and its societal function. Lynn Froggett argues in the chapter "The Museum as a Third Space – a Special Kind of Object Relating" that the institution of the museum and its traditional raison d'être, preserving artefacts and conveying their cultural significance, can be encouraged to translate conscious and unconscious experiences into learning processes for new user groups. First, the chapter demonstrates, through an example of media-based museum activity, how an artefact, a tea set, at the same time materializes a historical context (British imperialism) and personal everyday life experience (the author's own memory of family tea). Next, the chapter presents a typical local museum and the institutional reform context that forces the institution to reinvent itself as a framework for local community development and social work, but without discussing the actual development of the institution. Instead a case is presented showing cultural experience processing through museum visits: a group of unemployed people conducts a workshop in creative writing on the basis of a photo installation in the museum. Froggett analyses their poetic texts, demonstrating that a new mental space for experience processing is being created through the experience of the exhibition. The analysis refers in particular to Winnicott's concepts of object relations and "intermediate space", but also Lorenzer's concept of the scenic nature of experience. The process can thus be seen as an example of the museum institution taking on a new role. By activating the visitors' emotional experiences, it can create a new space for learning and ultimately for social practice in the local community.

Juxtaposing Winnicott and Lorenzer is interesting in itself. The intermediate level of society, i.e. organizations and institutions, has been handled in different ways in those research traditions which have contributed in particular to the development of the psychosocial approach presented in this book. Somewhat simplified, it can be said that the continental tradition has been particularly interested in the relation between societal conditions (including family structure) and psychodynamic dimensions in the significance of cultural and aesthetic phenomena, as well as particular mentalities. However, group and organizational psychology and the psychodynamic dimensions of institutions have played a significant role in British psychosocial research. There are, of course, many overlapping issues and interests, e.g. about the psychodynamic aspects of workplaces and work relations, but a significant amount of theoretical work has been necessary in clarifying which of these theoretical differences could be attributed to specific research areas and/or fields of practice to which the theorization and empirical results were committed.

PART 4: UNDERSTANDING SUBJECTIVE DIMENSIONS OF POLITICAL PROCESSES: IDENTITY AND POLITICS

Towards the end of the last century, references to identities and values in policy formation and justification seemed to gain a new significance in political processes. Identity politics was not exactly new, it had played a central role in ethnic and gender equality struggles for decades, but the dissolution of the cold war blocs gave way to new questioning of national identities and nation-based states. There was a tendency to deal with identity politics in a moral key, discussing the justification of (national) identities, or in terms of political science, analysing technically the influence and effects of identity processes in political processes. Both are of course relevant, but hardly sufficient to understand the diverse and intense development of identity based politics. We came upon this issue as a side effect of developing an interdisciplinary psychosocietal approach, and realized that this approach might help to understand the genesis of identity politics and its roots in everyday life experiences.

In the year 2000, a small group (Kirsten Weber, Thomas Leithäuser, Jessé de Sousa of the University of Brasilia, and myself) held a conference on "Interculturality, identity and social prejudice" in the Inter-University Centre in Dubrovnik. This conference worked out as an interesting sharpening of the questions of theorizing and studying the psychodynamic dimensions of collective social processes and cultural clashes. As a result, it was decided to organize a similar conference in 2001 with an emphasis on an interdisciplinary exercise in the interpretation of the psychodynamics of identity processes and social prejudice. The 2001 conference established the *International Research Group for Psychosocietal Analysis* which has since then been developing with an annual conference in Dubrovnik and a number of networking activities (guest lectures, joint research projects among some of the members, etc.). Generally the research group was founded on the basis of the idea that the mediation between societal (historical) processes and psychodynamics might bring decisive insights into some of the "mundane" social processes that each of us was working with elsewhere, being scholars of learning research, social work, health professions, organizational development and cultural analysis. The main topics for the work of the research group therefore came from everyday life in each of the three initially contributing countries, Germany, the UK and Denmark.

In a paper for a research seminar on social prejudice in Fortaleza, Brazil, I wrote the following: "Lately political and social processes seem to depend much more strongly on culture and identity than in the classic modernization process of industrial capitalism and the national state. Maybe it is more true to say that this relation has become obvious: the modernization itself dissolved traditional bonds and modes of shaping identities, including the nation state as a "natural" horizon, and political interaction increasingly involves asynchronous cultural and psychological encounters. It has become obvious, and at the same time very challenging to the rationality of modernized societies, that the social psychology of identification and of social prejudices are powerful building blocks in political processes – and hence also objects of manipulation.

In Europe we have several recent examples of violent political processes that seem mainly based on (cultural) identity (beside the historical one of anti-semitism and anti-romanism). One is the politicization of the anxieties and experiences with work migrants and refugees into *xenophobia*. The other one is the process of dissolution of the former *Yugoslavia* which has taken the shape of a religious and ethnic/national feud.

The political exploitations of 'identity' call for theoretical and political reflection. They might be seen as the most 'prominent' examples of, and also results of, the fact that cultural encounters and interferences have become an all-embracing aspect of everyday life. Broader examples are inter-cultural conflicts within a society, the fuelling of national or state conflicts with cultural meaning, or in the inclination to articulate identity as grounds for resistance to 'development', new technologies and changing social structures.

This political development is but one reason to focus on subjective aspects of culture and identity, in order to search for the mechanisms that can lead to either cultural enrichment and learning processes (inter-culturality), or to defensive consciousness and aggressive delimitation (social prejudice). It calls for examination of the links and mediations between everyday life social practice, identity building, and the subjective construction of socially active orientations, and not least a real historical approach in order to overcome reductionist explanations of present behaviour and orientation by projected historical legacies and/or essentialist concepts of identities".

These observations dating back around the millennium actualized a challenge for understanding the social psychology of relatively abstract national and religious identities and differences. The new type of politics, instead of struggles over resources or power and domination in the competition between systems, seemed to engage people much more directly and also to raise new questions of legitimacy. In this context the ubiquitous presence of the remnants of the Yugoslav war was of course a tragic and alarming reminder that identity formation was connected with strong feelings and might have powerful political consequences. Being in post-Yugoslavian Croatia, we could not avoid seeing the interpretation of the local history of civil war as a challenge for understanding those dynamics of everyday life which had led to the disastrous conflicts "out of the blue". It seemed obvious to work on that particular theme just within the Inter-University Centre of Postgraduate Studies. IUC had been a meeting point for "concerned scholars" who worked for an international dialogue during the period of the cold war, some in the form of peace and conflict research and some by organizing conferences and collaboration of critical scientists across the east-west-divide, and we were a group of critical social scientists who wanted to reactivate this practice after the Yugoslav civil war. Some of us had had continuous connections with colleagues and friends in Yugoslavia, and were, retrospectively seen, also identified with the Yugoslavian development of an independent socialism which, in spite of an authoritarian political regime, was culturally modern and free for its citizens. It had been painful to follow the rapid destabilization after Tito's death in 1980. Accumulated debts led to economic decline and inflation; gradually an ambience of crisis for the very legitimacy and sustainability of the federative state emerged – and nationalism began to surface in Croatia and Serbia. Paradoxes stood lined up: Yugoslavia was a highly profiled state, had broken out of the communist bloc, co-founded the movement of non-allied states, and had been able to secure its own socio-economic development. As a state it was a careful construction of ethnic, national, religious and regional balances; it was a modern society, open to international cultural influences, and people integrated and even married across those divisions. Yet the dissolution process seemed to be driven by, or at least taking the form of national and religious segregation and hostility. It seemed like a 'pathological' cultural development where the hitherto existing culture lost its effectiveness as a moral source in everyday life. The usual interpretation of the history was that previously repressed cultural orientations re-surfaced. Hence the question, here and elsewhere: What are the forces of cultural identity that seem to prevail over social and economic interests and contemporary realities and experiences?

The Yugoslav catastrophe still appeared around the turn of the millennium as an unlikely exception in the midst of Europe. There were lots of challenges to empathy and analysis. One of the chapters in Part 4, "Identity, Learning, and Social Prejudice", is an updated version of the paper whose preamble was quoted above. I wrote it as an immediate reflection on the surprising experience I myself had been through in frequent visits and contacts with networks of colleagues and friends in Yugoslavia from before the civil war.

In relation to the development of methodology and our usual focus on everyday life, it was also a kind of alternative case, a theoretical exercise based on an endless and complex source material, in opposition to the usual procedure focussing on well-defined set of empirical data.

The psychosocial analysis of this case pointed to a dynamism that later proved to be less of an exception. Questions of culture and national identity had been blocked during the cold war. In the western societies, the modernization process in the post-war period produced a dynamics of emancipation that was articulated in subcultures of e.g. youth and women and in consumerism. But politically the definition of freedom (which was largely adopted by the opposition in the Eastern Bloc) was mostly reduced to the anti-communist struggle. After the dissolution of the Soviet state, the Baltic countries were liberated from Russian dominance, but simple conflicts about Russian minorities flared up, while others just remained unresolved, as in Ukraine until today. Others have become more complicated and ambiguous when national identities re-emerge inside existing states, e.g. the Catalans in Spain, or in state conglomerates, such as the Scots within the UK, not to mention a number of other potential national minority issues. Identities that for decades appeared to be obsolete suddenly popped up as themes of mobilization in political conflicts – even sometimes leading to extreme hatred and violence.

But beside the nation-state issue we have seen surprisingly strong political identifications in several versions, which have broadly defined the political scene in Europe. For this reason, I also returned to the analysis of the Yugoslav case and recently discussed it again at the research group seminar in 2018. The dynamism that seemed to manifest itself in the Yugoslav conflict and which has since proved to be of decisive political significance is an issue of identity that not only appears in the relationship between nations and states. It has been particularly important in the relationship between peoples and population groups, partly independent of states. The politically most comprehensive impact of this issue is probably the relationship between population groups in multicultural societies and the relationship of the "existing population" to (war) refugees and immigrants.

Even before the migrations after the millennium, Britain was a multiethnic and multicultural society. Linden West has contributed to the book with an exemplary analysis of his birthplace, the formerly flourishing industrial city of Stoke-on-Trent. Here, radicalization and polarization have taken hold with the industrial decline and the establishment of a relatively numerous immigrant group organized around the Islamic religious community and the mosque. In this environment, fundamentalist Islamists face xenophobic British natives. Islamism has on the surface a religious foundation but Linden West seeks to understand more generally the dynamics which generate the firm belief in possessing an ultimate truth. He works with narrative interviews with local Islamists and shows how the individual story itself carries the interviewee's wider experience. With reference to Axel Honneth, he analyses how the experience of non-recognition at the personal level is connected with the awareness of wider misrecognition, epitomized in the genocide against Muslims in Bosnia which is interpreted as religiously motivated, committed by Christians. West applies psychoanalytical thinking to the interpretation of how this cultural experience, as a result of dependency and anxiety as to the complexity of the world, becomes a totalitarian assertion of possessing an indisputable truth which he refers to as "omniscience". The rest of the chapter revolves around the conditions for resisting totalitarian self-confirming identification. In opposition to this dynamic, he posits, through historical reference to the British workers' movement, the struggle against absolutism through democratic dialogue involving the cultural and psychological acceptance of the experience of others and the preliminary and relative nature of all knowledge.

Another theme of identity politics has evolved in relation to immigration, where war refugees are typically confused with migrant workers and others. The greatly increasing numbers of refugees from wars in Syria and Somalia, repression in the Middle East and Africa and work migrants from inside and outside the European Union have given rise to a wave of xenophobia. Although there is, of course, a rational core of social interests and concern for the sustainability of European welfare systems, it is quite obvious that the fear of strangers has an emotional intensity that does not correspond to real rational concerns. Understanding the material economic and social preconditions for this potential is, on the one hand, a way of understanding what troubled waters right-wing populists are fishing in. But it is also a source of a deeper understanding of the subjective aspects of how "ordinary people" feel threatened, not just physically, economically, or in relation to employment, but threatened in their identity and dignity.

THE DEFENCE MECHANISM AND ITS POLITICIZATION

The two cases included in this part of the book both deal with situations where strong group identifications are built on apparently unrealistic or disproportionate perceptions of social relations. The analysis of the Yugoslav conflict primarily points to a political exploitation of a social psychological defence reaction. The core of the understanding of the incomprehensible explosiveness is a psychodynamic interpretation of the feelings of ancient violations and new threats that in a moment made neighbours enemies and led to a radical dehumanization of their mutual perceptions. Something similar is true in the context of refugees and migration, as a political mobilizer for far-right nationalist parties and movements and sometimes also violent extremists. Linden West's chapter shows that the basis of Islamist fundamentalism is also feelings of lack of recognition and a similar sense of threatened collective identity.

A fairly common and well-known defence mechanism like "splitting", where relations are seen in exclusively black-and-white patterns, is activated on a collective level, and leads to the establishment of a strong group identity defined by hostility to other groups. The psychodynamic mechanism seems to be a quite simple one that already Freud was observing: individuals unconsciously seek to avoid anxiety by collectively identifying with some object, projecting any evil on other groups, and also feeling freed from individual responsibility. Acknowledging "the other" being different is no longer an opportunity or enrichment, but a threat. Even when more or less misinforming interventions are taken into account it seems to presume a radical detachment of the feelings from experiential content. Alfred Lorenzer coined the concept of cliché for such emotional reactions that have been detached from their original experiential content, but also have nothing to do with the actual situation. The psychosocial analysis seeks to understand the specific social and historical circumstances that make this dynamic comprehensible.

The analyses presented here show that unconscious subjective reactions may have severe or even disastrous societal and political consequences, when defensive psychodynamics for some reasons prevail, but also that psychodynamics are historical and specific to societal circumstances.

Linden West writes beautifully about the efforts of the historical education of workers to expand the tolerance to ambivalence and uncertainty. It is hardly coincidental that he chooses the historical reference to a context in which openness and confidence in the future was strong; the reality in contemporary societal situation is quite different, anxiety and uncertainty prevail, political forces wishing to exploit these emotions are very strong, and therefore also the unconscious defenses accompanying them. The two presented examples of a psychosocial interpretation of political processes are both about identity processes in which unconscious emotional forces are activated creating regressive, reactionary dynamics. But identity is not generally a cliché in Lorenzer's sense, it may of course be based in experience of belonging to a region, a language, a culture or a tradition and is a normal basis of orientation in a global and changing world. Identification is a coordinate from which one can experience the world and meet others as a subject. It is also a human right and codified in international law as the self-determination of peoples. One can easily argue that a well-integrated identity is the best prerequisite for openness, tolerance and learning ability. So why does it in specific cases work out as a cliché? It depends on the interactive relation of subjective experience. What matters is which conscious and unconscious impulses are activated through the encounter with others and with the world. Under certain social and political circumstances identities are destabilized undermining confidence in oneself and others This is where these realities are vital also for learning possibilities.

So beside the critical analysis of the regressive dynamics psychosocial research can also show ways in which an inclusive and containing social environment may support people's ability to realize and deal constructively with threats, learn about them and change them without resorting to defense mechanisms that distort observations of reality. This requires research that empirically analyse how specific individual and collective learning processes take place in different contexts and with people from different backgrounds. For example one can mention the ambiguity attached to protest movements which, based on authentic experiences, protest against elites while at the same time they are attempted to be orchestrated by populists. But even when they offer national conservative, xenophobic or fundamentalist politics, one should empirically seek to interpret what is grounded in experience and what is manipulation.

Although conservative and xenophobic identity policy prevails at present, there is at least one example of a political mobilization that seems to be based on authentic life experiences which should be mentioned, even though we do not have a research-based presentation of it in this book.

It is the #Metoo eruption and movement. It seems to be a belligerent example of socially repressed experiences that have been "stored" in women's bodies and psyche, usually individualized and presumably partly as an unconscious dynamics that has profoundly influenced women's perception of the world and of themselves. When these experiences become politically articulated, this enables both cognitive and emotional recollection of events that have marked them strongly. There is no doubt that individual women have retroactively changed their feelings and understanding of their own lives, and this will also decisively change the societal framework of gender and individual interactions in the future. At the same time, the actual communicative and political process of #metoo is a muddy stream which, in addition to righteous resentment and a new assertion of the right to integrity, also contains elements of splitting and xenophobia (feminist essentialism and demonization of men, individual injustices) and is thus exemplary of the complexity of the relationship between the unconscious and the conscious formation of experience.

A psychosocial research strategy that is theoretically aware of, and methodically seeks to interpret the meaning of, unconscious dynamics in everyday interactions and relationships may provide a more nuanced approach to the understanding of political processes. But I also see it as a confirmation that one can thereby understand the processes of learning embedded in subjective life worlds and experience. This means exactly not didactizing them or predicting the direction of the process, but to understand societal nature of adult education and lifelong learning. Individuals are continuously exposed to a condition of learning. Technological advances and globalization cause a developmental pressure that is a very direct driver for adult learning processes, which take place in practices, imperceptibly and necessarily even long before they are recognized and may or may not become organized education. We acquire new knowledge and new skills, change our attitudes and values, develop new identities, and sometimes also become better at understanding and tolerating that others are different. However, the emotional and cognitive effort may sometimes become too burdensome, and it is therefore crucial how this general developmental pressure is interpreted, by both individual learners and groups of learners, often unconsciously and before it is recognized. Learning can be stimulating and developing, or overwhelming and threatening, and individual and collective life histories may account for the way it is experienced, projected in their futures and influencing the content of learning processes. The problem that was about individual developments of professional identity in Karsten Mellon's and Sissel Finholt-Pedersen's projects is therefore also about, for example, the development of a professional field and its social function. In short, the social situation and the political thematization are in play together with the conscious and unconscious psychosocial dynamics and identity process of individuals and social groups and influence the motivation for and direction of learning processes.

PART 5: A PSYCHOSOCIETAL APPROACH TO LEARNING – A PROCEDURE FOR A MATERIALIST THEORY

The last part of the book, Part 5, consists of a single chapter presenting a theoretical and methodological framework for a psychosocial research approach. It has also been published in the online magazine *Forum: Qualitative Sozialforschung/Social Research.* It is primarily a methodological article. But by referring to Lorenzer's socialization theory it also provides a missing link in the reflection of subjectivity, conceptualizing both the object of the in-depth interpretation, namely the subjectivity of everyday social practice, consciousness and cultural artefacts, and the interpreting subject, the researcher, him/herself. With this material theory of the subject the methodology is a preliminary – procedural – opposition to an exclusively or primarily cultural understanding of the societal nature of subjectivity as we know it from the linguistic turn in the social sciences, in positioning theory, and in discourse analytical criticisms; each of these approaches problematizes the modern understanding of the subject without taking the step out of Cartesian idealism. It is a core aspect of this opposition that the materiality in terms of bodily life, dependence, historical temporality and social practice precedes the culture of the idea and language both in individual life and social development (Negt & Kluge, 2014). But it is not an "undialectical materialism" (unfortunately the corresponding positive concept is so politically compromised that it can hardly be used to express the opposite). The optimistic experience is that the socially unconscious in a given society contains resources for a dynamics that is not easily predictable, cf. #metoo. On the societal level, one does not understand revolutions until they have happened, but they could not have happened without unfolding unconscious psychodynamics and social agency that were not transparent at the time. On the individual level, learning processes and identity development take place in unpredictable directions and leaps. Therefore, understanding the socially unconscious must have the nature of a negative theory and a methodology fit for carving out the future of mundane present everyday life.

REFERENCES

Adorno, T. W. (2001). *Negative dialectics*. Retrieved from http://www.efn.org/~dredmond/ndtrans.html

Alheit, P. (1994a). *Taking the knocks:Youth unemployment and biography: A qualitative analysis*. London & New York, NY: Cassell. Retrieved from http://www.worldcat.org/oclc/32190708

Alheit, P. (1994b). *Zivile Kultur.* Frankfurt am Main: Campus Verlag.

Alheit, P., & Dausien, B. (2002). The "double face" of lifelong learning: Two analytical perspectives on a "silent revolution". *Studies in the Education of Adults, 34*(1), 3–22. Retrieved from http://www.worldcat.org/oclc/425480992

Becker-Schmidt, R. (2002). Theorizing gender arrangements. In R. Becker-Schmidt (Ed.), *Gender and work in transition. Globalization in Western, Middle and Eastern Europe* (pp. 25–48). Opladen.

Becker-Schmidt, R., & Knapp, G.-A. (1987). Die doppelte Vergeselschaftung – die doppelte Unterdrückung: Besonderheiten der Frauenforschung in den Sozialwissenschaften. In L. Unterkirchner & I. Wagner (Eds.), *Die andere Hälfte der Gesellschaft*. Wien: Verlag des Österreichischen Gewerkschaftsbundes.

Billett, S. (2001). *Learning in the workplace: Strategies for effective practice*. Crows Nest: Allen & Unwin.

Connell, R. (2007). *Southern theory: Social science and the global dynamics of knowledge*. London: Polity Press.

de Sousa Santos, B. (2014). *Epistemologies of the South. Justice against epistemicide*. Boulder, CO: Paradigm Publishers.

Dewey, J. (1971). *Experience and education*. New York, NY: Collier Books.

Dybbroe, B. (2002). "You've got to give all the love you have, and yet consider it to be a job" – Care work in a gendered and life-historical perspective. In C. H. Jørgensen & N. Warring (Eds.), *Adult education and the labour market VIIb*. Roskilde: ESREA/Adult Education Research Group, Roskilde University.

Dybbroe, B. (2012). Work identity and contradictory experiences of welfare workers in a life-history perspective. *Forum: Qualitative Social Research, 3*.

Fejes, A., & Salling Olesen, H. (2010). Editorial: Envisioning future research on the education and learning of adults. *European Journal for Research on the Education and Learning of Adults, 1*(1–2), 7–16. https://doi.org/10.3384/rela.2000-7426.relae1

Jütte, W., & Lattke, S. (2014). *Professionalisation of adult educators – International and comparative perspectives.* Frankfurt a.M.: Peter Lang.

Jütte, W., Nicoll, K., & Sallling Olesen, H. (2011). Professionalization – The struggle within. *European Journal for Research on the Education and Learning of Adults, 2*(1), 7–20. https://doi.org/10.3384/rela.2000-7426.201121

Klein, M. (1975). *Love, guilt and Reparation and other works 1921–45.* London: The Hogarth Press.

Knowles, M. (1980). *The modern practice of adult education: From pedagogy to andragogy.* Chicago, IL: Follett.

Knowles, M. (1984). *The adult learner: A neglected species* (3rd ed.). Houston, TX: Gulf Publishing.

Kondrup, S. (2013). *Unskilled work and learner identity* (Vol. 26). 7th European Research Conference, The Research Group in "Working Life and Learning". Retrieved from http://eric.ed.gov/?q=Changing+Configurations&id=ED546478

Larsen, L., Salling Olesen, H., & Tsanaka, M. (1998). Young women's views of work and education. In P. Alheit, S. Papaioannou, & H. Salling Olesen (Eds.), *Education, modernization, and peripheral community.* Roskilde.

Lave, J., & Wenger, E. (1991). *Situated learning: Legitimate peripheral participation.* Cambridge: Cambridge University Press.

Leithäuser, T., Salje, G., Volmerg, B., Volmerg, U., & Wutka, B. (1977). *Entwurf zu einer Empirie des Alltagsbewusstseins.* Frankfurt: Suhrkamp.

Lysgård, S. (1961). *Arbeiderkollektivet.* Oslo: Universitetsforlaget.

Merrill, B., Galimberti, A., Nizinska, A., & González-Monteagudo, J. (2018). *Continuity and discontinuity in learning careers.* Rotterdam, The Netherlands: Sense Publishers.

Mills, C. W. (1959). *The sociological imagination.* New York, NY: Oxford University Press.

Negt, O. (1964). *Soziologische Phantasie und exemplarisches Lernen.* Frankfurt: Europäische Verlagsanstalt.

Negt, O. (1999). Adorno's Begriff der Erfahrung. *Das Argument, 28*(229).

Negt, O., & Kluge, A. (1972). *Öffentlichkeit und Erfahrung.* Frankfurt: Europäische Verlagsanstalt.

Negt, O., & Kluge, A. (2014). *History and obstinacy.* New York, NY: Zone Books.

Negt, O., & Kluge, A. (2016). *Public sphere and experience toward an analysis of the Bourgeois and Proletarian public sphere.* New York, NY: Verso Books.

Nicoll, K., & Olesen, H. S. (2013). Editorial: What's new in a new competence regime? *European Journal for Research on the Education and Learning of Adults, 4,* 103–109. https://doi.org/10.3384/rela.2000-7426.relae7

Ostrouch-Kaminska, J., & Vieira, C. C. (2015). *Private world(s).* Rotterdam, The Netherlands: Sense Publishers.

Rosenthal, G. (1995). *Erlebte und erzählte Lebensgeschichte.* Frankfurt a.M.: Campus Verlag.

Rubenson, K., & Salling Olesen, H. (2007). Theorizing participation in Adult education and training. In *Meaning, Relevance and Variation – 2nd Nordic Conference on Adult Education Research.* Linköping. Retrieved from http://rucforsk.ruc.dk/site/da/publications/theorizing-participation-in-adult-education-and-training(bce9fc6b-facc-49b4-9e36-69d14f76b8a2)/export.html

Salling Olesen, H. (1985). *Voksenundervisning, hverdagsliv og erfaring.* Unge pædagoger. Retrieved from files/2436/save_zotero.html

Salling Olesen, H. (1989). *Adult education and everyday life.* Roskilde: Adult Education Research Group, Roskilde University.

Salling Olesen, H. (1994). Qualifying adult women for employment. In T. V. Klenovšek & H. S. Salling Olesen (Eds.), *Adult education and the labour market.* Ljubljana: Slovene Adult Education Centre.

Salling Olesen, H. (1996). Experience, life history and biography. In H. Salling Olesen & P. Rasmussen (Eds.), *Theoretical issues in adult education: Danish research and experiences.* Frederiksberg: Roskilde University Press.

Salling Olesen, H. (2006). Beyond the abstractions! Adult education research from idealism to critical social science. *International Journal of Lifelong Education, 25*(3), 241–256. Retrieved from http://www.tandfonline.com/doi/abs/10.1080/02601370600697128

Salling Olesen, H. (2007). Theorising learning in life history: A psychosocietal approach. *Studies in the Education of Adults, 39*(1), 38–53.

Salling Olesen, H. (2011). Exploração do sujeito problemático: história de vida, subjetividade, experiência de vida = Exploration of the problematic subject: history of life, subjectivity, life experience. *Educação, 34*, 137–146. Retrieved from files/2443/search.html

Salling Olesen, H. (2012). The societal nature of subjectivity: An interdisciplinary methodological challenge. A psycho-societal approach in empirical social research. *Forum: Qualitative Social Research Sozialforschung, 3.*

Salling Olesen, H., & Leithäuser, T. (2018). Psycho-societal interpretation of the unconscious dimensions in everyday life. In K. Stamenova & R. D. Hinshelwood (Eds.), *Methods of research into the unconscious. Applying pscyhoanalytic ideas to social science* (pp. 70–86). London & New York, NY: Routledge.

Salling Olesen, H., & Weber, K. (2002). Chasing potentials for a adult lerning. Lifelong learning in a life history perspective. *Zeitschrift Für Qualitative Bildungs-, Beratungs- Und Sozialforschung, 2*, 283–300.

UNESCO Institute of Lifelong Learning. (2016). *Third global report on adult learning and education: The impact of adult learning and education on health and well-being; Employment and the labour market; and social, civic and community life*. Hamburg.

Volmerg, B., Senghaas-Knobloch, E., & Leithäuser, T. (1986). *Betriebliche Lebenswelt. Eine sozialpsychologie industrieller Arbeitsverhältnisse*. Opladen: Westdeutscher Verlag.

Weber, K. (1995). *Ambivalens og Erfaring. Mod et kønsdifferentieret læringsbegreb.* Roskilde: Adult Education Research Group, Roskilde University.

Weber, K. (2007). Gender between knowledge economy and every day life. Change or reproduction. In L. R. West, P. Alheit, A. S. Andersen, & B. Merrill (Eds.), *Using biographical and life history approaches in the study of adult and lifelong learning: European perspectives* (pp. 91–108). Frankfurt a.M.: Peter Lang. Retrieved from http://forskningsbasen.deff.dk/Share.external?sp=S2a211580-52ae-11db-ae81-000ea68e967b&sp=Sruc

Weber, K. (2010). Aggression, recognition and qualification. On the social psychology of adult education in everyday life. *RELA European Journal for Research on the Education and Learning of Adults, 1*(1–2), 113–129.

Weick, K. (2009). *Making sense of the organization: The impermanent organization.* Hoboken, NJ: Blackwell.

West, L. R., Alheit, P., Andersen, A. S., & Merrill, B. (Eds.). (2007). *Using biographical and life history approaches in the study of adult and lifelong learning: European perspectives.* Frankfurt a.M.: Peter Lang.

PART 1

LEARNING, EXPERIENCE, AND THE UNCONSCIOUS: THE PSYCHOANALYTIC INSPIRATION

KIRSTEN WEBER

1. AMBIVALENCE AND EXPERIENCE

Un-Conscious Dimensions of Working Women's Social Learning

PRE-CONDITIONS OF EVERY-DAY LIFE COMMUNICATION AND SUBJECTIVE, GENDERED APPROPRIATION OF EVERY-DAY LIFE'S AMBIGUITIES[1]

You may approach the unconscious dimensions of learning processes by observing the communication of everyday life. Among the less acknowledged truisms in the academic learning discourse is an assumed pragmatic precondition: that people individually perceive what they see and hear, and that they – belonging to a common culture – see or hear much the same thing. This pragmatic precondition of communication in every-day life is particularly important in formal learning situations, in teaching and education. Here inter-subjectivity and communication are (considered) the logical foundations of the effective communication of the subject matter (other people hear what you say), of the learning of the individual (they understand what is communicated), and not least that learning can be managed and controlled. Neither are, however, self-evident – nor is the accordance between the content of perception and the emotion that follows. You do not necessarily notice if your reaction is aggressive or negative. You just move on. You seek some meaning or structure, in the world as such as well as in yourself. Dealing with social reality in every-day life you adapt – and you adapt what you see and hear. Only when an individual psychological disposition leads to significant deviance in perception is it noticed, only then is it defined as such: deviant.

Thomas Leithäuser (1976) speaks of the "general vagueness of the communication of every-day life". The vagueness concerns substance and social reference, and it is only recognized as such when an external view searches for a general cultural meaning – which in turn cannot be found. Communication takes place in a field defined around the "lowest common denominator" of observation, between the substance that the communication is explicitly about and the subjectivity and experience of the people involved. The same vagueness is also referred to as practical intuition or "tacit knowing" (Knapp, 1989; Polanyi, 1967). In many ways a pragmatic, a practical advantage (like not perceiving misspellings in effective reading) but downright destructive when it leads to a simplistic misperception of a complex reality.

© KONINKLIJKE BRILL NV, LEIDEN, 2020 | DOI: 10.1163/9789004420274_002

The difficulty of perceiving otherness, the different or novel, and its specific qualities and ambience, arise when people within a shared – collective – situation react in individually different manners, while – for whatever reason – the discrepancy is not articulated. Instead, some emotional complementary compensation takes over, so that recognition or silencing and denial in various and changing combinations sustain one another.

Subjectively most of us know about this, e.g. from the experience of leaving a social context with a feeling of vague discomfort that you rid yourself of in order to "get on with it", but it also figures as a collective mechanism defining collective issues of considerable importance. One example, mentioned by Regina Becker-Schmidt, is the political experience of Nazi Germany, hardly ever spoken of. Why should we? Indeed!

The vagueness in communication is on the one hand the glue which keeps everyday life together by hiding difference and enabling the process of "getting on". On the other hand it is the medium in which sometimes the recognition of difference and ideas of a new practice may arise. On the one hand perceptions of details in everyday life are kept in place in a world view, on the other hand individual perceptions of difference can mature until they become conscious experience and even articulated.

Gender being an organizing component in a world view means that this space of implicit meaning is also the social space in which the development, establishing, and change of social gender roles emerge.

When a sufficient number of people begin attaching new perceptions and new phenomena to the meaning of gender, e.g. when the "special thing about women" no longer referring to the feminine mystique, but paradoxically to its counterpart: the double work of family and wage labour (not much mystique there!)

Such new cultural meanings are articulated only with some anxiety, for not only must you take possession of a whole new world, you must also rid yourself of a number of well socialized routines, including well-defined parts of established every-day life. But when silence is broken and the complementary balance between such emotional dispositions likewise, energy so far locked up may well emerge.

Gudrun-Axeli Knapp (1989) points out the unconscious dynamic of communication in a slightly different manner, by its effects on the social level. She directly addresses the somewhat mysterious and indefinable question: why women's psychological resources can – for apparently any length of time – remain invested in sustaining a subjectively unbearable situation, and then at times to suddenly re-appear as potential for initiatives of change. Becker-Schmidt draws a parallel to victims of domestic violence: women who may suddenly, without warning, take initiatives of dramatic change – the "straw that broke the camel´s back-wise". Knapp however, focuses on the gendered nature of the working *capacity*. It is, she argues, perceived and assessed as a neutrum, a non-gendered matter. While in reality it arises from, and is solidly integrated into the triad of historical femininity: it is *different* (from the cultural mainstream male work capacity), it is *particular* (in the sense that it possesses its very own cultural qualities) and it has culturally and economically *lower value* (ibid., p. 300). The triangle of difference, specificity and lower value becomes obvious when women's manifold perceptions and broad experience meet with every-day cultural communication which comprise few of those – and addresses even fewer. Presumably most women recognize the experience of *having dealt* successfully with a problem, – the success however, appearing to be culturally invisible, simply because nobody else recognized the problem as such. Or the other way around: being the only one *to face* a problem, which nobody else wanted or dared to address. An example might be that of the woman arguing the subjective necessity of part-time work (a point of view never popular in the male dominated labour movement) while at the same time being under pressure to stay at the trade union meeting where she is formally "necessary", despite her need to pick up her children from day care – i.e. "just because" of her children. Behind the apparent contradiction of being important and necessary and lack of self-confidence respectively lurks the defining T.U.-gender stereotype: the full time, skilled, white, male worker. Women's experience remains inarticulate in the vagueness of every-day life communication (Leithäuser) or as tacit knowing (Knapp and Polanyi).

The learning potential does however, arise from this very contradiction: women are practically systematically down-graded, assessed as the lesser – as well as being idealized, even idolized. This socially well-established ambivalence is perceived and embodied by the individual woman, and it is well integrated in the general social idea of what it is to be a woman. Knapp sees this as a surplus production of meaning, a benefit, which she discusses in Polanyi's terms of tacit knowing (implizites Wissen). She thus philosophically generalizes a (power-) critical point often voiced in the earlier stages of gender research (compare Baker Miller, 1976): that dominance produces an implicit and sometimes not conscious dependency for the dominant party, so that "no king is a master to his servant". Consistently, Knapp points to the fact that women's tacit knowing is more accessible than men's, produced as it is by the current clashes between experience and the numerous social clichés that in every-day language define the idea of a woman. Women, so to speak, approach their real experience when they express their tacit knowing. Whereas men must let go of their experience for they have to recognize that their spontaneous activities are only possible because they hold special privilege. Knapp comments:

> Women know (implicitly) that they are different –and better (!) – that they act differently and wiser, and they are well aware that they know more – more than either the ideological idea of female essence, the socially allotted space of action or the labour market imagination of their abilities. That knowledge itself may well form the core of the idea of autonomy in as much as it contains the structure of the elimination of the non-identity. (Knapp, 1989, pp. 301–302, author's translation)

Tacit knowing is equivocal because in communication it facilitates a more general definition of the ambivalence, and thereby becomes a foundation of action, a potential means of self-regulation. It does not simply *reflect* the objective historical situation, in a double sense it *creates* it. Partly as a particular and individual subjective change, partly in collective forms, where symbols become collective and where subjectivity co-constitutes culture and society.

If you define tacit knowledge more precisely in terms of social psychology you will see that it is the very capacity to attach emotionally to objects (an object in the psychological sense comprising tools, humans or relations … you name it) that enables the particular capacity of human communication. Making objects of elements in the outer world is the raw material of the special human capacity, formation of and communication by symbols. This capacity is in our language, in creativity as well as being made collective by habits, reproduced historically by culture (cf. Nielsen, 1993, pp. 103 ff). Symbols as such do not produce consensus. They function well in communication even if ridden by prejudice or articulated in clichés. Which is not least a relevant point in the context of women's learning: only shared cultural symbols – here defined as clichés – are at hand for women to organize self-images and experience. In a contradictory way women's learning processes – acquiring symbolic knowledge – also limits their experience of reality significantly.

So tacit knowing is a dimension of oppression. Partly because of its substance, "what it knows" – it defines reality for you whether you ask for it or not. Partly because being tacit is one way of not being social, of denying oneself. At the same time, however, cognitively it sees through oppression, and psychologically/emotionally it separates the *recognition of* oppression from oppression *itself*. Thus individuals may rid themselves of oppression, know themselves as different from it, not allowing themselves to de defined by it. At times tacit knowledge just confirms a status quo, but it may as well become a potential for the hesitation, the search and the eventual break-up. Knapp by the way, ventures to define the historical role of gender research as a doubling of this relation.

The concept of *consciousness of everyday* life was introduced by Thomas Leithäuser (1976). It comprises a mutual collective recognition of individual defence – "that's the way we do it around here". Its methodology is based upon a social psychology understanding of group-processes. Where Becker-Schmidt's concept of learning refers to the learning in everyday life interaction Leithäuser develops a historical or epochal concept of learning and blocking of experience. Since the 1970'ies it has formed the basis of an extensive qualitative research strategy that exposes and thematises the individual subjective blockages in the context they arise from (Leithäuser, Salje, Volmerg, Volmerg, & Wutka, 1977; Volmerg, Volmerg, & Leithäuser, 1983). Methodologically the focus is on development of the thematised group discussion, and later on establishing a study groups based learning activity in the every-day life of the enterprise, approaching good oldfashioned political enlightenment and general adult education (Senghaas-Knobloch & Volmerg, 1990; Volmerg, Senghaas-Knobloch, & Leithäuser, 1986). A similar theoretical framework is characteristic of the research on unemployment and trade-union consciousness by Christine Morgenroth (1989, 1990).

The common denominator for these references is the psychoanalytic dimension in the understanding of subjective learning. Faced with contradictions people will invariably relate to external stimuli as well as their respective internal resources. The interplay exposes individual lines of memory – and different degrees of pleasure or displeasure. Every perception, the key to the outside world, is subjectively defined, i.e. it is (also) emotional – co-defined by images, imaginations, sensations. Subjectivity regulates itself, defense is at constant work. It is possible to develop an awareness of them and a certain degree of management as well. Social learning is among other things, defined by the capacity to distinguish and manage these dynamics, as well as by defining your own role.

So managing emotions requires analytical thinking! *Affect* and *emotion* must collaborate with *attention* for only then do we "think" – as Becker-Schmidt has it. In that sense "thinking" is inter-woven with emotions, consciousness is multidimensional. In the subjective world of the individual all objects in the physical world possess a certain, particular value, it comprises specific psychic energies that altogether influence our perception of the immediate every-day world. That is why we can be annoyed or content – instead of simply registering the world as a matter of fact. Objects, persons, situations are not just facts or structures, they trigger off emotion as well. To understand the outside world you must learn to distinguish movement in your own inner drives or wishes – such as anxiety of being ignored or let down, aggression, desire – from the objects they attach to, and whose perception they define.

Becker-Schmidt refers to the well known child in the Danish tale of the emperor's new clothes, the child (most often referred to as a boy?) who cries out that "he's got nothing on, has he!" Subjectively learning is slightly more complex than the child's exposition of the collective taboo, the emperor's nakedness. Not least in a learning perspective, per se a perspective of progression, the question of the genesis of psychological defence of individuals arises as a theoretical agenda in its own right. The dynamic of learning is self-regulatory, so you can never know when an individual/a woman choses to do something about her situation. The process of separation from the positive dimensions of ambivalence take on different forms.

THE UN-CONSCIOUS RESOURCES OF LEARNING: DYNAMICS OF DRIVES, LIFE HISTORY OR EVERY-DAY LIFE? THE IMPLICATIONS OF BASIC CONCEPTS FOR (THE UNDERSTANDING OF) LEARNING AND BLOCKING OF LEARNING

So far I have implicitly assumed that the un-conscious plays an important role for the formation of adult experience. However, the application of psychoanalytic insights always raise questions and disagreements about the relation between adult everyday life and childhood experiences/life-history. Which dimensions are decisive, which are at all important? This question must be faced before addressing how (much) learning blockages actually mean in the formation of experience.

By focusing on the concept of ambivalence Becker-Schmidt sets off from classical psychoanalysis. She picks up the concept from Joseph Breuer, who writes about conflicting emotions in terms of ambivalence, and about conflicts of will *against* an impulse *to* take action in terms of ambi-tendency (Becker-Schmidt, 1982, 1993). She adds the concept of inconsistency referring to conflicts that are handled cognitively. According to her Freud simply takes over Breuer's concept and defines it in terms of "an economy of the drives", which implies that Freud sees ambivalence as co-defined by developmental stages. It is founded in specific stages as a dimension of the appropriation of reality. On the other hand, however, it is "just another example" of the latent conflict between libido and thanatos. Becker-Schmidt, however, explicitly denounces this (drive-)reductionist understanding – she is concerned with the relation of ambivalence to external problems: what happens when subjectivity meets with reality and with contradictions which are also life conditions. For that reason she refers to Sandor Ferenczi. He held a somewhat higher interest in the social context and in the ego, than in the economy of drives "as such", let alone the sexual drives. He spells it out directly saying that you can process contradictory emotions in the interaction with reality. When ambivalences founded in life history are activated, they lend energy to the present ones, and are processed in the interaction with present realities.

Morgenroth (1990, p. 49ff) states something similar: She uses the classical concepts of transference and counter-transference, which – she pragmatically remarks – constitute most human communication. The nature of human relations is generally a systematic, trans-individual pattern of countertransference. Social patterns of communication are at the same *time produced by* the manifold of human communications – as *regulating* them. Some things are articulated, some are not, but yet another category is what *cannot* be articulated. It just happens. This explicitly goes for every-day-life communication, not addressing clinical circumstances. Again we notice a re-interpretation of psychoanalytic thinking into social psychology. The patterns of transference are solidly founded in affective psychic dynamics which co-define action as well as the expression of emotion, also to be noticed in language. On the social surface you register only some inhibition in individuals' self-regulated articulation of needs and wishes – hesitation, silence, interruptions, or the socially more visible, break up of habits and cultural conventions.

This is not solely a theoretical assumption – it is notably empirical. Figures of consciousness, modes of opinion, etc. can all be understood *in the context of the text*, produced for the purpose. Both Leithäuser et al. and Morgenroth based their theorizing on interpretations of interview texts. The concept of language game forms the framework for understanding, inspired by Lorenzer (1970). Becker-Schmidt makes current use of quotations to illustrate her point (Becker-Schmidt & Knapp, 1985, 1987b; Becker-Schmidt, 1982b; Becker-Schmidt, Knapp, & Schmidt, 1984). Her reference is a quite general psychoanalytic one – which, incidentally, annoys Alheit and Dausien (1985, p. 33) as they consider it a most basic limitation in the theoretical basis. Terminology-wise Becker-Schmidt's differentiation between inconsistency, ambi-tendency and ambivalence approaches a more traditional disciplinary view of the psyche as composed by cognition, personality and emotion – it does, however well reflect the scope of action available to the individual in a society defined by division of labour, thus representing some subjective reality. The differentiation is a culturally functional fact, which is why it is theorized as a critical point: The concept of ambivalence must be seen as conceptualizing an actively appropriated and subjective dynamic structure, produced in inter-action with reality – and its contradictions, e.g. those between work-life and family-life as well as contradictions within each (Becker-Schmidt, 1982a). The theoretical distinction between cognitive and motivational structures also reflects the working women's situation, divided as it stands – be it more or less action-oriented, more or less reflected. This is well documented in her work over the years (Becker-Schmidt et al., 1984). Her concept of social learning and her later revision of it into more of a social-psychological manner, re-introducing Freud's concept of "Nachträglichkeit" (deferred action) to understand life history and biographies underlines that she employs these inspirations to develop a *social psychology* (Becker-Schmidt, 1991, 1993a, 1994).

In spite of similarities in the interpretational approach between Becker-Schmidt, Leithäuser and Morgenroth their ideas of the nature of the "damages" of the capacity to experience, not least how serious they should be considered, or how "deep" they are, differ. Leithäuser et al. (1977) tend to assume that inter-action in the social situation in itself produces the "un-conscious scenes" – the psychological impact that may or may not be relevant to the specific social reality it is embedded in, or which it is "just about"! They hereby assume that present day interaction may activate as well as complement defences. The very situation activates *common* psychological conflicts which is subjectively supporting, and may help "thematising" – i.e. recognizing the conflict and building a relevant experience of it. The potential experience – making a theme of it: "thematising" – arises not alone from the "out of the blue" un-conscious of the individual. It arises gradually in the very process of social experience.

Up against this Morgenroth denounces any text-analysis not founded in a broad understanding of individual life experience, which according to her is what actually lends its energies to any social inter-action. Even in groups – and maybe not least in groups – individuals can only contribute bits and pieces from what they have learned, from what they know. Experience may well be, and it most often is, in-articulate (language-wise) – but it still rules. Accepting the importance of a life history dimension in the formation of experience does not permit or imply any sort of "surplus" production of meaning – group dynamics or otherwise. In the last analysis common psychological figures like "regression" would never have become within any reach of understanding if the group or the situation per se, set the frame of understanding. Which, as she sees it, is the case with Leithäuser et al. Applying Wilfred Bion's (1961) concepts enables an understanding of how the communication in "basic assumption groups" is structured by unconscious dynamics more or less independent of the explicit agenda of the group or its rational background. Following

Bion the justification for using the group as a therapeutic space in point that a transaction between unconscious psychodynamic agendas and the rational reality may take place. The characteristics of groups in this analysis emerges from the interplay between individual dispositions brought in from elsewhere, and the group process enables changes in this interplay (Bion, 1961; Morgenroth, 1990, p. 42). Similarly with Becker-Schmidt, Bion sees the influence of unconscious dynamics as inhibitions for learning and experience building, but the cultural content of the social interaction in which these dynamics are activated are having much less attention.

The point from classical psychoanalysis is that group processes cannot be understood as merely everyday life practices. They are decisively drawing on infantile psychic fixations which are then mirrored into the group. Morgenroth's analyses of the life world of unemployed people are e.g. not illuminating the substance matter that group discussions deal with, but how the group members deal with them, how they see themselves in relation to the group, and which consequences it has for their selfunderstanding. In Leithäuser et al.'s analyses everyday life factory work reproduces itself in an specific level of collective psychic defence in groups at each level of the workplace hierarchy. This reveals defences, but at the same time they are analyzed as specific defences in relation to specific work conditions (Volmerg et al., 1986).

The different theoretical weighting of life history vs. situational influences in the experience building which is a recurrent theme in theorizing consciousness, including education discussions, are depending on different psychoanalytic inspirations. Leithäuser et al. are closer to Lorenzer, emphasizing the group and the social interaction. Morgenroth and Becker-Schmidt are closer to Freud and emphasize the individual: But Becker-Schmidt rather than a clinical interest applies a direct political perspective on her material, investigating why and how people (here: women) act or do not act. In Becker-Schmidt's perspective: learn and act on their contradictory life conditions.

I my own work the everyday life and social psychology approaches of Leithäuser et al has proven to be most useful. On the one hand I find the psychoanalytical foundation unique and necessary, but in the field of investigation, learning processes, and more generally growth of human autonomy, is always mediated by a social environment and a relation to culturally defined contents. In education and teaching is may be intentionally constructed environment but the point also holds for learning in other social situations in which agency is necessary, and in which experience depends on the interplay between individual psychodynamics and a social and culturally determined context. Becker-Schmidt's explicit positioning of the concept of ambivalence in a social psychology context enables a theoretically sophisticated analysis which comprises individual psychodynamic structures, the interplay of these dynamics in groups, and the social practice in its necessary relation to social reality.

These theoretical considerations have been developed in conjunction with empirical analysis of a number of trade union and work related issues, focused on education and learning. Although we have in these analyses we have in some cases worked with in-depth hermeneutic interpretations drawing on an understanding of drives as well as referring to the impact of childhood experience, they have not been prevailing, and I follow Becker-Schmidt in her idea of "liberating" psychological analysis from a "drive-oriented" approach. Such an approach is valid, but not the only central dimension of experience, and may sometimes shadow over other dimensions. Besides, my focus on education and the according nature of the texts produced determines that they cannot always be fully opened in all dimensions – and certainly not by me.

However: When the psychoanalytic concepts are liberated from their drive-oriented tradition, the concept of psychological ambivalence is opened to understanding the relation to contradictions in the social world. So the concept of "Nachträglichkeit" (deferred action) (Ferenczi, 1972b) can be seen as the psychological operation that rearticulates experience, impressions and remembrance – at a later stage in life and on the basis of new experience. In the re-interpretation "ancient experience" gains a new significance, indeed they are simply activated: they re-appear at a conscious level enabled by new related experience. Becker-Schmidt stresses that the "liberation" from the dynamics of the drives does not imply any kind of secondary rationalization let alone harmonizing of life historical ambivalences. On the contrary: individual – adult or elderly – experience is a pre-condition for successful integration of previous experiences (Becker-Schmidt, 1991, p. 167). If people get stuck with fixations from precious life it may rather be because their life courses in all their complexity have prevented a conscious approach to retrospective subjective understanding of "your own life". This is particularly true for women because the gendered experience, especially when un-pleasant or even nasty, are culturally depicted as any other sort of difficulty: a woman may think that it's all about her class, or her race, or her generation. Even with successful women at university such assumptions prevail! It is difficult – even for privileged groups, and maybe in a specific, complex manner – to acknowledge the "triadic traces of the very definition of (gender) identity": difference, specificity and low self-esteem – because gender is a central dimension of identity and social roles difficult to get at reading distance. It is possible to see oneself as a historical "product" in almost any other dimension than that of gender – the (non-)problem is generally seen as an individual one.

THE RHYTHM OF EXPERIENCE: REALITY, EXPERIMENTS AND SEPARATION

Theorizing social learning within a theoretical discourse of experience we emphasize the embedding in social practice – and hence relation to historical and currently changing social reality (Salling Olesen, 1989, p. 8ff). Change, however, requires subjective engagement, so the mediating concept could well be the psychoanalytic concepts of testing reality, "Realitätsprobe". It refers to the fact that in order to deal effectively with reality, reality must be subjectively differentiated and appropriated. Thus social learning can be defined as an ever expanding capacity to test and deal with reality, as an understanding of your own inner life world in an interplay with external conditions. You must learn to distinguish between your own experience of reality and outer world reality and to never under-estimate the mutual tension.

So social learning comprises two dimensions (Becker-Schmidt, 1987a): The ego must recognize *its inner reality* as levels of phantasies, imaginations, tensions of drives, and defence mechanisms, all potentially relevant for agency. Some are not conscious and many remain unconscious. At the same time the ego must grasp *outer* reality as objective and goes beyond individual control – and is not fully transparent. Inner and outer dimensions interact, and the process is a confrontation of power and conflicts, also when not registered consciously. Conflicts are mostly not enacted but are kept socially invisible, i.e. in culturally tacit knowledge. The social and material world seem to obey a causal logic and to adapt to rational human action, be it pragmatic, striving for survival … it seems to be under the control of the rational subject. However, the subjective perception of reality is permeated by emotion and phantasy, and the psychological process that precedes agency is much more complex. Thematizing the complexity and contradictions of emotional and cognitive truths is a precondition for social learning, a dynamic process driven by emotion and cognition, reference to and appropriation of reality. You learn when consciousness is activated, becomes aware of its perceptions sand subsequently deals with their direction and interest. In that sense thinking is developed when you reflect how you "feel about it".

In further detail Becker-Schmidt describes thinking and learning as chains of tentative imaginative agency – indeed you could say *that experience is built up by series of such tentative imaginations* – striving to determine whether you prefer the well-known to the un-known. Strategies for the future are developed on the basis of experience. The point is similar to the "theme/horizon"-figure in Leithäuser's theory of the consciousness of everyday life, in which horizon defines the scope of potential experience and theme is directing attention within it. Reality is widely perceived in terms of more or less adequate transference, and in Leithäuser's critical presentation the psyche/consciousness of every-day life is relentlessly and systematically seen as comfortable, lazy or at best: pragmatic. "Reduction" is indeed a central sub-category of an "ontological syndrome": the consciousness of every-day life with its lack of capacity to recognize the genesis of things perceived, let alone their potential for change. The point is that the practical, reality-oriented functions of cognitive reduction (such as managing complexity, doing one thing at a time, etc.) is corrupted by defence mechanisms that permeates perception itself – in all dimensions. It infiltrates the experience of time, the perception of space, the cognitive organization. According to Leithäuser et al. the fundamental historical reason for the loss of memory and the lack of future orientation lies in outer reality, in the development physical and psychological condensation of time of everyday life in confrontation with various standing offers from culture and media as far as defining your life history is concerned. Such a condensation lies behind the "normal pathology", while the narrowing of physical and psychological space in every-day life is more important for the development of patterns that are directly pathological: individual break-down and collective neuroses. Both are confronted with subjective and objective shifts of horizon that cause either the common – reductive – pragmatic orientation or, indeed, the other way around: learning, experience. The latter demands that some energy has been set free …

It is actually a point with Becker-Schmidt that the psyche does not want to be exhausted. She refers to Bernfeld's term of its "conservatism". Curiosity is a challenge to this specific characteristic of the psyche: It takes energy to approach something that you do not know of. Consequently over-coming this must be gradual, taking subjectively suitably measured steps when appropriating new land, indeed a "tentative imaginative action". You try out yourself against this un-known reality and carefully you assess its nature. It is structurally like a research-process – and the very idea that research as such is inter-woven with and doubles common strategies of thinking is in accordance with Freud – and by the way generally acknowledged in developmental psychology in all schools of the discipline – e.g. Bruner, e.g. Piaget. Thinking cannot be understood out of context, without considering what it is *about*. Thinking develops/expands when the psyche carefully and gradually activates the senses and the general attention, approaches and then again withdraws from the new reality. What in education we address as "thinking" is thus in itself a dynamic inter-play of affective reactions, handling the irritation of the yet un-known, and renewed reflection – enabling a gradual accept of a new (aspect of) reality. Ziehe and Stubenrauch (1982, p. 101) refer to such a progression – and, respectively, regression – as a rhythm of learning to the infant's fear of dedication and separation respectively – each navigating principles of security versus risk. Thus experience and learning presuppose framework where progression and regression may alternate in a self-regulated way:

> What we emphasize is the capacity to live through both poles of extremes: the utter dedication and the utter alienation. It is about a decisive shift of balance towards one of the poles, a temporary excess without losing neither the connection back nor the possibility of returning to the other pole. (1982, p. 104, author's translation)

If successful, the ego will accept unpleasantness, and not need to suppress it. Reality is accepted as you distinguish yourself from the process – and the various elements in it – for finally re-possessing the world. Comparing your inner images with the images of the outside world, you accept that they differ. The comparison and the recognition of the discrepancy is painful because it comprises a confrontation between wishes and reality. On the other hand, however, ridding yourself of illusions is liberating. Emotions tied to the illusion can be dealt with, trigger off new emotional energy, that is not just re-distributed – finding new objects – but actually transformed, change qualitatively. The world is perceived anew, and as we are talking about subjective reality we may sum up: The world IS new, it is re-born.

Alfred Lorenzer, in his theory of socialization, also thematizes the process, e.g. using the critical concepts of cliché and formation of symbols, which are particularly relevant for interpretation methodology (Olesen & Weber, 2012; Salling Olesen, 2012). However, addressing "learning" Lorenzer applies the Winnicott concept "transitional object" (Davis & Wallbridge, 1981; Winnicott, 1958) to throw light on the adult learner. Transitional objects may be an artefact, a situation, sensory-symbolic inter-action forms. On the surface you deal with them un-problematically but at the same time, all along the pragmatic communication of every-day life, they establish connections to un-conscious, suppressed meaning. This meaning is dealt with automatically, the sub-conscious and un-manageable finds a format that can be integrated into everyday life communication, creating the material basis for its becoming conscious and integrated, object of psychodynamic regulation. The-classical psychoanalytical references are of course dreaming and playing. It is implied in Lorenzers thinking that current social conventions in a similar manner can work organizing on the entire psychological household, individually as well as collectively. This is how he founds his "psychoanalytic social psychology". At the same time cultural expressions define, regulate and manipulate psychological dispositions – as do the physical spaces of every-day life, as does the media, art and culture in the broadest sense. It is all about transitional objects when every-day life runs smoothly – but there is something dangerous inside it ... This version of a fundamental psychoanalytic inspiration which also allows Becker-Schmidt to go beyond the perspective of the clinic – is basically enabled by Lorenzer's theoretical development of a psychoanalytic analysis of culture, what he called in-depth hermeneutics (Lorenzer, 1970; Lorenzer & König, 1986; Olesen & Weber, 2012).

Lorenzer's concepts – of the linguistic articulation of sensory experience and of destruction of symbols into signs or clichés – are integrated in the concept of consciousness of everyday life. In terms of the latter the psychological process we here refer to as social learning is the step from dependency, from defensive mechanisms of transference within individual schemata of theme and horizon – to thematization (Leithäuser, 1976, pp. 112–119). You can look at individual learning as well as group communication in this manner, and the mode of analysis grasps well the role of the unconscious in the life of organizations (Lyth, 1988). The overcoming of dependency, the separation, is described by a somewhat macabre image, *sequestration*, a self-mutilation like an animal gnawing itself out of a trap by splitting off a wounded limb. It is the recognition of the necessity of sequestration, the recognition of ambivalence, through a detour around the double negation (It is not true that it does not hurt) that enables the appropriation of reality.

The hypothesis, or maybe rather the hope, might be that the recognition of ambivalence develops the capacity to deal with conflict and that it will furthermore be a spark to ignite the will to re-orientate. The spark may enlighten something different, trigger off a positive anticipation, imagining something better. How does this motivation for change at all arise?

It is a complex process. Becker-Schmidt refers to a classic case in developmental psychology, whose structure she ventures to generalize (Becker-Schmidt, 1987, p. 62). It is about R. Spitz' experiment with children's experience (of toys): When a child loses a toy he/she is paralysed and momentarily not able to act. Sometime however, the love for the lost object returns and gradually it expands, gets larger than the bother of the trouble it will take to recover it. This, we may assume, is when the child stops crying and begins to look around. The inner image of the toy is not sufficient stimulation for action, it is pre-conscious and can only become exposed if it is emotionally occupied. The child must anticipate a connection between the image and reality. It compares well with an electrical impulse made useful in interaction with a slice of reality needing energy. The libidinous drive (needing to be near, approaching an object) is de-sexualized, the aggressive attachment (the impulse to grasp, to destroy, to liquidate) neutralized, and the emotional energies are transformed into construction, creativity. Spitz claims that drives are so undifferentiated in the infant that it does not master any proper libidinous material. It does not suffice that the child has learned to combine the image of the object with the object itself – i.e. that it perceives the relation between language and reality correctly. For cognitive and affective processes respectively obey different orders of development and they must be synchronized before the child can develop a sense of reality. A certain amount of tolerance of letting go and lose is required as well as some capacity for imagination and future orientation.

With this in mind the classical experiment, also discussed by Freud and Piaget, about hiding a toy under a pillow deals with the need for the child to distinguish between the image of the object and the object itself – as well as distributing positive and negative impulses adequately, and endure the absence of the toy while aware of the future gratification. Such capacity to uphold different and contradictory engagements to the same image (in Becker-Schmidt's terminology: tolerance of ambiguity) is the precondition of the child being able to solve the complex task. The point of the experiment in a Piaget'ian sense is a matter of object permanence, but in this context the point is that the child may also recognize that the world is not just good or bad, white or black, but comprises many shades. A central point in developmental psychology, here used to expose similar structures and dimensions in experience building processes in adult life. Complexity itself certainly calls for humility. But it also offers a possibility of grasping the variety and the manifold differences that constitute learning blockages and resistance in adults.

So I have defined levels of psychodynamic pre-conditions and reasons in that particular field of formation of experience that has to do with the capacity for subjective change and future-orientation – for hope. The correspondence between thinking and emotional separation is no absolute thing, above history let alone a general human condition. It is enabled by – and indeed becomes necessary – while inner conflicts and societal antagonism interact in ambiguous constellations. For instance this is what happens when at times the individual (woman) find it hard to believe in the legitimacy of her wishes: Does she perform a legitimate protest against an un-willing resignation – or is she simply not able to face that illusions are illusions? This question is answered time and time again by any number of conscious minds – minds in constant development.

AMBIVALENCE AND DOUBLE DENIAL

Departing from women's every-day lives, in social reality, the outer contradictions, the changes of time, space and function that constitute the reality scene that give rise to ambivalence, are easily identifiable. It is simply a woman's modern every-day life, double work and double attachments of domestic work and wage labour. On a general, abstract level you may see it as a confrontation between societal and nature-given, historical dependencies in various complex combinations – specifically and individually about motherhood and wage labour. Not just a "choice" but a social destiny with a double bind as a psychological effect. Social contradictions hit women's psychological resources in a cruelly direct manner: On the one hand "women" appear to secure a minimum of existential human communication. On the other hand through experience of separation, doubled over and over in life history, women are systematically socialized into abstaining. To pin point it: In our culture women are socialized as different, particular, and of a lower value – which is why women must time and time again give up themselves to enter into passable social roles. Reality itself produces ambivalence. This is why Ferenczi's concept of affirmation of unpleasure ("Unlustbejahung") is particularly relevant – comprising the drives, but more oriented towards social reality. On the other hand adult women's experience can hardly be grasped without accepting that social contradictions are mediated in infantile or childhood experience. The fundamental structure of the drives is still co-determining the process (cf. above).

Women's "double societalization" is real. Contradictions in female every-day life and life-history, the complexity and special "nature" are rooted here. To-day women's every-day lives comprise private as well as professional contexts (Becker-Schmidt, 1982b; Becker-Schmidt & Knapp, 1987a; Knapp, 1990).

"So they must not only answer to contradictory demands of the spheres of family and work life. There are more potential conflicts. For both central fields of women's lives are in themselves contradictory" (Becker-Schmidt, 1993b, p. 80, author's translation).

Accordingly the experience of reality is packed up and stored behind complex patterns of psychological reaction – in psychoanalysis known as neurotic ones. If, however, you focus on the learning potential, you may observe that the sensory experience of reality – the very substance of political experience – is a precondition for learning and must be un-packed in the process. One level is to simply state, to name the contradictions, the next is to trace them emotionally. As pointed out these two dimensions presuppose each other.

In a comment to a Danish translation of Freud's *Das Unheimliche*, Visholm (1998) refers the point of retrieving the earlier well-known, but now repressed, directly to

Freud. He moans that it never occurred to Father Freud him-self to establish a societal perspective on the set of problems. Visholm discusses the psychological category of the uncomfortable (das Unheimliche, literally un-homely). He further claims that sociological and historical analyses of home – and homeliness – establishes a solid material basis for understanding what makes something un-homely, creepy – the development of neurosis – and the other way around, its eventual dissolution.

> Just as you can dissolve a paradox that ascribes contradictory qualities to the same object by dissolving it in time, you can dissolve it by separating it in terms of space or persons. (Ibid., author's translation)

So where Becker-Schmidt uses of the concept of deferred action to transgress and expand her analysis of women's everyday lives, Visholm as a psychologist must – like Leithäuser and Morgenroth – put his attention to Freud's ideas of continuity in psychological reactions throughout the life history, that may also be applied on a horizontal cross section of everyday life.

Freud's point is that faced with meaningless ideas and futile activities you must trace the – long gone? – situation where the ideas were well motivated and the activities had a purpose. I.e. liberate a historical insight from its current re-interpretations and "take it back where it belonged". As for women's experience the process is obviously doubled along with critical events in the life course: Motherhood and wage-labour each in their own way sustain women's capacity to endure and integrate – both spaces provide pleasure and dis-pleasure – in the general social spheres of work and family-life/motherhood respectively. Both spheres offer pleasure and displeasure. Within the culturally prevalent images of femininity as well as in the individual woman's self-identity the dimension of pleasure is prevalent: "We want it all!" – or an existential and political choice is imminent (as in recent debate of potential autonomous motherhood vs. dependency on a husband).

Women of the mid-age generation, and maybe also the younger ones, "put up with quite a lot" (cf. Nielsen & Rudberg, 1994; Prokop, 1981). There are generational variations of women's subjectivity, caused by different conditions of socialization. However, the conflict between needing autonomy and identity respectively, appears constant. The capacity to endure this is founded in the separation of actual experience including the according reaction from – stirring of – the silent knowledge and phantasies. Learning needs to build on an un-raveling of this process. Again Becker-Schmidt takes up a concept from Ferenczi, namely the "acceptance of un-lust/displeasure". It is about experiencing displeasure, denying it, and integrating it – in order to later re-trace displeasure through denial of the denial, i.e. to locate experience and sensation in their own time and space, in every-day life as well as in life history – whereby their subjective meaning is made relative, and energy is set free. It is by meeting up with the objective, societal framework around the psychological ambivalence, that the so-called tolerance of ambivalence is established and a realistic orientation towards the future becomes possible.

Affirming the un-pleasure (die Unlustbejahung) is, according to Ferenczi, a specific human perception of social circumstances in a diff way from psych– a capacity of distinguishing between social and psychological circumstance. If drives, e.g. sexual drives, are not met people will normally suppress the wish that provokes the frustration, i.e. suppress the un-pleasant situation it-self. However, what takes place here is an active acceptance of un-pleasure – the problem(a phenomenon) that has been stated in different ways by Becker-Schmidt and by Negt and Kluge (1972) as well as by the women we interviewed in our empirical research in Danish trade unions.

Freud (1943) defined denial as a transitional phase from ignoring and recognizing reality. His classical example is that of sibling rivalry: from "I am not jealous" to "it is not true that I am not jealous". The example demonstrates that recognition of displeasure must go through two denials in order to become subjectively true. Firstly un-pleasure must be faced, and then suppression (or the attempt at suppression) must be suspended. Denial must be denied – or negation negated.

Adult people master that, particularly so in the therapeutic space. Ferenczi points to the double negation taking place in those phases of analysis where transference is predominant: That is when ambivalence is recognized because transference yields "comfort" or release. The clinical point being that only if the principle of reality is stabilized in subjective experience – taking over the function of "comfort" – will the analysis succeed. If you stay in the identification with the analyst, in the transference, you will regress into denial, i.e. denial of the denial = repression. If the analysis is successful the reward is liberation from guilt and repetitions. The positive outcome, the recognition of the reality of un-pleasure can only be achieved through the double negation.

According to Ferenczi reality is at first denied because it is un-pleasant. It is attributed a negative pre-fix! That this is possible is in itself based on an important step in the development of the child – when play and its symbolic dealing with reality and un-pleasure was no longer sufficient. Denial does not imply that you make something non-existent. Un-pleasure – and what's causing it – is the substance of denial, its raison d'être. All present consideration of experience, drawing on psychoanalysis, builds on what Ferenzci explicates: Pursuing experience leads to reality. If you face un-pleasure it becomes the motor behind "experience" being a political and critical category – cf. the general perspective of critical theory, that critique is a mode of thinking, a mode of existence.

In the first place the sense of reality is provoked by the real world not simply yielding to individual will. It requires facing infantile sensation of omnipotence. This comes in different forms – symbolic, gestic, physical – in the infantile imagination, and facing it yields varying degrees of frustration or satisfaction. Typically you adapt to the circumstances where satisfaction is met. The real actors stand out from the context, e.g. "mother" changes from a psychic image associated with satisfaction of needs and drives, to a real existing person also negatively connotated – e.g. reacting to other phenomena in the world than the child him/herself (Lorenzer, 1970). The child has to look for a de-tour to its fulfilment of wishes, because the direct route is infected with un-pleasure. However, exactly as the direct, un-pleasurable route the de-tour goes through anger, rage, aggression and fear – as well as through love for the caring adult. Different emotions are experienced in relation to different aspects of the situation, at different times and also under different circumstances. All this experience – out of its original time and place as it is – must be co-ordinated. Abstaining from and thriving on the world are two aspects of the person – who, at the same time, remains him/herself. That is not so easy.

Also in adult learning you can trace how conflict-ridden and dramatic it is to cope with contradictory emotions. They may be sexually, erotically tinted because of their relation to early objects of desire. Often emotions turn into their opposites, causing confusion and guilt. Destructive emotions may turn autonomous and direct themselves against the very person originally meant to receive the positive emotions. When a target of desire is at the same time desired and feared most likely one of these emotional poles will be repressed. In any case the object must be protected from the destructive impulses These in turn can only be integrated if the autonomy of the individual is respected, and if the positive gains prohibit their growing autonomous (the destructive impulses).

So where individuals gain status of object, ambivalence signifies the current presence of contradictory efforts and emotions – e.g. love and hatred. As the drives are developed through their various stages, the contradictory emotions can be distinguished – but then blur under new conditions. This may be the explanation of women's statistical over-representation in the diagnoses of severe psychic diseases. In this context, however, the ordinary learning processes of ordinary women are in focus – and so the development of the drives as such gets less attention than their social circumstances.

As an outset Ferenczi focuses on emotional conflict founded in the early mother-child relation. What is of interest here is especially the learning processes that serve self-preservation (ego-drives), rather than psychosexual development as such. This is why his concepts of accepting un-pleasure fall within the discourse on women's experience in the complex outer world of every-day life. While the principle of desire operates at an un-conscious level and seeks immediate reduction of tension and wish-fulfilment, the principle of reality will detect the situations in the immediate outer world that does actually satisfy these. Like Freud, Ferenzci assumes that the sexual drives are more subject to the principle of desire than they are to the ego-drives/self-preservation. The latter is easier "educated" as it allows itself to be governed by the principle of reality. The ego is closer to reality, it is more dependent on it than have either the ego-managed or the un-conscious sexuality. In the psycho-analytic frame of understanding – which is in itself not a subject for discussion here – this has a double cause: One is that sexuality is less dependent on reality (it can be satisfied auto-erotically), another is that it lies suppressed during the entire period of latency – and so it simply does not enter into contact with reality. It is thus a central point, borrowed from Ferenzci, that a sense of reality arises from seeking pleasure and avoidance of un-pleasure respectively – a point that strongly supports the social dimension of the concept.

As discussed above, though on a broader scale, the preconditions of experience are present in situations where firstly you are not powerless, and so potentially disposed for identification with an aggressor, secondly you are challenged in a combination of sensation/analysis, facts/intellect, comfort and safety/emotionality. Ferenzci's concepts grasp exactly the psychodynamic dimension of the basic pre-condition of experience. The concept of experience is defined as an analogy of the test of reality – survival. The basic example is hunger – hunger being the most fundamental expression of self-preservation. It cannot be satisfied by imagination. Ferenczi simply has it that for instance "enjoying your food" would be impossible if food were always and unlimitedly available. Desire is a product of experiencing needs, of lacking and missing something. The positive experience of social, material reality must be appropriated through negation: "A reality that does not conflict with human wishes or needs cannot become experience" (Ferenczi, 1972a, p. 204).

The "obstinate reality" is the occasion for experience. It causes the immediate will of your own ("Eigensinn") as Negt and Kluge articulates it in their book title (Negt & Kluge, 1981, 2014). Immediate sources of satisfaction are invisible – quasi-natural, not to be recognized. The significantly hostile or non-pleasant we repress. What is accessible on condition – those we appreciate. Distance and ambivalence are simply the necessary pre-conditions for object cathexis, for a sense of reality (Becker-Schmidt, 1993a, p. 84; Ferenczi, 1972a). Actually Becker-Schmidt comes close to reducing the adult to the abstract "developing child" in psychoanalysis. For she concords with Ferenzci in this: Those or that which satisfies us, we love, but they/it do(es) not belong to us, and so we also hate them/it. For the child such things achieve status of an objective world, and only solely because it sets the outside world. For adult women this emotional ambiguity has become "natural": It constitutes subjectivity as well as do family and wage labour. When psychic energy is stuck in ambivalence it remains suppressed, and women's lives are – in Lorenzers‘s terms defined by clichés. In such cases women navigate in "social topoi" (Negt, 1964) like e.g. "oh, well, can't win them all … that's life …".

As mentioned above in her later writings (1993, 1994) Becker-Schmidt supplements the concept of ambivalence with the psychoanalytic concept "Nachträglichkeit" (deferred action). It sums up the fact that through present experience the subject may subjectively change the nature of earlier experience. It comprises all the points of attempting to define a social psychology of psychoanalysis and for an accordant theory of learning. Firstly that identity is no given or absolute thing locked by early experience, that it is not located in one specific area, and secondly that "the active structures in the sub-conscious … are results of the confrontation between former and present experience" (ibid.). The interplay between experience from different stages of life – from themes of life-history – cannot be isolated from neither the basic dualism of drives nor from the psychosexual stages. The prime example is the interplay between the oedipal phase and puberty, the process where the transcription of earlier experience – now deposited in memory and as phantasies – is concordant with the individual meeting with a new psychosexual stage. This concept of "life history synthesizing" (Becker-Schmidt, 1994) is further applied to the experience of various social situations, stages of life and forms of oppression. This perspective may develop our understanding of subjective concepts of social time –in the sense of its becoming collective.

The approach is quite an optimistic one. Defining the potentials of a future orientation of the life perspective she sees any positive attachment as a potential for the future, and in any anticipation the remembrance of a life once successful. To emerge the traces of remembrance must be activated by the positive energies embedded in the ambivalence. The capacity of patience, to allow imagination the time needed to visualize the desirable life – interpreting it in terms of the delay of deferred action (Nachträglichkeit) – is the tolerance of ambivalence. It is an important point in Becker-Schmidt's theory of gender relations that ambivalence is not an outcome of the contradictions in women's lives, it is also enriching women with this autonomous capacity, which is a historical characteristic of femininity. The tolerance of ambivalence implies that even after long periods of crisis such a potential may break through its (historically allotted) structure and change into its opposite, into experience and action.

Active and passive extremes may threaten your life – as mania or a depression. The utterly good and the utterly evil cannot produce experience. A "healthy mix" of frustration and gratification is the pre-condition for development (Freud), learning (Ferenczi), social learning (Becker-Schmidt) or formation of experience (Negt).

EXEMPLARY LEARNING AS CULTURAL CHANGE

The paradox behind part of the discussion so far – the discussion of the subjective conditions for social learning and experience – is the historical fact that the more pronounced the societal organization of every-day life gets – the more ontological and a-historic, without any past every-day life will appear to the individual.

The importance of individualization – or the thesis of individualization – is theorized in various manners in current theories (e.g. Beck, 1983; Giddens, 1991; Ziehe & Stubenrauch, 1982). However different categories of analysis and however different they prioritize various dimensions – all refer to changing preconditions of every-day life. The theory of everyday life from Lefebvre to Leithäuser also shares this observation. But instead of seeing the process as a reduction of social determination of the individual it is rather seen as an increase. The deeper human lives, sense and emotion are societally defined, the more individualized will the individual *appear*. Societal development actually liberates or detaches the individual from his or her self, in the form of the pragmatism of the consciousness of every-day life.

This process of individualization is of course a core issue for education in the trade union movement, we have been researching. Its educational ambition is to stimulate social learning of workers and their representatives on the basis of their own experiences and interests. Trade union education should be the educational framework which enables social learning. This implies a view of Trade Union education as historical processes in their own right, not just secondary supplement to general or professional education. The crisis of legitimacy in the labor movement was perceived as a problem of mediation between participants' individualized everyday life and their basic (collective) attitudes. So when every life experiences are articulated and confronted with attitudes the fundamental ideas of the labour movement will become active in the experience of everyday life. The labour organization and education respectively was perceived as the culturally explicit framework that at the same time produces a collective tacit knowledge about societal and social conditions and a setting for its potential articulation in policies of the union. It lifts the search for the potential of historical experience to a collective level, where the search itself is a part of a cultural and political movement. The formation of experience becomes more than a degree of individual enlightenment. However, in this process the organization as such would also be exposed anew, it would become an object of experience, it might change – provoking a psychological defence.

So social learning points beyond itself. Individuals and social context change. Organizations, including educational institutions, may be influenced. In the Danish discourse learning mediating individual, cultural and societal dimensions has been conceptualized in terms of "exemplary learning", and with Negt's development of Wright Mills' concept of "sociological imagination" (Becker-Schmidt, 1987; Leithäuser et al., 1977; Leithäuser & Volmerg, 1988; Salling Olesen, 1989). It has been integrated with a substantial understanding of (learning by) experience – in contrast to other popular, less political, but also dialogically oriented didactical concepts. Becker-Schmidt seems to be in accordance with Negt. Only she reaches the position by other – psychodynamic and historical (women's history) – routes than do the gentlemen themselves.

However neither Becker-Schmidt nor Negt appear to have found a comprehensive psychological principle of construction that enables and supports experience processes, they have mapped out some necessary dimensions. The connection between the specific experience and the wider societal reality as such, between current observation and wider reflection is established by raising questions about sensory experience versus conceptualization, by changing perspective and by establishing new relations. Maybe we should simply accept Becker-Schmidt's agreeing with Walter Benjamin in reserving the concept of imagination for that specific capacity.

On a more general level, placing the discourse as a contribution to the theory of knowledge, we find the concept of experience paralleled by the concept of abduction. Scientific knowledge – at least in the social and human sciences, is produced in processes which generate knowledge by interpreting specific experiences in a process that Peirce gave the logical label abduction – transgressing the dichotomy between deduction and induction – but which remains an issue for discussion among philosophers (Douven, 2011). Abduction presupposes that (the process) of experience enriches an observation by an addition of meaning or by the expression of a silent, implicit or contingent knowledge. Meaning explicitly comprises the view of the interpreting subject. Research experience must therefore reflect the time and place of the researcher, his/her individual perspective, at the same time placing it precisely in time and space. Social space comprises the traditional discourses of the scientific community as well as the present social and political world (Becker-Schmidt, 1987; Leithäuser et al., 1977; Leithäuser & Volmerg, 1988). I shall now summarize – as a sort of utopian horizon for political learning.

Exemplary learning requires confrontation with individual and culturally collective defence mechanisms. "Hesitating" in the space left between one's own mixed emotions and reality itself asks for attention to both. It does not go without saying that attention is to what is actually going on, let alone how one feels about it. Even the basic level of "what do I see" – "what's my experience" can be difficult to approach, let alone answer for. That can be argued theoretically, but it is also a commonplace in everyday life in adult education. Most people are dependent on their own experience – (we) need to interpret the world as such in terms of what we know of. If so the world as such, the empirically accessible facts, are reduced in terms of individual schemata of theme and horizon. In a life history perspective this of course has to do with each individual childhood history – integrated however with the general patterns of socialization and culture of up-bringing of the historical period of our respective childhoods. If as a child – when encountering the world – you were forever met with a warning of something forbidden or dangerous it is no wonder that later in life you – un- or sub-consciously – choose to stick to strict definitions of the world, to set horizons – and to identify the un-known in terms of the well-known. Clinically or educationally this may be professionally reduced to a personal quality or resistance – but it should rightly be understood in conjunction with earlier experience – such as losing something dear (remember "sequestration"). Children may well unlearn curiosity – substituting it with routines. And while this concept can well be discussed theoretically at length Becker-Schmidt simply states: "routine – that's having ended up in a trace without curiosity" (Becker-Schmidt, 1987). A person who is an expert in terms of his/her own personal life may well be unable to learn, let alone grasp other peoples' perspective.

The robust nature of adult attitudes may well be rooted in dependency on personal experience, the experience having fortified itself against challenge. Personal experience may actually turn authoritarian, it may establish it-self as a common reference, a criterion of truth or correctness – systematically avoiding criticism, developing absolutism and rigidity. This is the very psychological state that Becker-Schmidt discusses as an inter-play between women's socialization through life history and complex everyday lives, and that Leithäuser discusses as a collective historical (epochal) form of consciousness – the consciousness of everyday life. Such a mental fortification will, however, always turn out to be just one pole in a contradictory consciousness – it presupposes that something is perceived – accordingly being potential experience, for the time being embedded in tacit knowledge.

So in a theoretical discourse experience does not just spring from people articulating their immediate emotions or sensations. Experience presupposes that you have access to what happens and what you feel about it, that no defences are at work. So it is not possible to assess potential for adult experience from appearances alone – although this is actually often needed in everyday life in adult education. Adults often appear quite robust – but the present discussion may add something to the understanding of resistance against progression in educational enterprise, be it about organization or substance. Hesitation can be a prerequisite for and an integrated dimension of experience, not least when tacit knowledge is problematized by a teacher, a school, or by an educational system.

Exemplary learning requires recognition of the social and societal – determining – framework. The comfort of dwelling in your own experience, in the immediate pleasure may actually be counter-productive to learning, not only for psychological reasons but for practical ones as well. Experiences must be digested. The substance of what they actually recall as well as their subjective importance. The societal impact must be critically analyzed. Experience with further ambition than what merely happened must transgress its empirical limits. Any section of realities of times, places and functions in every-day life houses a determining connection to a social and societal logic. Thus experience of a generally accepted reality will always point to a wider context, to social reality as such. This is what Negt's concept of exemplary learning is about (1964) as well as Negt and Kluge's idea that self-regulation produces coherence, consistence – continuity based on recognized discontinuity (Negt & Kluge, 1981, 2014). When conscience is conscious of itself, reflects upon itself. What Hegel labels as the dialectic movement of consciousness relating to itself, when subjectivity deals with itself and its relation to the outer world. When left alone experience withers. It must move between the two poles: the object in question and its being reflected, between self-awareness and the reality it copes with. The subjectively remarkable individual case and the social and societal context it needs to be recognized in to gather meaning at all. Consciousness changes in movement between subjectivity and the objective. Not only does the perception of reality change, consciousness it-self is transformed, it is kept floating – as is its very object.

Exemplary learning is not often educational or pedagogically initiated. It rather contributes to a development of a theory of consciousness and subjectivity in its own right. The concept does, however, imply important insights into the pre-conditions of education and learning. Furthermore the subjective perspective provokes a number of critical points regarding the field. On a general political level, as well as on a level of gender politics, the analysis demonstrates that perception and experience of conflict is a central prerequisite for learning – a central point in Negt's (version of the) concept of exemplary learning. It moderates the common-place that any experience may be developed exemplarily – on the other hand pointing to the inevitability of experience. It cannot be skipped. For it renders it realistic to carry the concrete appearances of reality through individual and collective/institutionalized defence – towards verbalization and potential awareness.

In educational theory as well as teaching practice it is hard to maintain the dimension of "openness", the floating nature of consciousness. Not only so because of the material determinations of education – qualification, discipline, etc. – is it hard for professional minds to contain these concepts. Maybe the "floating" dimension is simply perceived of as a negative one, too informal, an absence of structure, whereby it loses meaning. The present discussion, on the other hand, attempts to demonstrate that a floating condition is loaded with content, with the energy of recognizing ambivalence as well as a contradictory reality.

The process of learning comprises both the direct, immediate experience, self-reflection, both the emerging into detail and the analysis of wider connections, abstraction and concretization, sensory experience and theory. None of these sources of experience can be dispensed with, and none can stand alone. Education may interfere, favour or prevent development. But the process as such is too large for the pedagogical space to direct (or so I hope).

Reversing a quote from Oskar Negt who is talking about the labour-movement: The women's movement possesses neither an immanent scientific nor an immediate pragmatic framework of ideas for its emancipatory goals. The same goes for theorizing learning (as opposed to teaching or education). In this sense formation of theory is in itself a learning process, where experiences are associated and combined in manners that provoke the social preconditions to be reflected.

By necessity exemplary learning is – by object and by content – a collective process. This is evident in Negt's earlier more explicitly societal concept of experience. Experience is the very mode of production where reality is dealt with, as well as the active reaction to reality (Becker-Schmidt & Knapp, 1987b, p. 68; Negt, 2001; Negt & Kluge, 1981, p. 25; Salling Olesen, 1989, p. 8). Experience must be individual, pass through minds and bodies – nevertheless it is digested and communicated by language and concepts, and so it is also cultural and collective. Exemplary learning will rarely be individual, concerning only one woman or man. If no sooner this becomes clear when you work for your own interest – for that is when you will unavoidably interfere with the needs and interests of others – in all the social spaces and spheres you move in. Self-reflection and political after-thought is the very medium where individual self-interest is transformed into solidarity.

Immediate experience does not, however, always expose the structure behind events of social crisis. We all go through a lot without recognizing the historical pre-conditions, etc. – but then again even the most peculiar events may "touch the edge of a relevant conflict" (Becker-Schmidt, 1987) – and when that happens we name the event "exemplary". The quality of exemplarity presupposes some subjective meaning as a necessary foundation for future perspectives and according action. Exemplary experience is striking – affectively and emotionally. It may trigger off dedication but it may as well result in paralysis of action, anxiety and depression. Objective conflict is only subjectively motivating when individual interests are at stake. Otherwise the conflict is of no avail. So ego interest and the underlying drives are necessary preconditions for social learning. Furthermore meaning is always *meaning to somebody*, to a specific subjectivity.

It is indeed possible to recognize one's own motives in a manner where they constitute social contexts, reach beyond themselves, and relate to other people's motives. Not least so if the tacit knowledge is articulated publicly. Even more so in a labour movement context where classical values such as collectivity and solidarity have often degenerated into clichés. Especially here the option of criticism is essential. It does put the (eternal) public communication of equality and gender privileges into perspective.

As a consequence exemplary learning turns out to be imminently critical of existing power relations. All social contexts that house social learning will be exposed anew and – more or less discreetly – pressured to change. Organizations too must appropriate new analyses of society – and thereby experience subjective loss, processes of separation. Organizations too must rid themselves of "parts of themselves". Not least so in highly hierarchic organisations like the trade union movement.

Collective experience does actually turn into cultural change as e.g. we witness in the recent debate of letting gender privileges go. Not that privileges should go as any abstract matter of principle – but they should be in accordance with change of social reality and in recognition of their potential. As a gendered political point this may be noted when private enterprise fails to recognize the potentials of women's experience in management and co-operation within enterprises. They tend to perceive only that they have to let go of well-known routines. Likewise most women find it hard to dispense with the emotional and social privileges of breeding children. Both issues are, however, doubled in our use of language as well as reflected in everyday culture. Our more or less automatic ascribing of qualities to gender is out of touch with reality. The culturally accepted and ascribed qualities fit into and inter-act with hierarchies of power and social status. "Gender" is not only a classification of characteristics – but a fundamental category that structure and reconfirm everyday expectations. "Asking why" immediately exposes that gender characteristics cannot be understood out of their historical context – and attempting an answer simply produces social learning. That's the curriculum!

Morgenroth (1989) illustrates this in her investigation of the German trade unions meeting with women's initiatives – establishing child care so that they can get to work – and the format of the initiatives: meeting and talking, including talking to people outside the movement, but to people who would actually further the women's cause. Besides actually establishing the kinder-garden they needed, Morgenroth's women colleagues also learned something about their Trade Union. They were allowed to express their competences, but they were invariably up against a masculinist organization which fundamentally co-defined both form and content of the work. So the women's qualification and the men's organization that cannot contain them lock up each other in antagonism. Until the women may, as it matters, re- or de-organize! In another context Morgenroth stated that "the future belongs to the women – also in trade unions" (Morgenroth, Negt, Hollman, & Niemeyer, 1992), and in her production continues discussing the "precarious relation between the genders in the organizations" (Morgenroth, Hollman, & Niemeyer, 1994).

This type of conflict, the "double ambivalence"(!) is a cultural process that strikes most women as a prerogative as well as an opportunity. It may be pin-pointed: Stay in the movement despite its negligence – or spite the movement and stand despised or even excluded. The situation may in itself appear promising in that collective and gendered needs can influence organizations and de-build hierarchies, but this organizational potential is too small. There are other possibilities, building on specific needs and demands in larger groups – e.g. with generational groups, professional groups, etc.

Changing historically produced patterns of gender is no simple enterprise. Essential dimensions of adult subjectivity are founded early in life, in primary socialization. It can be retrospectively activated, become subject to "Nachträglichkeit", retrospective activation or deferred action, but they are still rooted early, pre-oedipally, that they are most likely to remain un-conscious.

This level is conceptualized by Nielsen and Rudberg (1994) as gendered subjectivity. As stated by Freud gender identity is potentially open and prone to further experience, however still inter-woven with its immanent and fundamental genesis. Both levels are integrated in psychological gender, constituting the level that may change through experience of ambivalence. This is why possible shifts in what we know as social gender roles are unlikely if not impossible without foundation in a formation of collective experience on the level of psychological gender or gender identity.

Nielsen and Rudberg (1989) pick up some related concepts directly from object relations theory. They define the experiential potential in women and men in the double definition of need for/anxiety at, respectively – autonomy and intimacy, both potential outsets for further experience. They label the male path "the ambivalent way" (Nielsen & Rudberg, 1988, p. 40) signifying a hesitant appropriation of intimacy which is rendered possible by recognition of autonomy and visible results of effort – thereby not having their fundamentally masculine identity questioned. The women's path they name "the paradoxical way" (ibid.) because women, as in their gendered identification process in the oedipal phase must pass through intimacy to autonomy – and vice versa. In short: Male version – recognize me and I'll love you. Female version – love me or I cannot recognize you. Both versions demonstrate that ambivalence is rooted in life history, its re-birth or re-construction in the confrontation with the social world and its decisive influence on the formation of experience.

Furthermore the authors stress that identity can be subject to historical change as a dimension of the transformation of living conditions as such (Nielsen & Rudberg, 1994). Current women-hood or femininity is a product of modernity and it is assessed that the generational transformation will – with a bit of luck – provoke a relational competence. This competence will draw on, but not change, the fundamental capacity for intimacy immanent in female gendered subjectivity. They also produce an impressive comparative study of generations and they hope – like Becker-Schmidt – that the transformations will provide better opportunities for the younger generations to fully realize the disposition for intimacy. Because of the transformations of gender identities and thereby the transformation of psychological gender as such. As well as found more general changes in cultural and social gender.

NOTE

[1] Translation of chapter from Kirsten Weber's doctoral work from 1995: Ambivalens og Erfaring. Mod et kønsdifferentieret læringsbegreb [Ambivalence and experience. Towards a gendered concept of learning] (chapter 3.3, pp. 71–99). The translation with minor adaptations was made by Kirsten Weber in 2015, and technically finished by Henning Salling Olesen after her death November 8, 2015.

The topic of the dissertation was women's learning in the context of Danish trade unions. Empirically the study was based in a major study of the education program established by LO, the Danish confederation of trade unions, which was carried out by a research group also including Anders Siig Andersen, Finn Sommer, and Henning Salling Olesen.

REFERENCES

Alheit, P., & Dausien, B. (1985). *Arbeitsleben. Eine qualitative Untersuchung von Arbeiterlebensgeschichten*. Frankfurt: Campus.

Baker Miller, J. (1976). *Toward a new psychology of women*. New York, NY: Beacon Press.

Beck, U. (1983). *Risikogesellschaft. Auf dem Weg in eine andere Moderne*. Frankfurt: Suhrkamp.

Becker-Schmidt, R. (1982a). Modsætningsfyldt realitet og ambivalens: kvinders arbejdserfaringer i fabrik og familie. *Udkast, (n/a)*, 164–198.

Becker-Schmidt, R. (1982b). *Nicht wir haben die Minuten, die Minuten haben uns: Zeitprobleme und Zeiterfahrungen von Arbeitermüttern in Fabrik und Familie: Studie zum Projekt "Probleme lohnabhängig arbeitender Mütter."* Bonn: Verlag Neue Geselschaft.

Becker-Schmidt, R. (1987). Dynamiken Sozialen Lernens. In R. Becker-Schmidt & G.-A. Knapp (Eds.), *Geschlechtertrennung – Geschlechterdifferenz*. Bonn: Dietz.

Becker-Schmidt, R. (1991). Continuity and discontinuity in women's life courses. In W. R. Heinz (Ed.), *Theoretical advances in life course research. Status passages and the life course*. Weinheim: Deutsche Studien Verlag.

Becker-Schmidt, R. (1993a). Ambivalenz und Nachträglichkeit: Perspektiven einer feministischen Biographieforschung. In *Was heisst hier eigentlich feministisch? Zur theoretischen Diskussion in der Geistes- und Sozialwissenscheaften*. Bremen: Donat Verlag.

Becker-Schmidt, R. (1993b). Ambivalenz und Nachträglichkeit. Perspektiven einer feministischen Biographieforschung. In M. Krüger (Ed.), *Was heisst hier eigentlich feministisch? Zur theoretischen Diskussion in der Geistes- und Sozialwissenscheaften*. Bremen: Donat Verlag.

Becker-Schmidt, R. (1994). Diskontinuität und Nachträglichkeit. Theoretische und methodische Überlegungen zur Erforschung weiblicher Lebenslaufe. In *Erfahrung mit Methode. Wege sozialwissenschaftlicher Frauenforschung*. Freiburg: Kore.

Becker-Schmidt, R., & Knapp, G.-A. (1985). *Arbeiterkinder gestern – Arbeiterkinder heute*. Bonn: Neue Gesellschaft.

Becker-Schmidt, R., & Knapp, G.-A. (1987a). Die doppelte Vergeselschaftung – die doppelte Unterdrückung: Besonderheiten der Frauenforschung in den Sozialwissenschaften. In L. Unterkirchner & I. Wagner (Eds.), *Die andere Hälfte der Gesellschaft*. Wien: Verlag des Österreichischen Gewerkschaftsbundes.

Becker-Schmidt, R., & Knapp, G.-A. (1987b). *Geschlechtertrennung – Geschlechterdifferenz. Suchbewegungen sozialen Lernens*. Bonn: Dietz.

Becker-Schmidt, R., Knapp, G.-A., & Schmidt, B. (1984). *Eines ist zu wenig – beides ist zuviel. Erfahrungen von Arbeiterfrauen zwischen Famrik und Familie*. Bonn: Neue Gesellschaft.

Bion, W. R. (1961). *Experiences in groups and other papers*. London: Tavistock Publications.

Davis, M., & Wallbridge, D. (1981). *Boundary and space*. Henning, this reference isn't complete!

Douven, I. (2011). Abduction. In E. N. Zalta (Ed.), *The stanford encyclopedia of philosophy* (Spring 2011 ed.). Retrieved from http://plato.stanford.edu/archives/spr2011/entries/abduction/

Ferenczi, S. (1972a). Das Problem der Unlustbejahung. In *Schriften zur Psychoanalyse bd II*. Frankfurt: Fischer.

Ferenczi, S. (1972b). *Schriften zur Psychoanalyse, bd II*. Frankfurt: Fischer.

Freud, S. (1943). *Die Verneinung. Gesammelte Werke Band XIV*. London: Imago.

Giddens, A. (1991). *Modernity and self-identity*. Cambridge: Polity Press.

Knapp, G. A. (1989). Arbeitsteilung und Sozialisation: Konstellationen von Arbeitsvermögen und Arbeitskraft im Lebenszusammenhang von Frauen. In U. Beer (Ed.), *Klasse und Geschlecht. Feministische Geselschaftsanalyse und Wissenschaftskritik*. Bielefeld: AJZ-Verlag.

Knapp, G.-A. (1990). Zur widersprüchlichen Vergesellschaftung von Frauen. In *Die doppelte Sozialisation Erwachsener. Zum Verhältnis von beruflichem und privatem Lebenstrang*. München: Deutsches Jugeninstitut.

Leithäuser, T. (1976). *Formen des Alltagsbewusstseins*. Frankfurt & New York, NY: Campus-Verlag.

Leithäuser, T., Salje, G., Volmerg, B., Volmerg, U., & Wutka, B. (1977). *Entwurf zu einer Empirie des Alltagsbewusstseins*. Frankfurt: Suhrkamp.

Leithäuser, T., & Volmerg, B. (1988). *Psychoanalyse in der Sozialforschung: Eine Einführung am Beispiel einer Sozialpsychologie der Arbeit*. Opladen: Westdeutscher Verlag.

Lorenzer, A. (1970). *Sprachzerstörung und Rekonstruktion: Vorarbeiten zu e. Metatheorie d. Psychoanalyse*. Frankfurt: Suhrkamp.

Lorenzer, A., & König, H.-D. (1986). Tiefenhermeneutische Kulturanalyse. In *Kultur-analysen* (Vol. 7334, pp. 11–98). Frankfurt: Fischer Taschenbuch Verlag.

Lyth, I. M. (1988). *Containing anxiety in institutions: Selected essays* (Vol. 1). Oxford: Free Association Books.

Morgenroth, C. (1989). Frauen sind keine Randgruppe – komplexes weibliches Arbeitsvermögen und das Recht des Besonderen. In O. Negt, C. Morgenroth, H. Geiling, & E. Niemeyer (Eds.), *Emanzipationsinteressen und Organisaationsphantasie*. Köln: Bund Verlag.

Morgenroth, C. (1990). *Sprachloser Widerstand. Fischer Taschenbuch*. Retrieved from http://rub.ruc.dk/soeg/kviksoeg/?query=3596102405

Morgenroth, C., Hollman, R., & Niemeyer, E. (1994). *Realistische Utopien – Beteiligungsgewerkschaften als Zukunftsperspektive*. Frankfurt: Fischer.

Morgenroth, C., Negt, O., Hollman, R., & Niemeyer, E. (1992). *Individuum, Geschlecht, Solidarität*. Hannover: University Manuscript.

Negt, O. (1964). *Soziologische Phantasie und exemplarisches Lernen*. Frankfurt: Europäische Verlagsanstalt.

Negt, O. (2001). Adorno's Begriff der Erfahrung. Das Argument. In A. Kluge & O. Negt (Eds.), *Der unterschätzte Mensch: Gemeinsame Philosophie in zwei Bänden*. Frankfurt am Main: Zweitausendeins.

Negt, O., & Kluge, A. (1972). *Öffentlichkeit und Erfahrung*. Frankfurt: Europäische Verlagsanstalt.

Negt, O., & Kluge, A. (1981). *Geschichte und Eigensinn. Zweitausendeins*. Retrieved from http://rub.ruc.dk/soeg/kviksoeg/?query=x100076725

Negt, O., & Kluge, A. (2014). *History and obstinacy*. New York, NY: Zone Books.

Nielsen, H. B., & Rudberg, M. (1988). Hur flickor blir flickor och pojkar blir pojkar. *Kvinnovetenskaplig Tidsksrift*, (1).

Nielsen, H. B., & Rudberg, M. (1989). *Historien om jenter og gutter. Kjønnssocialisering i et utviklingpsykologisk perspektiv*. Oslo: Universitetsforlaget.

Nielsen, H. B., & Rudberg, M. (1994). *Psychological gender and modernity*. Oslo: Scandinavian University Press.

Nielsen, H. K. (1993). *Kultur og Modernitet*. Århus: Århus Universitetsforlag.

Olesen, H. S., & Weber, K. (2012). Socialization, language, and scenic understanding. Alfred Lorenzer's contribution to a psycho-societal methodology 1. The landscape before and around Lorenzer Forum. *Qualitative Social Research/Sozialforschung, 13*(3), Article 22.

Polanyi, M. (1967). *The tacit dimension*. London: Routledge.

Prokop, U. (1981). Sehnsucht nach der Volkseinheit. Zum Konservatismus der bürgerlichen Frauenbewegung vor 1933. In G. Dietze (Ed.), *Die Überwindung der Sparchlosigkeit. Texte aus der neuen Frauenbewegung* (pp. 176–202). Darmstadt.

Salling Olesen, H. (1989). *Adult education and everyday life*. Roskilde: Adult Education Research Group, Roskilde University.

Salling Olesen, H. (2012). The societal nature of subjectivity: An interdisciplinary methodological challenge. *Forum Qualitative Sozialforschung/Forum: Qualitative Social Research, 13*(3).

Senghaas-Knobloch, E., & Volmerg, B. (1990). *Technische Fortschritt und Verantwortungsbewusstsein. Die gesellschaftliche Verantwortung von Ingenieuren*. Opladen: Westdeutscher Verlag.

Visholm, S. (1998). Overflade og dybde. Om projektiv identifikation og det modernes sociologi. In *Det uhyggelige*. Viborg: Politisk Revys forlag.

Volmerg, B., Senghaas-Knobloch, E., & Leithäuser, T. (1986). *Betriebliche Lebenswelt. Eine sozialpsychologie industrieller Arbeitsverhältnisse*. Opladen: Westdeutscher Verlag.

Volmerg, B., Volmerg, U., & Leithäuser, T. (1983). *Kriegsängste und Sicherheitsbedürfnis. Zur Sozialpsychologi des Ost-West-Konflikts*. Frankfurt: Fischer.

Winnicott, D. W. (1958). Transitional objects and transitional phenomena. In *collected papers: Through paediatrics to psycho-analysis*. London: Tavistock Publications.

Ziehe, T., & Stubenrauch, H. (1982). *Plädoyer für ungewöhnliches Lernen. Ideen zur Jugendsituation*. Reibek: Rowohlt.

REGINA BECKER-SCHMIDT

2. THE RELEVANCE OF BIOGRAPHICAL STUDIES FOR EMPOWERMENT STRATEGIES

INTRODUCTION

Although it is common sense that women's work is influenced by globalization processes, their socio-psychological impact is scarcely investigated. Little attention is paid to the subjective implications of the notion "women's work as an ensemble of different forms of practices". The personal importance of the combination of domestic and professional work is, so to speak, "a dark continent". Are the experiences women make with different forms of work either positive or negative or do we have to anticipate an emotional entanglement of attraction and defense? In addition: we don't know very much about the psychic energy that women have to summon when they are forced to give up routinized balances. That is necessary, when shifts within the labor-market alter women's work under the pressure of world-wide economic competition.

Before I present a socio-psychological approach, which throws light on the inner dynamic of women's working experiences, I want to make some brief preliminary remarks. I think that insights into the feelings and perceptions of women, concerning their working conditions as a whole, are relevant for discussing adequate empowerment strategies. Women who switch from domestic (subsistence) work to market mediated work and back again are confronted with challenges, conflicts and constraints which men don't have to bear in the same way. Disadvantages women suffer due to their gender are not only based on unjust distribution of paid and unpaid work, but also on a disrespect of the psychological burden resulting from their multi-orientation which tries to integrate both family subsistence and professional career. The neglect of their physical and psychological exertions belongs to the indifference which characterizes andro-centric or patriarchal gender orders which is accompanied by a disregard for human needs in the capitalist organization of work. If we want to understand women as vulnerable and simultaneously steady subjects, who are willing to fight for their rights, we have to acknowledge their biographies as processes of lifelong learning. But lifelong learning for me does not only mean always having skills in the newest standards of know-how, above all technological know-how, but also not forgetting cultural achievements, human claims and personal dreams. At the risk of being diminished by economic rationalization these dimensions must always be revitalized.

© KONINKLIJKE BRILL NV, LEIDEN, 2020 | DOI: 10.1163/9789004420274_003

We have to be aware that women bridge what is societally divided – the public and the private sphere as well as productive, reproductive and regenerative activities. This recombining of the separated social practices takes place in an invisible and silent way. There is no public discourse articulating women's efforts and the efficiencies of these efforts for society. Empowerment activities can make both the burden and the social value of this knotting of divided sectors transparent. This knotting guarantees the maintenance of social life.

That is for me the frame of a political psychology and sociology with practical ambitions, in which the investigation of female biographical studies should be embedded.

SPECIFIC CONFLICTS IN WOMEN'S ENSEMBLE OF WORK

From a feminist perspective, analyzing women's work biographies has not only to do with objective life conditions, but also with the conflicts which shape experiences. That is especially important for the understanding of coping strategies women develop in their life courses. Whether women are able to combine various form of work or not depends on the objective and subjective possibilities to deal with controversial life conditions. The fact that women's work is an ensemble of *different* social practices does not only imply double or triple burden, but also the capability to endure contradictory demands. So the burden of women has a quantitative side (domestic work plus child care plus paid work) and a qualitative side. On a qualitative level, time pressure and the necessity to change priorities when switching between different working places is an extremely hard psychological effort, e.g. attitudes concerning child care differ deeply from demands of performance required in a factory or a firm. In the first case you must have the ability to let time flow playing with the kids, in the second case you are not allowed to waste time.

A special conflict in women's work biographies is discontinuity. Women more often are forced to interrupt their careers, because there are phases where duties in the family are prevalent. Although the unemployment rate of men is increasing in countries where male dominated industries (e.g. mining and steel industries) have been abolished, we can recognize that women more often are fired or put off to a lower position when paid work is generally shrinking.

Changes in the ensemble of women's social activities and shifts of their positions in the labor market, unemployment and migration are evident indicators of alterations due to national and international economic, political and cultural developments. We have a lot of data which prove such alterations. But they are aggregated on such a high level of objectivation that they are too abstract to see the conflicts these changes cause.

The balances women have built up in the past while dealing with domestic unpaid and market-mediated work have to be deconstructed and reconstructed when alterations in the combination of their social activities occur. Shifting from areas of the formal to the informal market, from highly qualified jobs to less qualified occupations does not only touch income and social prestige. In any case, a revaluation of positive and negative aspects within the new situation has to be undertaken in order to regain routine. So the need to reorganize balances in changing constellations is a challenge and a strain in women's biographies.

I draw the following conclusions from these considerations: only if we know something about the personal importance the different forms of work have in women's lives, only if we know in which ways women assess their divergent practices and how they find criteria defining pro and contra in each part of their work, can we look – together with them – for measures to improve their living conditions.

CONTRADICTION AND AMBIVALENCE: AN APPROACH TO UNDERSTANDING WOMEN'S WORK BIOGRAPHIES

The following approach is won by doing biographical studies. Between 1980 and 1986 I made – in cooperation with colleagues and students – 60 in-depth-interviews with working class women (Becker-Schmidt et al., 1982, 1983, 1984, 1985).

Some years later I worked out together with Angelika Wetterer a similar approach by interviewing female and male social scientists.(Becker-Schmidt & Wetterer, 1990). Christel Schachtner used the so-called "Hannover Ansatz" to understand the conflicts of female and male computer programmers (Schachtner, 1993). Later our approach was used to guide a gender oriented study in the Life History Project at University of Roskilde, Denmark (Weber, 1995). One phenomenon, we found out, corresponds with results of other independent studies. Beyond class and country specific constellations one common trait you can see is that women react with ambivalence to contradictory demands they are confronted with in paid and unpaid work. They assess the different forms of work by comparing and contrasting them. The deficits experienced in the private sphere are compensated by experiences in the public sphere and vice versa. I will give you three examples.

A working class woman I interviewed some years ago articulated a dilemma she cannot solve. She wants to have a family and to participate in the labor force at the same time. She said: "Only one kind of work is too little, the combination of paid and unpaid work is too much". Although her working place (putting together little thin plates, which form a piece for television receivers) is extremely monotonous and restricted, the idea of quitting the job makes her nervous. It is not only the money she cannot renounce. There are intrinsic motivations which drive her to persevere with the working place in the factory. She loves her little daughter and seems to have a good relationship to her husband. "But if I would stay every day at home – without my colleagues, without the feeling that I am a good worker and co worker I would get depressive". She hates the time pressure in the factory, but she likes the possibility to assess her work by holding the norm. For her it is a satisfying feeling that she has produced the number of pieces she has to produce in a shift. "You know,

I can see what I have done, I can compare my performance with the performances of the others – at home nobody comes and gives me a feedback for my work. You have cleaned a room and after some time it is dirty again. That's boring". Housework is endless. She criticizes the gender segregation in the factory. "All our leading hands are men. I think that's not fair. I am as competent as they are". When her husband proposes to buy a new TV, she makes the decision. Her comment: "TV – that's my thing". She appreciates the freedom at home, to have some self-determination: "When I see the laundry, I can say – oh, today I am not in the mood to iron, I will do it tomorrow. In the factory that is impossible. On the other side: when I leave my firm, all work there is done. When I come home and see the laundry from yesterday, I think: "If you don't do the work now, the household will become a mess". She is angry that she has to take more responsibility for the domestic work than her husband. Gender-based division of work very often causes conflicts. "I cooked a soup, so that he and our daughter had something to eat, when my mother could not be at home at noon. But then he burned the soup. So next time I had to write a note and put it next to the kitchen-range: "Please, do stir".

Monika Goldmann and Ursula Muller had interviews with sales-women. For them time pressure is also the worst stress. "When I come home, I am so exhausted that I need regeneration time for me. But then there are my husband and my child. And they keep me busy. So I ask myself, whether I should switch to a part-time job". An extremely long work day, bad regulation of breaks, bad climatic conditions, the need to stand the whole day – those are the burdens sales women have to bear. On the other side, they like the interaction and communication with the clients. "To find something for them they like is a real pleasure". In the field of selling we can see special conflicts: the pressure to be polite to clients with bad behavior and the obligation to sell things even knowing that they do not fit to the clients.

Ambivalence is the result of these contradictions. The positive experiences, contrasted with the isolation at home, stimulate the desire to hold onto the job. The negative experiences nourish the wish to stay at home (Goldmann & Müller, 1986). Christel Schachtner pointed out another ambiguity which programmers articulated. They are proud to fulfill a creative profession. They like to develop programs suitable for their clients. They are fond of the logical procedures they have to deal with. Team work is highly valued. But there is always the fear of not catching new developments and becoming old-fashioned. Team work and competition lay very close together. Female and male programmers are threatened by the next generation, which is younger and fitter than them. Female programmers are aware of a special problem: the effects of "deformations professionelles". They recognize the temptation to handle private problems with the same logic as computer programs.

THEORETICAL AND METHODOLOGICAL CONSIDERATIONS

Before representing a summary of results won in studies dealing with women's work biographies, I want to mention some theoretical and methodological requirements.

1. We have to avoid a theoretical short-coming, when we want to bring together socio-economic conditions and cultural traditions which frame women's indoor and outdoor work (capitalist norms of performance, gender-based division and segregation of work, unequal assessment of female and male social activities) and the psychic dynamics which unroll in view of attracting and deterring dimensions of labor. Although both levels – the objective and the subjective one – are reciprocally mediated, they do not follow the same logic. We cannot grasp contradictions and incompatible issues which are specific for the outer and the inner realities of a person, if we derive subjective reactions directly from objective constellations or if we see objective conditions without any relation to human actions.
2. We have to take into consideration breaks and imbalances in biographical processes.
3. Similar living conditions do not necessarily imply similar psychological reactions. So we have to search for analogies *and* deviations with the same attention while studying the work experiences of divergent social groups of women. Ambivalence seems to be a common trait in this field. But the pro and contra, which give the different forms of work their special weight, varies from case to case and the disposition of women to cope with ambiguity differs from person to person as well. One woman may hold together negative and positive aspects of her various social activities following her experience that staying at home is too one-dimensional for her. Another may split her ambivalent feelings by forgetting the pressure of paid work at home or letting behind her family troubles while working in the public sphere. A third may harmonize the pain of double burden in order to stick to an internalized double orientation. A fourth may give more weight to the negative dimensions of professional work just to get rid of the impression of being tom up. And we know situations in developing countries where the gaps between processes of modernization in the market-mediated world and the traditional structures in religion and family are so insuperable that women perish who try to bridge them. Those divergences depend on country, class and ethnic specific contexts as well as on socio psychological back-grounds. So we cannot construct a universal theory or develop an omniscient compendium of empirical data which represent all kinds of biographies. But we can conceptualize relatively complex models which are suitable for an exemplary approach and which are open for modifications forced by comparison.
4. We have to break with the idea of "identical individuality". This construction belongs to the European philosophy which is signed by andro-centric and bourgeois concepts of a rational subject which masters reality. We have to see that even when individuals do have the feeling of personal continuity and undividedness their personality is stamped by non-identity: there is no consciousness without unconsciousness; we are often confronted with a divided will; we have to give up plans we have identified with and to cope with unfulfilled wishes. Beyond this:

subjects don't want to be simply and solely individuals. They need communities, connections and forms of cooperation.

5. "Work" in the sense of "living labor" has another meaning for human beings who want to be active in public spheres than for managements which reduce "living labor" to an exploitative source of profit. Capitalist rules pervert cooperation into competition. The organization of labor has to serve the accumulation\of surplus value. Of course, people work for money. They are instrumentalized for money and they instrumentalize themselves for money. That's unavoidable in market-mediated world-systems. But we should not oversee intrinsic motivations which are addressed to work. Even under work conditions with alienating effects, certain implications of "living labor" cannot be totally suppressed[1]: motion and emotion stimulated by corporeality and practical-communicative spirits. Production and services done for others are connected with the idea of consumption, not with the intention of profit making.

So remnants of liveliness and social commitment survive. These moments of human potentials paradoxically support an organization of work which requires subordination. This reflection emphasizing the divergent importance of labor for employees in comparison with employers is especially important for the understanding of women's work.

As their social activities are embedded in private and public contexts there is a constant flow of meanings loading both forms of work reciprocally with hopes and disappointments. This reciprocal loading is nourished by the changes between the indoor and outdoor working places and the memory of activities performed in former life phases.

Domestic tasks, subsistence work and child care include corporeality and community – at least under the condition, that community is not reduced to the core of a two generation family, but encompasses a wider horizon of kinship and neighborhood. Work organized in such contexts has its own weight as long as it secures the existence of a family. But modernization and rationalization which hallmark globalization processes do not only alter the labor market. These trends penetrate into privacy, too. The family loses more and more of its former functions: production of goods, socialization of the next generation after childhood, connecting the private with the public in acts of hospitality, mediation of cultural practices. On the labor market "living work" has become a commodity reified as other things. But in comparison with domestic work it is paid and gives the wage-earner the role of a bread-winner.

So the prestige of domestic work is weakened. This development provokes women's decision to look for market-mediated work which promises a salary, recognition as a co-worker, as a producer of goods for a common use and as a member of a public space.

These aspirations rush together with the rules of profit oriented labor: limitation of corporeality, regulation of sensuality, fragmentation of actions. But these experiences lose their harshness in comparison to the degradation of women as housewives, their isolation at home and their dependence on the bread-winner.

The discrepancies between expectations and the shocking reality may be especially hard in contexts of migration or getaways from rural to urban areas with different work traditions.

Let me finish these general reflections with a last methodological consideration.

If we want to acknowledge work experiences women make going from one status passage to the other and switching between different working places, then we should let them be the experts of their everyday lives. That means: we have to listen to them and not to follow our own ideas constructed through the optics of lenses which are spoiled by otherness. Self-reflection and empathy are required to overcome this bias. Scientists have to bridge the gap between theoretical and methodological knowledge, which is necessary for the conceptualization of an investigation, and the experiences of those they want to interrogate

Another epistemological claim is a thorough concept of the questionnaire guiding the in-depth interviews. It must be open for all aspects of domestic and professional work including their reciprocal relations.

There is a tendency in the traditional main-stream of social research, which is oriented around the principles of natural science, to look for consistent results. The devise is "either/or". Contradictory comments seem to be unreliable. But in view of women's living conditions, which are characterized by controversial structures and demands, we must be aware of unstable reactions that correspond incompatibilities. So the interviews must be conducted to allow women to express objective inconsistencies in a contradictory way. They should have the opportunity to change their perceptions according to altering contexts and to see situations from different angles.

So a questionnaire suitable for women's work experiences has to combine three approaches. First: in retrospect, we have to grasp the influences of the past. Former events have another meaning seen from the present balance than they did years ago. Second: It is necessary to focus the interviews on the most important issues which mark women's present work life: family and professional career. But – and that's the third methodological requirement – these centers of investigation cannot be treated as isolated parts, discussed one after the other. As they are interrelated within the life courses and as experiences alter their content following altering contexts women must be encouraged to change their perspectives. Working women talk about domestic tasks in another way when they see them from the angle of outdoor labor and not only within the frame "family". And vice versa: positive and negative aspects of market-mediated labor gain other facets when discussed in the context of domestic work than within the thematic center "professional performances and demands". The ambivalences which occur are results of two psychodynamic processes: the one can be seen as a reaction to immanent frictions women are confronted with in all their work areas; the other is shaped by contrasting them. Women try to bargain the costs and advantages of the two possible decisions: to stay at home or to combine paid and unpaid work.

Women's Work: A Model for the Analysis of Complex and Multi-dimensional Social Problems

Let us remember the connections women's work biographies are embedded in.

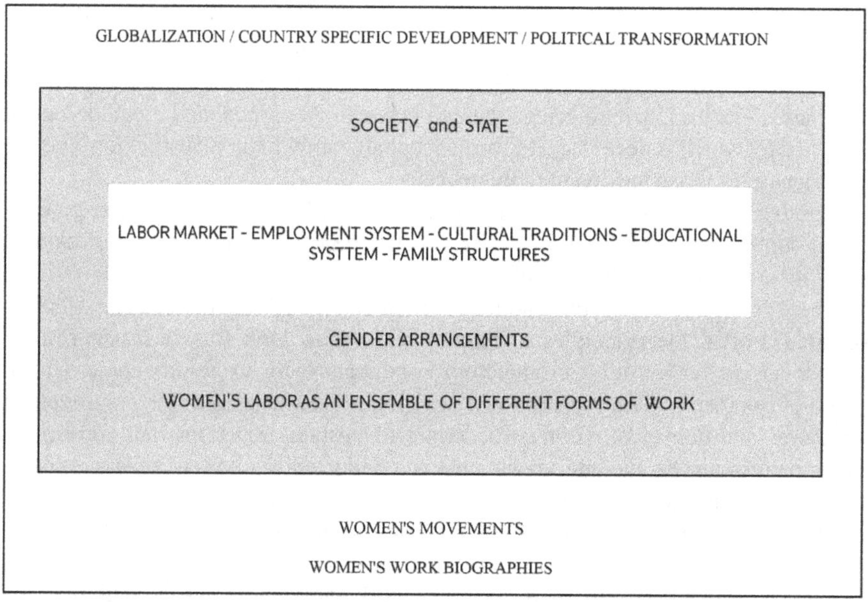

Figure 4.1. A summarizing model

In the following passages I want to show interdependencies between objective and subjective life conditions and the psychodynamics due to discrepancies in both contexts.

In order not to overcharge the formalized summary, I chose a simple model which deals only with two dimensions of women's work: domestic and work in firms.

I will begin from the perspective of a present stage and add then a short biographical retrospective.

I have pointed out the contradictions women have to cope with within the family and professional work.

Let's repeat the incompatible issues of firms.

In all profit-oriented firms, two contradictory claims can be found:

accumulation of profit (dimension of quantity)	↔	Production of commodities for the consumers (dimension of quality)

This implies two other contradictions on the level of work performance

The organization of labor has a strict time regulation, but requires through performances		
high outpur under timepressure	↔	no waste, skilled work

The profit-oriented arrangement of cooperation causes

competition (challenge of personal ambitions)	↔	solidarity (reciprocal) help to lessen bad working conditions

The structural contradictions lying on a more abstract level are recognized via controversial demands. They cause ambivalence.

The institution "family" which frames domestic work is marked by structural contradictions, too.

family as a private realm (degrees of self-determination domestic work the satisfaction of human needs)	↔	family as institution which is responsible, for public affairs (maintenance of the population by procreation and the regeneration of "living labour")
domestic work societal necessary work	↔	underestimated, unpaid work
promise of leisure time	↔	second working place for women
privacy as sphere of intimacy	↔	isolation

In the private sphere women are also confronted with controversial demands due to structural contradictions which cause ambivalences.

to accept gender-based division of labor	↔	performing paid work, just like the husband
to be responsible care work although	↔	family life is a shared goal of a couple
promise of leisure time	↔	second working place for women

We have to be aware of two dimensions of contradictions:

We have recognized incompatibilities within family and firm, but also those between the differently structured institutions: exploitation of "living labor"/ regeneration of life; paid/unpaid work; private/public.

So we can reconstruct the positive and negative aspects of ambivalences.

Outdoor work means

time pressure	↔	feeling to be a good worker
exhausting work	↔	transparence of conditions and work norms
indifference against individuality	↔	acknowledgement salary
competition	↔	cooperation, communication

Indoor work means

being part of relationships	↔	domestic work is vanishing while it is done
satisfying human needs	↔	unpaid, unequal division of work
being one's own mastress	↔	being surrendered to patriarchal authority

In addition we have to consider the following dynamics.

First: experiences made in the firm affect women's attitudes towards the family and vice versa. I quote the working class woman we have already noticed to illustrate this fact. "This morning I said to my boss: 'I can't stand your treatment of me. Do you deal with your wife at home in the same manner? I don't think you would dare". Interactions taking place in the private sphere serve as measurement for human behavior in the firm. And vice versa: forms of recognition experienced in the firm are standards for behavior in the family. My interviewee encounters her husband with a self-confidence she has won in the firm. One day he didn't want to help her clean the dishes. She shouted: "If you want to play the pascha here, you will see no penny of my earnings in the future".

Second: there is a correspondence between the evaluation of paid and unpaid work which is faned by comparison and contrast. The results of comparison and contrasting decide on the weight the different forms of work are assessed with.

AN EXTRACT FROM A CASE STUDY: "DEFERRED ACTION"

When interpreting interviews I had with working women I stumbled upon a mechanism to deal with disguised conflicts which belonged to former life phases. The conflicts had to do with dreams or wishes which could not be realized at the time they occurred. Although they were of great relevance for the interviewed persons they disappeared. But by reading their life stories very thoroughly I could find traces of them in other life passages. The wishes had changed, but certain motivations were re-conceivable. I knew this phenomenon from Freud. He called it "Umschrift" ("retroactive interpretation" or "transcription") and characterized it as follows: it is a mental operation through which past experiences, impressions and desires, which must be suppressed out of inner or outer reasons in the life span when they emerged, are reactivated later on. That what seemed to be lost reappears in a new significance and in new psychic dimensions. It is as if the dreams and desires had wintered in the realm of the unconsciousness and waited there until the time is ripe for their fulfilment. The wishes do not reappear in the old form but better adjusted to the outer and inner reality. Freud assumed that there are situations in our biographies in which we do not understand why we are not allowed to do this or that. So we have no target for resistance. Growing up, we learn to cope with obstacles. The conflicts which could not be solved in former life phases can be solved later on and the suppressed desires can then be accepted. I adhere to Freud's explanation that experiences are reinterpreted retrospectively when a state of consciousness or a context of meaning has been established which allows us a more productive exposition with the old conflict. Freud invented for this psychic operation the notion "Nachtraglichkeit" ("deferred action").

The mechanism of deferred action makes new assessments possible and in turn also releases new impulses to act. From the present falls light into the past and the energy bound in the unconsciousness is freed for the future.

I will give you an example taken from a case study.

Mrs. X dreamt in her childhood: as an adult she would be a driver of a bus. She would be an employee of a tourist agency and drive people through foreign countries.

The dream disappeared in school time. Her teacher said: "That's no profession for a girl".

Mrs. X did not understand why a woman should not be able to drive a bus. In this age gender based segregation of work was not yet mentioned. But as she recognized that her dream was an offence to her teacher she forgot about it. But the wishes which had driven the dream stayed in her, unconsciously. The desire to move, to have adventures and to be free remained unimpressed.

As a teenager, she dreamt of having a motorcar, a black leather suit and a boyfriend sitting on the back seat.

When she had a boyfriend who was accepted by her parents her father financed a motorbike. But the friend drove the motorbike and after an accident the fun was over. The dream of a motorcar representing the old desires had to be deduced to a motorbike. And Mrs. X made a new experience which touched a former disappointment: Women are not allowed to do the same as men do. There is a gender-order: not women but men drive busses and motorcars. This knowledge transformed her drives: the wish to transgress gender-orders joined the desire to be mobile, to experience motion and adventures.

After her schooling, Mrs. X worked in a car factory. After two years of piece work, she passed the park of transporter vehicles. She decided to get her driver license for a fork-lift truck. She got it. But as she was a woman she was only allowed to drive a little fork-lift truck. She convinced her colleagues who worked together with her in the park to let her drive a bigger one from time to time. One day she appeared in her boss' office and showed a new license: one for a bigger transporter. At last she got the permission to drive it.

We see: psychoanalytically oriented social science can help to find hidden potentials in women's biographies which can be reactivated and which can stimulate motivations concerning vocational training or emancipation from patriarchal power structures within the private and public sphere. When we wish to encourage women to go their own way in an independent manner, it is perhaps helpful to know that dreams constituted in former times, let's say childhood, are not lost when women are forced to give them up. They are laid down in a realm where they are not controlled by the principles of reality: that's the psychic space of unconsciousness. As the unconsciousness holds contact with the consciousness, old dreams can be modified with the development of a person. So I think that dreams are relevant forces for the will to change unjust life conditions.

NOTE

1 This is no anthropological remark. We know from the Nazi-regime, that the human basis of living labor can be denied to a degree that exploitation implies killing. But the capitalist has to respect liveliness. As "living labor" is an instrument of profit, it needs – like a machine – some care.

REFERENCES

Becker-Schmidt, R. (1990). Umschrift und Nachtraglichkeit in Biographien von Soziologinnen. In I. Sommerkorn (Ed.), *Lehren und Lernen in der Soziologie heute. Aktuelle Fragen zu einem alten Problem* (pp. 100–126.). Berlin: Sigma Rainer Bohm Verlag.

Becker-Schmidt, R., Brandes-Erlhoff, U., Knapp, G. A., Rumpf, M., & Schmidt, B. (1982). *Nicht wir haben die Minuten, die Minuten haben uns.* Bonn: Verlag Neue Gesellschaft.

Becker-Schmidt, R., & Knapp, G. A. (1986). *Arbeiterkinder gestern, Arbeiterkinder heute*. Bonn: Verlag Neue Gesellschaft.

Becker-Schmidt, R. et al. (1983). *Arbeitsleben – Lebensarbeit*. Bonn: Verlag Neue Gesellschaft.

Becker-Schmidt, R. et al. (1984). *Eines ist zu wenig – beides ist zu viel*. Bonn: Verlag Neue Gesellschaft.

Goldmann, M., & Müller, U. (1986). *Junge Frauen im Verkaufsberuf. Berufliche Sozialisation, Arbeits- und Lebensperspektiven*. Berlin/Köln/Mainz: Schriftenreihe des Bundseministers für Jugend, Frauen und Familie.

Schachtner, C. (1993). *Geistmaschine. Faszination und Provokation am Computer*. Frankfurt a.M.: Suhrkamp.

Weber, K. (1995). *Ambivalens og Erfaring* (Dissertation). Roskilde University.

Wetterer, A. (1990). Frauenthemen und Themen von Frauen in der Soziologielehre. In I. Sommerkorn (Ed.), *Lehren und Lernen in der Soziologie heute ...* (pp. 127–1467). Berlin: Sigma Rainer Bohm Verlag.

THOMAS LEITHÄUSER

3. EVERYDAY LIFE AND THE SOCIETAL UNCONSCIOUS

In social science theory and empirical social research, in which I include social psychology, there is scarcely any discussion of the phenomenon of everyday life. This was quite different in the 1960s, 1970s and 1980s. The concept of everyday life did not pass through the mesh of the scientific division of labour. Rather, it was a precious discovery that both theoretically and empirically helped to develop cross-disciplinary social research.

EVERYDAY LIFE AS AN OBJECT FOR SOCIAL SCIENCE

Today there is a critical need for this type of research. Everyday life presents a jumble of societal, political and psychological problems; antisemitism, racism, populism, nationalistic and patriarchal prejudice, the media game with its fake news, etc. all appear as phenomena of everyday life. They penetrate the consciousness of everyday life, condense into cognitive and emotional patterns in our everyday experiences that exert ever more influence on the political and social agency of political parties, groups and individuals. This also includes the systematic trivialization of horror stories about Nazism in Germany from 1933 to 1945.

Everyday life is a difficult societal, political and psychological terrain which requires new research and critical political activity in order to counter the early stages of a destruction of liberal and social democracy. Sociological and social psychological research into the authoritarian personality on a psychoanalytical basis (Adorno, Frenkel-Brunswik, Levinson, & Sanford, 1950), which took place in the Frankfurt Institute for Social Research in the 1950s, and previous and current social psychology research in the field of the psychology of prejudice, such as Allport's work "The Nature of Prejudice", are once again becoming socially and politically relevant. Particularly important for the understanding of the contemporary rejection of everyday life in the USA and Europe is Erich Fromm's comprehensive, psychoanalytically-based work *Arbeiter und Angestellte am Vorabend des Dritten Reiches* (translated as *The Working Class in Weimar Germany* by Barbara Weinberger). This study shows how rapidly well-established political (democratic and socialist) ways of thinking and attitudes in difficult times can be manipulated into right-wing radicalism and populist consciousness and agency. Everyday forms of consciousness become unstable and receptive to aggressive propaganda.

© KONINKLIJKE BRILL NV, LEIDEN, 2020 | DOI: 10.1163/9789004420274_004

The dispositions to learning, to education and to identity development which pervade our everyday consciousness are being reshaped and discouraged by regressive mechanisms of repression. Out of the darkness of a societal unconsciousness rise archaic phantasies of violence, which had already seemed to have been overcome since their domination of the propagandistically manipulated everyday life consciousness in Nazi Germany. Nationalistic ideologies again seem acceptable and presentable. Modern everyday life consciousness reveals many faces. The backward-looking ones prevail over the progressive ones. Enlightenment becomes perplexed (cf. Leithäuser, 1976).

EVERYDAY LIFE CONSCIOUSNESS AND IDEOLOGY

In referring to forms of everyday life consciousness, we do not envisage fixed and structured forms. The image is rather that of a container with porous, perforated walls into which all kinds of intellectual rubbish can sink while driving out well-considered thoughts, or of the emergence of a type of intellectual hodgepodge. Such everyday life consciousness easily escapes critical reflection. Yet it also has its own wilfulness. We often find an approach to a form of dogmatic philosophizing, setting up ideological assertions proclaimed with excessive eagerness; these are wrong and obscure, mostly uttered angrily and provocatively, yet almost unshakable. That is the nature of fake news.

Everyday conversations are characterized by a seemingly self-evident use of language. The participants mostly assume that the words they use are understood in the same way by the others. There is little discussion around the meaning of words. Questions like: What do you mean by that? rarely appear. Listeners mostly assume that they inevitably understand everything in the same way as the speaker. In everyday conversation, the participants tend to mutually confirm what is and what is not, what ought to be and what ought not to be. Talk in an everyday context mostly provides assertions and confirmations, and much less questioning and critical reflection. Truths are asserted, not sought jointly. What is sought is agreement with the assertions. We mostly find language games of gossip and chit-chat about immoral and moral events. Such language games satisfy a malicious pleasure by degrading, unveiling and exposing, while pretending to be serious criticism. Such degrading, unveiling and exposing may be understood as psychological defence mechanisms and the repression of truthfulness and serious insight. These mechanisms also create an unconsciousness instead of a critical acknowledgement of societal reality. They constitute what Erich Fromm calls the "societal unconscious". Everyday life is a glittering mosaic of practical activity, tempting consumption, tediousness, sleepiness, insipid daydreams, but sometimes also a flash of an idea about what is not, but could be, a wickerwork of shadowy prejudices, opinions and vague hopes. Opinions, prejudices and ideologies connected by segments of various religions together provide the mosaic of everyday life consciousness. It is not an individual consciousness, but belongs to groups, collectives, cultures, and entire societies.

THE SOCIETAL UNCONSCIOUS AS AN IDEOLOGICAL FILTER

For many people, everyday consciousness is not at all self-evident and unproblematic. It has a powerful unconscious side, which social psychologists and psychoanalysts describe as the "societal unconscious", an area of psychological repression.

> I would call the areas of repression found in most members of a society 'the societal unconscious'. These elements suppressed from people at large represent content that must not become conscious for members of the society if the society with its particular contradictions is to function smoothly. (Fromm, 1962, p. 96)

With this concept of "the societal unconscious", Fromm seeks to connect the Marxian concept of ideology with the Freudian concept of repression. For Freud, repression is a mechanism where the individual makes something unconscious, while Fromm sees it as a mechanism whereby society makes something unconscious. A society develops social and moral laws, norms and rules that sanction and prohibit (consciousness of) those elements which would disturb the smooth functioning of society. Such elements are filtered out by means of opinions, prejudices and ideologies. Fromm writes about the categories of thinking and feeling: "Some categories like time and space may be universal, common to all people. Others, like causality, may be valid categories for many, but not all, types of conscious perception. Yet other categories have even less general validity and vary from one culture to another. In any case, perceptions can only become conscious if they can be related to and fitted into a conceptual system and its categories. This system is itself a result of societal developments. Every society uses its ways of life and its types of relating, feeling and perceiving to create a system of categories that determines the forms of consciousness. This system could be said to work as a societally conditioned filter. A perception can only become conscious if it passes through this filter" (Fromm, 1950, p. 323). Opinions, prejudices and ideologies, as described above, are just such filters for everyday life consciousness. These filters are inserted into in social and political frameworks that prescribe possibilities and constraints for everyday thoughts and feelings. This takes place in a self-evident manner, quite beyond any critical, enlightening reflection. Each society defines, according to its development, such frameworks that make it difficult to expand the horizon of experiencing and thinking, and difficult to take charge of one's own thoughts and uncover one's deeply personal feelings. We might also call these ideological frameworks that take a hold in societies. Where such frameworks are lacking, they tend to be frantically sought after.

Their aim is to provide a sense of security in societal coexistence. Cognitive science uses the term "framing" to describe these attempts to set norms for consciousness. Cognitive scientist Elisabeth Wehling has illuminated these partly conscious, partly unconscious framing mechanisms in her book "Politisches Framing, wie eine Nation sich ihr Denken einredet – und daraus Politik macht" (Wehling, 2016). A translation is forthcoming, entitled "Political framing: A cognitive scientist's guide to how a nation turns language into politics". She writes: "Frames are activated in the brain through language. They first assign a meaning to facts and then arrange them by relating the information to our bodily experiences and our accumulated knowledge about the world. In this way, frames are always selective. They highlight certain facts and realities and let others fall by the wayside. They thus evaluate and interpret. And once they have been activated in our heads, in e.g. a public debate, they will guide our thinking and acting, without us even noticing" (p. 18). The current populism and the political game with its fake news represent a broad field of framing. The US President Donald Trump has entered the political stage as a master of populist framing. His celebration of his nationalist slogan "America First" is not far from the "Deutschland über alles" (Germany above all else) of the National Socialists of the 1930s and 1940s. Today's political struggle in Germany increasingly involves the power of definition of framing the "homeland". If we include the Wehlingian research concept of framing in the Frommian investigation of the "societal unconscious", we can understand frames as ideological filters, which regulate our thinking and imagining and the social mechanisms of repression and drive them into the unconscious. In this form of regulation, Trump's policies attempt to suppress the politics of globalization and multilateralism with nationalist phrases and bilateral deals. In the long run, this will probably not succeed. This is because the ideological filter of nationalism is no longer self-evident enough. One self-evident frame in business is the distinction between employer and employee (in German, literally: "work giver" and "work taker"); thus work is understood as something that can be given and taken. Those who possess the means of production are described in natural language as "work givers", while those who have no means of production are seen as "work takers". Such an understanding of the division of roles in work is currently not called into question. It has become an unconscious frame in society, an ideological filter that barely allows for consciousness or critical reflection, unless in an ironically meant role reversal, as suggested by Elisabeth Wehling: "One could equally well say that those who perform the work are the "work givers" and conceptualize the receivers of this work as the "work takers" (Wehling, 2016, p. 132). But how, we may ask, does framing filter out conscious and unconscious parts of thinking and acting? Fromm would probably seek to understand framing as a process of adaptation to the constraints and opportunities of social reality. Framing is the result of the socialization of individuals into society. This socialization begins, as Fromm understands it as a psychoanalytical social psychologist, in the earliest mother-child relationship, and as we know today, even in prenatal developmental processes in the womb. The physical and psychological development of an individual can never be completely separated from his/her social development. It is an interdependent, differentiating developmental process which Fromm addresses as a basic, bodily, emotional, and cognitively intimate social relationship, unlike traditional Freudian psychoanalysis, which would examine it as concerning the development of a single individual. Fromm's research perspective is genuinely social-psychological, not individual-psychological.

SOCIALIZATION OF THE SOCIETAL UNCONSCIOUS

To further clarify the "societal unconscious" and its entanglement in everyday life, I would like to refer to the psychoanalytical socialization theory of the psychoanalyst and social researcher Alfred Lorenzer (see Salling Olesen & Weber, Chapter 12). Similarly to Erich Fromm, Alfred Lorenzer has a theoretical orientation towards Marx and the critical theory of the Frankfurt Institute for Social Research. Erich Fromm also belonged to this institute in his early days and played a major part in the development of psychoanalytical research in the institute. Lorenzer also sees the constitution of human consciousness and its differentiation into conscious and unconscious from the early stages of psychological development as a social process. Fundamental to the forming of the psychological structure of each individual is the mother-child relationship, which Lorenzer calls the "mother-child dyad". A central concept for Lorenzer is the "form of interaction", which he uses to describe the initial symbiotic, emotional and cognitive relationship of the mother-child dyad, which becomes differentiated in the course of the child's development. This process is by no means devoid of conflict. It constantly requires new agreements on forms of interaction between child and mother. The early symbiotic stages of development, when the child experiences the mother as part of itself, include phases of separation of the dyad, in which the child can gradually experience itself as a being that is independent of the mother. This process of socialization is a process of agreement on continual new forms of interaction that differentiate the mother-child dyad, to the point of detachment of the child from the mother to become a separate individual. This socialization (which involves language development) also causes the differentiation of consciousness into conscious and unconscious parts. Thus, forms of interaction that have become obsolete in the socialization of the child are not simply deleted. Rather, they are repressed and condensed into the unconscious level of consciousness. In frequent repetitions and variations of mother-child interactions, they attach themselves to forms of interaction, a relational context of lactation and weaning, play, strictness and force, conflicts and reconciliation, whims and fancies. Last but not least, this includes the "fort!" and "da!" game, made famous through Freud's analysis, where the child enjoys making things disappear and finding things. Such forms of interaction shape the everyday life of the mother-child dyad and the family. In the mother-child dyad, the ability for everyday life is socialized with all its apparent self-evidence and contradictions. Consciousness has its foundation and genesis in everyday family life, an everydayness that continues into the working lives of adults and is decisively effective in the general societal and political reality, as characterized above.

DEEP HERMENEUTICS AS A METHOD FOR RESEARCHING EVERYDAY LIFE

Everyday life is a story of relationships that settle in the societal unconscious, and it requires its own social research. Since it concerns the phenomenon of the unconscious, this research needs a psychoanalytic orientation without any therapeutic intent. Its findings should rather enlighten a political and social practice which aims at the improvement and enrichment of human coexistence. Such research can learn much from individual psychology-oriented psychoanalysis, which still today draws on Freud's therapeutic experience and his theoretical (meta-psychological) elaborations, but later differentiated into different schools. All these psychoanalytic schools can inform social research of the societal unconscious. However, such research must develop a methodology appropriate to its research topic. Its methodological setting is not the therapeutic conversation with a couch and armchair, a patient forming associations and an interpreting analyst. Its method is the open interview where interviewee and interviewer meet on an equal footing.

Alfred Lorenzer has developed an independent interview method of this type, which he called deep hermeneutics (as presented elsewhere in this volume by Salling Olesen & Weber, Chapter 12). These interviews are not about tapping into information and knowledge. They consist of a mutual exploration by interviewee and interviewer; here the interviewee's words have priority, but the interviewer should not hold back his views on the topic either. It should not be a heated argument based on fixed points of view, but an exploratory conversation. The interview partners will tend to become a research team. The aim is to discover and analyse the frames and ideological filters of the societal unconscious of everyday life. Deep hermeneutics is a qualitative research method that is considered to be part of the empirical hermeneutics of social research. In every empirical research project, the methodology has to be justified in relation to the object of study. There are now qualitative, empirical-hermeneutic research projects in several countries, including Denmark, the UK and Germany. In Denmark, it was Kirsten Weber in particular whose research promoted the study of everyday life with its unconscious aspects. I dedicate this essay to her memory.

REFERENCES

Adorno, T. W. (1950). *The authoritarian personality*. New York, NY: Harper and Row, Publishers.

Allport, G. W. (1954). *The nature of prejudice*. New York, NY: Doubleday and Company, Inc.

Fromm, E. (1950). *Psychoanalyse und Religion, Erich Fromm Gesamtausgabe, Bd. 6*. Stuttgart: Deutsche Verlagsanstalt.

Fromm, E. (1962). *Jenseits der Illusionen. Die Bedeutung von Marx und Freud, Erich Fromm Gesamtausgabe, Bd. 9* (E. Fromm, Trans., 2001). Stuttgart: Deutsche Verlagsanstalt.

Fromm, E. (1980). *Arbeiter und Angestellte am Vorabend des Dritten Reiches, Erich Fromm Gesamtausgabe, Bd. 3* (E. Fromm, Trans., 1984). Stuttgart: Deutsche Verlagsanstalt.

Fromm, E. (1984). *The working class in Weimar Germany* (B. Weinberger, Trans.). Leamington Spa: Berg Publishers.

Fromm, E. (2001). *Beyond the chains of illusion. My meeting with Freud and Marx*. Continuum Impact.

Leithäuser, T. (1979). *Formen des Alltagsbewußtseins*. Frankfurt a. Main: Campus-Verlag.

Lorenzer, A. (1972). *Zur Begründung einer materialistischen Sozialisationstheorie*. Frankfurt a. Main: Suhrkamp Verlag.

Wehling, E. (2016). *Politisches Framing, Wie eine Nation sich ihr Denken einredet – und daraus Politik macht*. Köln: Herbert von Halem Verlag.

PART 2

UNDERSTANDING INDIVIDUAL LEARNING AND LEARNING CAREERS IN LIFE HISTORY

KIRSTEN WEBER

4. AGGRESSION, RECOGNITION AND QUALIFICATION

On the Social Psychology of Adult Education and Learning in Everyday Life

FROM "WIDER BENEFITS" TO "ACKNOWLEDGED COMPLEXITY"

Adult education can surely be shown to possess a number of "wider benefits" for individuals, employers and society. A cool-headed academic approach should, however, not jump to such demonstration without reflecting on the nature of more traditional benefits – such as motivation and learning. The historical framework for giving substance to the benefits of education are more complex than ever before, as current internationalisation and (discourse of) globalization does indeed point to. Education is not about skills and qualifications only, but about identities and lifelong development of capacities and attitudes. And is it, one may ask, subjectively exclusively a benefit to engage in such processes? Even in Denmark, who possesses a well developed system of general and labour market education, motivations are not always so positive as the tradition of enlightenment would assume.

For the structural paradoxes behind the expanding and programmatically optimistic adult education sector are of course perceived more or less directly by participants. In Denmark we empirically register considerable enthusiasm about education – often with women – or downright refusal of it – often with men, if the training in question is not directly relevant for work or employment. Below the surface more mixed and complex motivations can generally be found, and in this chapter I shall indeed focus on two populations, whose subjective motivations for participating in their respective formally qualifying educational programmes were certainly explicitly ambivalent both cognitively and emotionally. And whose contradictory motivations were constituted by perceptions and experiences deeply personal and individual, yet collective and historically significant. This chapter was written for the ESREA triennial conference "Wider Benefits of Adult Learning" in Lisbon 2001.

EMPLOYMENT DEMANDS EDUCATION

So my empirical material, the texts to be discussed, are two. One is produced in a thematized group discussion by a group of adult men – long term unemployed skilled workers along with ex-UN soldiers out of a civil job – who went through a two year training programme for jobs within care. They did so with a view to *obtain permanent employment* as wardens in a psychiatric hospital – by tradition a man's job. The other text is produced in a group interview by a mixed gender group of adults working in youth clubs – but not possessing any formal qualifications within social pedagogy. They completed a two year part time programme especially designed to match their job, which they kept during the entire period of training, but *which they would lose if they did not complete the training.*

Both texts were produced as empirical data in evaluation projects concerning the respective educational programmes.[1]

So the empirical populations are exemplary objects of the current function of adult education which is to not only supply the qualifications allegedly needed in the jobs available, but to furthermore constitute the space where fundamental changes of work identity and general future orientation may develop. The subjective journeys of the skilled painter or welder and his class-mate, the soldier just returned from Kosova, towards identification with the professional standards of the caring professions – and the shifts of life perspective of the hairdresser towards becoming a social worker, are considerable ones.

So the explicit ambiguities voiced to the researchers[2] were to be expected. Both groups – and their colleagues – had good reason to be concerned about their future employment, income and social status. They were explicitly dependent on the specific economic organization, designed to keep them on track, of their programmes. The instrumental attitude was forever popping up … interrupting and disturbing the agreed agenda, which was that of subjectively relevant and societally demanded qualification. Much fussing and complaining in the texts can be attributed to the labourious psychological processes harmonizing the basically compulsory participation with the self-identity as autonomous adults, of managing the competing motivations of infantilisation and boredom versus the obviously interesting – at least occasionally! – substance of the educational discourse and the subjective need to attribute some kind of meaning to the perspective of doing this job for a considerable number of years, if not for the rest of one's life.

The fact that the educational programmes were subject to evaluation probably accentuated the perception of this implicit motivational conflict.[3] The participants did not think of themselves as contributors to educational evaluations or to any other major political problems, and anyway the message to research subjects[4] is always a double one: in the context the research subjects are the most important people on earth, the chosen, those receiving attention – while at the same time they might immediately and with no special effect on the research agenda be substituted by somebody else.[5]

The subjective conflict outlined is interesting and its analysis can yield considerable inspiration to improvement or renewal of educational settings. The focus of this particular analysis, however, is on a number of "uncouth" outbursts of aggression, on collectively agreed statements about others, that were surprising and disquieting even in the relaxed and permissive context of research interviewing and discussion.

It may be argued that such outbursts belong to ordinary human communication and that they should be condoned. Every text production comprises irrelevancies, and is it not the function of the researcher to sort this out, to get the discussion back on the track, to condense the objective and impartial? In my approach: Not necessarily so! The very organization of the research group building on existing social organization aims at bringing out the explicit as well as the implicit substance and the legitimate as well as the illegitimate psychological energies immanent in the social setting. The presupposition is that "thinking is a highly emotional affair" (Becker-Schmidt, 1987), that factual and functional attitudes and opinions are products of multidimensional subjective processes that are cognitive, social, emotional as well as physical – and furthermore that the group processes contribute to the exposition of this complexity. The irrational, even the idiosyncratic, surplus is an invaluable spur to research. This is a point highly relevant for our conceptions of learning, e.g. in that it approaches the everyday situation in education where teachers and administrators often face diffuse complaint (cf. Weber, 2001b). I shall return in some detail to the theoretical framework, once I have presented the texts and my provisional analyses.

THE BODIES IN THE DEPARTMENT – ON THE PERCEPTION OF FEMALE SUPERIORS

During the thematized group discussion on the qualities of work – taking place immediately after a practice period in the hospital departments – life the following passage[6] occurs. It is one out of many where the perception of women become the defining theme of the discussion, and where the men in education for social- and health assistants denounce their female colleagues whose "cunt prat" or "cucumber cackle"[7] they overtly and explicitly detest:

> Steen: "Is there anything you've been provoked by, when you got out [in the departments of the hospitals KW]?"
>
> Mads: "That the women have so much power. It scared me somewhat in the first place [I was in KW]. There were two men there, and I saw very little of them, and the rest … they were women. It's just *a bit* strange, to sit there, among all those women, and to hear nappy-talk, and *birthings*, and all the time, you know, that sort of thing …".
>
> Lars: "Exactly!"
>
> Mads: "Like food recipes, clothes and make-up. It's simply impossible to join in. A man might as well keep his mouth shut".
>
> Steen: "So there is a culture in the place that you feel you don't belong to?"
>
> Mads: "But, yes, you know, I would actually like to talk. They are very nice, the women are, but it sort of scares you a bit, that there are just so many women

sitting there, you … you don't really have anything grand to contribute, you know … at least I feel I don't".

Lars: "I'll certainly confirm that … when they sit around talking about how sore their nipples are … from breast-feeding, you know."

Loud laughter around the table.

Peter: "Well, I was thinking, that it's something that affects the patients, these things, when we were talking about all that cuckoo …".

Several people make confirming noises.

Peter: "I said: "Actually, you know, it might have benefited the patients, all this time here!" … just wasting away every morning. All year round. Year out and year in. There's a bloody lot of resources there that just … and fuck the patients anyway".

Lars: It's also because there are some departments that are very particular about it, that now we have a break, isn't it? "Now we cannot talk anymore!" And it's psychiatric people around here, people that you cannot just treat like that, I feel".

Peter: "Like "Please hurry up and eat up, so that we can lay the table for us!". That way, that there attitude, I really can't stand".

Lars: "I remember that I was obliged to hold my breaks along with the rest of the regular staff. In that there women's department that I was in. Erh … and a … we only had that half hour break the whole day. And a, it [the work KW] was all about sitting and drinking coffee and chatting with patients and the like. And then, you know, I liked it, to go upstairs to play table tennis [with patients KW], in order to, sort of, get some exercise, you know. It was rather nice, you know, to just, like … instead of sitting down all the time. But they wouldn't have that. I was to sit down and have my break along with the rest of them, because, as they put it, it was about … and it did happen too, that they talked about patients, and the like. So it was important that we were there".

Peter sighs audibly.

Lars: "But I never experienced, not once, that the actually did talk about patients. It was always about those, well … those women's things".

Facts and Fiction

If we look first at the *factual content of the passage* the first striking thing is the very first reply by Mads, the willing admission that the most provoking thing about practice periods in psychiatric departments is not the psychiatric patients, the sometimes violent confrontations, the strenuous working conditions and night shifts – but "*that the women have so much power*". The general idea of the health sector is that the medical profession, the doctors, occupy the executive layers of the organization, both administratively and medically, and the statistical truth is that doctors are most often men.[8] The next striking thing is that the concrete exemplification of the alleged exertion of power is women who sit and talk – in general cultural terms that is the most powerless of images! Sitting, not moving; talking, not acting; self-contained, not directed against others. Furthermore the power talk is about children and childbirth – the latter certainly in a fundamental sense a powerful thing, but as a topic of conversation one could hardly think of a less belligerent one.

Further on in the passage a number of allegations are made about the staff wasting a lot of time on their job, not caring about the patients, being overly obsessed with negotiated rights such as regular breaks, and even being bossy towards patients as well denying trainees their breaks and lying about their professional commitment, alleging to speak professionally when in fact they are chatting about themselves. Of course we are in no positions to deny that these accusations may be true, but the assembled recriminations seem more fit for a political vendetta against the growing public sector than for a discussion of the learning experience of would be social and health assistants. Which is what is actually is.

On the other hand the passage conveys a culturally plausible image of female work place culture, which is indeed what the interviewer hears and interprets as an experience of exclusion on behalf of the men. This active definition of the initial tale is accepted – even to the degree that the men state their own innocence: they do want to talk! And to the degree that examples of explicit humiliation is given: a man has been denied the right to stand up and leave the table, he has been put in his place as if he were a child.

So on the referential level the passage is about women who talk about women's things and who do their job poorly, and about oppression and humiliation of men by women.

Communicative Dimensions

As the transcription hopefully communicates the passage was spoken with dedication and eagerness. Mads' opening answer is somewhat reluctant, only speeding up towards the end. The "somewhat scared" and the paradoxical "a bit" (strange) in fact means very much so, and furthermore Mads' comes up with a proper linguistic innovation the the phrasing of "birthings" thus stressing the strange quality of the situation, attributing a connotation of active giving birth, instead of just referring to childbirths as events of the past, and maybe even signifying that – at least for him – new experience is being formed in the situation. His experience is immediately confirmed (by Lars), elaborated ("food recipes, clothes and make-up") and followed up (by Lars: "sore nipples", "breast-feeding"). Later on the example of the female staff disregarding the patients is about taking the space for their own eating, and the scene where their power is exerted towards the trainee is that of "sitting and drinking coffee".

So the general characterization of the women's talk has to do not only with activities that are culturally connotated as belonging to a women's realm of experience, it also specifically about body, reproduction (babies sucking, women eating and drinking, food-recipes, babies' faeces), intimacy (mother-child dyade, sore nipples), and decorating the body (clothes and make-up) with a view to looks and possible seduction.

The general perception of the women is of their number (all those women, so many women), power and possession of space (the women's department) and the notion of their (in)activities is its all-consuming nature (all that cuckoo, all this time, every morning, all year round, day in and day out, bloody lot of resources, all about sitting and …, sitting down all the time) – concerned about themselves.

The general image of the men, on the contrary is that they are few, and not seen, that they might as well keep quiet, and that they do not have anything grand to contribute (or feel they don't). When Peter introduces the patients' perspective he not only offers a rational and professional framework for the dissatisfaction of the men, he directly inverts the psychologic states of the staff and the patients in that it's the staff's talk that is "cuckoo", not the psychiatric patients. Who are, in their turn, "affected", need the "time to benefit them", are degraded and neglected, and who "cannot just be treated like that". In short, the patients are characterized as suffering much in the same way as the men themselves, and their liberty to move about are even envied and sought for (in joining the table tennis).

As the men are thus denied their space they focus on and specify what they are not able to do: they are not able to contribute anything grand (as implicitly a man should presumably do) and they are not allowed to be physically active (rationalized into "getting some exercise" by Lars. As a result they are left to allege that they'd like to talk (i.e. do as the women do), to feel, to think, to be there. Paradoxically, what happens in the group discussion is actually that the men adopt the female standard of talking about themselves as well as mutually confirming their professional interest – taking on what is formally the women's obligation.

The conclusion of the passage holds special interest: The statement that the female staff is basically not concerned with their work "not once did they talk about the patients" is a direct contradiction of the preceding "it did happen too, that they talked about patients, and the like". The self-contradiction is triggered off by the colleague Peter's non-verbal reply. Peter's sigh seems to imply "they would *say* that, wouldn't they". The reference disturbs the by now established rational message and the shared emotional content of the communication immediately causes it to be censored.

Threatening Femininity

During the passage the emotional experience of being threatened, excluded and belittled, as well as being exposed to women's intimacies, is supplemented by a rational and professional concern about the patients. In the context, however, it is obvious that the patients are not analysed in their own right, but serve as objects of projection of the men's own perceptions and needs. The total image is that of the men being surrounded by and engorged by female passive-active flesh to an extent that it becomes necessary to break away, to get up and out. If the interpretation of the men collectively wishing to be reborn out of this institutionalized womb, the perceptual version of the scene of their labour market integration, is perhaps a dramatic one, it is, none the less, the one that emerges to the empathic reader sympathising with their lively and indignant communication.

As space for articulation of needs is denied they return in a rationalized (re)version. Accordingly the experience of women as strange and powerful self contained bodies is collectively confirmed, only to be stored in the experience of each man, ready to be activated in other situations of confrontations with women.

THE MISFITS IN THE CLASSROOMS – ON THE PERCEPTION OF PASSIVE CLASSMATES

During the group interview on possible improvements of the education for social work in youth clubs the following passage occurred.[9] It is just one example, and a fairly moderate and well argued one too, of participants talking derogatorily about their fellow students. The textual reproduction does not signal the speed of the lines or the vibrating anger of the group, nor does it catch the vehemence of the initial statement by Anna – on the factual surface she is simply stating:

> Anna: "There is one thing about the club education, though, and that is that when you start, that is on the first day, and people introduce themselves ... and it happens both here and on other courses ... you often hear that people are subject to rehabilitation [i.e. being supported by labour market authorities because of physical or social handicaps KW]. And it is maybe 15 or 20%, that represent, in a class, that actually **is** that. It's not as if there's any wrong in that, mind you, and I do agree that it's a fine thing to be social and to help a lot of people, but I do have a feeling that if you can't become anything else, or if you are unable to keep the job you once have, then you can always become a club pedagogue [Danish: Klubpædagog, the name of the un-skilled social workers in youth clubs KW]. And I can't help feeling that the education sort of falls down a bit because of that".
>
> Kenneth: "Not just those that have a bad back, but if they have problems that cannot be combined with our profession, then I think it's wrong. And there is much debate about it around, actually!
>
> Des: "Yes, but that is because people are so different here, and because their background is so mixed. And of course there are some that are not so used to these here things. To formulate things verbally or in writing, that is – you

can feel that, it's all very different, and the teachers must pay attention to the differences. And sometimes you feel that it's … a bit heavy … there must be space for all".

Anna: "And I absolutely do agree that there must, and I would not think it wrong if it were only a few, but it's many (…) And there's nobody around to look after people who maybe have a hard time. But I do think that the general level sort of drops because of that (…)".

Kenneth: "But they are allowed in along the same lines as everybody …".

Peter (interrupting): "No, no, I don't think so. There is a lot of people who do not have enough points, but who get in because of their background. It is basically a downgrading of our trade".

Anna: "That's my point. That's what I'm getting at. I think that the education is degraded".

Kenneth: "You get a world of problems later on, when you get out, when you have problems with yourself, and then have to work with other people who have problems. That's where it is bound to go totally wrong".

Val: "I don't think it's acceptable. I don't think we should just live with it, for I consider our way of working an important part of the life of young people. We are there to help them, and to guide them, and to instruct them, and it simply cannot be right that there are some people who have problems themselves, and who cannot tackle their own problems, and then to go in and work with children and youngsters (…) And for anybody to just come in from the street, apply for a club job, and the get it, because we need staff. That's dangerous, I feel".

Kenneth: "I agree. It cannot be right that any number of nut-cases can get into this. It's not that they are dyslectic, it's not that. (…) You can get a diploma here even if you have a severe alcohol problem. There are people here who have really grave problems with themselves … with alcohol or with other things … and it's them that a lot of people want out".

Peter: "But don't people sort that out for themselves?"

Val: "No, I'm not sure, because there are some who'd say that: I need to hang on to this because I need the 10.000 kroner every month. And there's no other way to get it".

Facts and Fiction

If we look, firstly, at the *factual content of the passage*, of the presentation of the educational context, a number of lines are arresting: The fact that some participants are subject to rehabilitation is verifiably true, but the registered number is exaggerated. Another stated fact is that some people are allowed in especially *because* they are handicapped, which is formally and empirically not possible. A third is that any nutcase can get in from the street and that you can get a diploma in spite of alcoholism, intimations that are basically unfounded.[10] On the whole the college is given little credit: It has few resources, it lets people in against rules, it accepts general dissipation, and hands out diplomas at random! This contrasts heavily with the explicit satisfaction with the education evident in other parts of the text.

So the impact of the passage is that the group – as opposed to the college – is concerned with a potential dilemma well known in education, namely how far a given education should accept participants that need special attention for social and health reasons, and that it is so concerned that some exaggeration is needed to convince the interviewer. The group is aware of this dilemma. Several lines meet with envisaged contradictions that they are discriminating people who do not deserve it, i.e. the bad backs and the dyslectics. The concern is on behalf of the status of the education, of the profession, and of the children and youngsters in the clubs.

Now, skilled and professional labour is actually in great demand in the Danish health and social sector. It is an acknowledged fact that there are "too many unskilled pedagogues" at work not only in clubs, but also in day care.[11] Furthermore the club sector by tradition recruits non-professional staff, and so it is vulnerable to general stigmatisation when staff problems occur – which invariably they do, as Kenneth confirms. So the arresting point here is not so much that the group points to a problem, but that in the public and administrative eye *they are themselves the very population that is problematic* in the sense that they are not formally qualified for their – societally important – job of socialisation and integration. That is why Danish municipalities demand that they complete the education programme that is the subject of our interview. Whether the individual participant suffers from a bad back or is recovering from drug abuse, whether he or she is in education – and working in the youth club – because he or she fell out of university, because the building industries are down or hairdressing is not much of a business these days – these facts are immaterial – both in the public eye, in the bureaucratic sense and as far as the educational measures are concerned. And contrary to the assumption of the group there is no documented covariance between rehabilitation, dyslexia, alcoholism and having problems with oneself.[12]

The concluding line, Val's accusation that the rehabilitating colleagues are strictly instrumentally, economically, motivated, is also strange. For it is generally agreed that more or less *everybody* in this education are dependent on upholding their income while they qualify. The education is designed for such people, for adults, with adult lives and obligations.

The characterization of the club pedagogue's task – as "helping, guiding and instructing" (Val) – is noticeable: It is true that working with the young is societally important,and that youth need reliable adults! But social advisors, school teachers and other professional groups would smile, to say the least, at the club pedagogue's ambitious self-understanding. Youth clubs do work with fringe groups, but much everyday life in youth clubs comprise a number of relaxed leisurely activities. Furthermore in the Danish context the references to the work as "profession" (Kenneth) and "our trade" (Peter) is peculiar. They signal a well defined line of work, social recognition and standards of quality – in short: professionality.[13] Actually the culturally established profile of the "club pedagogues" is that of the informal, comradely and loyal companion – undisturbed by professional distance, defying control and disciplinary dimensions of the job. This collective understanding of the sector is confirmed throughout the present project, and although it may be said to make a virtue out of necessity, it appears well founded in the subjective experience of the staff. If this syndrome is perhaps also nurtured by subjective and objective inferiority, it is at least a popular one … but it is remarkably absent in this passage. Here we meet professional concern only.

One interesting feature of the dialogue is the way factual corrections are turned around and used to opposite ends: The group denies the fact that the rehabilitating colleagues are allowed in along the general rules (as suggested by Kenneth) and it refutes the possibility that they might themselves be capable of assessing their competence (as imagined by Peter). Both attempts at modifying Anna's initial definition of the problem are used to further degrade the colleagues.

Finally the group builds consistent argument that people who "have problems with themselves", i.e. who are psychologically unstable, should not work in the caring professions, concluding that they are only in it for the money, anyway. The preoccupation with the psychological resources is a valid and recurrent debate all over the social and health sectors, and it does possess its own relevance in this short-term educational programme. But there is little, if any, reason that this general problem should arise in the context of the discussion.

So even at the surface level, where the text is confronted with the reality it refers to, the text has little value of information. In a positivist sense the group is not reliable. On the other hand the group is remarkably at ease with itself, it is in relative agreement – it is obviously telling us something important.

Communicative Dimensions

So how does the group go about it? Which features in their way of talking and which figures of speech convey the message to us? As above, the lines are spoken rapidly, with a high level of dedication, and there is a generally positive and corroborative atmosphere. People are eager and responding, almost echoing, and the energy grows steadily throughout the quoted passage.

As it turns out Anna's opening statement sets a theme, and also launches a pattern of formulation that are kept up by the group during the paragraph. Anna repeats a lot. She uses a number of parallel, slightly droning sentences, as well as literal repetitions. She feels, even if she allegedly doesn't want to – thus calling for explication of this conflict between emotion and rational argument. The theme is that of *the others*, developed as a definition of *intruders*. The imagery of intrusion is supplemented by that of the education *falling down*, and the general framework of *right and wrong* is introduced.

The intrusion is defined by the "wrong" presence of the others. Their getting *in*to the introduction is echoed all through: they make the *space* heavy, they are allowed *in* wrongly by the system, they go *in* the work, and they get *into* this, until at last they are wanted *out* – of the education, to prevent them from getting out in the workplaces.

Anna's perception is that the education "falls down a bit" as if the education might fall on her and bring her down. This is no error of translation, she actually uses this slightly awkward, very concrete image. Combined with the inevitability of the feeling the fear of falling is frightening. "A bit" is a paradoxical colloquialism, literally modifying, but substantially augmenting. It is echoed in the space getting "a bit heavy" (Des), and in the "sort of" dropping level (Anna herself). Finally the image is qualified in the "downgrading of our trade" (Peter) and the "degrading of the education" (Anna herself).

The theme of right and wrong is paradoxical from the outset: Anna distinguishes in the peculiar way that something is wrong (the number of participants in rehabilitation), which there's "nothing wrong in" because it's social and helpful and (therefore) right. It is within this paradoxical framework that she must modify her statement, she "can't help" feeling, despite herself. In her second remark Anna reiterates both structure and content of the first: She confirms her original "nothing wrong", assessing that "absolutely" must there be space for all – only not for all, because there are too many. She accelerates the discomfort by denying her own reassurance of the right, that she thinks wrong, you cannot do *that much* right, too much right makes wrong, and she substantiates her point by alluding to the (too small) resources of the college, again ending up in a down falling image, this time of the education dropping. The wrong is first substantiated by Kenneth, modified (into difference) by Des, enhanced by Kenneth (into totally wrong), civilized as well as dramatized (into not acceptable as well as downright dangerous) by Val, and confirmed (it cannot be right) by Kenneth, who also elaborates qualitatively as well as quantitatively on the danger: the intruders are nut-cases, they come in any number, their problems are severe and really grave, and the problem is alcohol as well as other things, intimating drug problems. The culmination of the definition of the wrong is the explication of the attitude of the others. They are dishonest, they are in the education on pretence.

Do Not Degrade Us!

Cris-crossing these consistent figures is the emotional presence of the "we" of the (insider) group as called upon by Anna's anxiety, as opposition to the others, who represent the explicit danger of the club-pedagogues being considered of no value ("if you can't become anything else") – a fear well-founded in the current hierarchies of the social and health labour market, a much wider problem with no direct connection to a possible number of misfits in the education. This is made explicit again when Anna – happily: "That's my point! That's what I'm getting at!" – answers Peter's "they are let in", where she also changes the "downgrading of the trade" to the "degrading of the education". She is herself *part of* the education, she is indeed *within it* in the very interview situation, so if the education is degraded, she is herself degraded. The unconscious thematic collusion of the group is: *We* do not want to be degraded. And at this point the more vicious attacks on the others (Kenneth's remark and Val's denunciation of their morals) have become legitimate. And the somewhat pompous sketch of our own importance in "helping, guiding and instructing" falls into place.

So the *real* danger is one facing the group itself, and the *unconscious* danger is that the degradation might be justified. After all "problems with oneself" and a fair amount of daily alcohol intake are not uncommon – neither with the population in general or with the low-skilled segment with an unstable labour market position that the group represents. Although in the interview situation the individuals come out as winners, there is no reason that they should not be as ambivalent facing the challenges of their job of social work as anybody else, and their labour market carriers are probably as mixed.[14] In structural terms the group represents one layer or level in a Chinese box, where income and cultural status form the objective foundation of individual and collective inferiority, substantiated by the imagined shortcomings of other professional groups.[15]

So as a result of the interview we have gained two results, neither of which are directly relevant to the evaluation project: One is that it takes very little to bring out an intolerant and aggressive attitude towards people with social problems in the club pedagogues to be – the exact opposite of what the educational impact should ideally be, and one which seriously questions the general suitability of the unskilled social workers to their jobs. I.e. the group manages to produce the exact opposite of their more or less conscious intention. Another is that the club pedagogues-to-be are in serious need of recognition. Below I shall discuss how and why the educational setting and the position of being a student may contribute to these two states of mind.

INDIVIDUALS, TEXTS AND GROUP DYNAMICS

The individuals who spoke the lines quoted were brought together in their special capacities as participants in an educational setting that was being explored and evaluated. They brought into the research setting not only their shared experience of the educations, but also the general experience of their everyday life and their respective life histories. In this respect they are representative[16] of the unskilled populations that in current years are more or less willingly training or retraining for the changing and increasingly qualifications demanding labour market. Their labour market experience is a mixed bag: this segment of the labour force is the one to immediately feel ups and downs of trades and the general economy. Participants' experience comprises a number of contradictory motivations. The jobs headed for are much wanted, if not for their content then for the income. The road to get there is, however, paved with a number of imposed regressions, the structural position of a pupil perhaps being the most basic and at the same time the most challenging.

So the general background of experience is contradictory – jobs wanted, training unwanted, followed by training accepted, and infantile position unwanted.[17] We are not surprised that there is an explicit need to let out some steam of aggression, for these adult pupils have surely had a number of reasons to be angry along their ways, and have not been offered appropriate arenas for voicing their experience and putting it into words.

The group communication will implicitly and sometimes explicitly appeal to each participant to search emotionally and cognitively for the shared experience of the group.[18] Of course the experience of the research setting is immediately shared, as is the implicit subjective pressure to contribute. The interview situation bears some structural resemblance to the teaching, which holds its own kind of pressure, and the teaching in its turn refers to the work situation, which holds another kind of pressure. It may even be argued that the interplay between these levels of experience of pressure is in itself anxiety provoking and will produce regressive resistance. So if there is anxiety around it is sure to be exposed, and as we have seen in the texts, it does, and it is managed by means of collective rationalization.[19]

So voicing shared experience referring to any of these levels invariably brings about qualities of perception that cannot be understood in terms of the factual events referred to only. The challenges of social work and dealing with patients have long ago activated emotions, strategies of action and understandings from other phases of the life course, from family settings as well as from other workplaces. In the communication a gradual and intuitive selection of experience suitable in the group takes place, and emotional qualities and intellectual insights are attributed to the common production of meaning. This does not happen randomly, but not in a purely rational manner either. Contributions are formed in a subjective navigation between the reservoirs of individual experience and the theme perceived developing in the group. In this respect the research setting actually reproduces a characteristic of everyday life communication, where the attitudes and emotions of people are often not articulate until they are offered a communicative arena, until they are voiced in a social situation. The group thus develops its own explicit meaning, drawing on dimensions of experience, and indeed formulations, from the individual participants, who in their turn have contributed, not what they are, who they are, or what they think, but what this setting and communication allowed them to feel, remember and articulate – and avoid. The meaning developed by the group is not simply the sum of the attitudes and opinions of the participants, nor are the participants victims of external group dynamics. The group produces a unique and original text that communicates shared experience, not exhaustingly so, but relevant and carefully voiced dimensions of experience.

RECOGNITION, AGGRESSION AND EDUCATIONAL RESULTS

The two empirical populations have produced texts that explicitly and implicitly voices the need for personal and professional recognition by superiors and by society. They have also “texted” a professional concern – for the well-being of psychiatric patients and for the reputation of the education for social pedagogic work in clubs – thus legitimizing not only their demand for recognition, but also their apparent emotional state of readiness to perceive degradation and humiliation.

In both cases, however, the groups verbalized their messages in a roundabout manner by abusing a specific population of others, indeed they collectively constructed the female nursing staff and the rehabilitating colleagues respectively, not only as less able populations, but as morally corrupt as well. The images produced and confirmed each correspond depressingly well with a number of cultural cliches active in popular or populist political rhetoric and in everyday folklore. As recognizable figures they serve to simplify and thus make bearable the complex and multitudinous experience of everyday life, and as organizers of subjective collective energy they contribute powerfully to corrupting political civilization and gender equality. It is safe to say that the attitudes texted above are not the intended outcome of the respective training programmes. They have certainly nothing to do with neither the formal curriculum nor with the intended communication of workplace culture or general political implications of being public sector social service staff. They even disavow the professional ethos that they serve to establish in the texts.

So have the educations been counterproductive? Is the educational outcome that poor? And are the individuals so politically blind (labelling socially deprived groups) and so male chauvinist?

Hopefully not. My exposition of the regressive images in the collective unconscious of the groups is on the one hand a research produced artefact that – on the other hand – exposes a potential of subjective energies, organized within the framework of the consciousness of everyday life (Leithäuser, 1977). A general cultural disposition to employ reductive schemes of understanding in complex and challenging situations is reproduced. The interpretation has focussed on the frightening aspects of the collective subjectivity – with good reason, I should think – but the texts themselves comprise reference to the contradictions reacted to. There is a framework of ambition of being and doing “right” in the club pedagogues’ discussion and beyond the aggression of the men in the psychiatric hospital we can actually detect some sound observation of a routinized and (too?) highly gendered workplace culture.

So the scapegoat figures of munching women and morally corrupt colleagues are also *inversions of a general humanist and/or professional ethic* – the claim that education and social work should be for the benefit of the users – children, youngsters, patients, etc. In fact random elements of such ethics are employed to construct the villainous images. And in present day institutionalised and bureaucratic public sector such ambitions, however fragmented they stand, are no irrelevant agenda.

My general line of arguments has been that the interplay between lacks of recognition at different levels of experience is decisive in producing the defensive reductions. So the experience atclassroom level does come into it.

So what characterises the classroom experience: A double agenda of accepting to be a pupil and a curriculum of welfare state legislation, psychology, pedagogy, cultural studies, etc. – very much about the very situation that is reacted to, but in both training programmes, in abstract and general terms. Indeed the men in the hospital faced a number of physics and chemistry lessons at the level of 7th grade, but that was difficult enough. And although teachers strive to meet the subjective experience of the work they are qualifying people for, they work within a set of rules describing the context of the education in terms of subjects and disciplines, not as experienced problems.

In educational terms these analyses thus point to the relevance of problem-oriented curricula, and to the need of explicitly reflecting the background experience and the subjective motivations of participants within the framework of education. It also reminds us that teachers should respect that subjective motivations are only one version of the multitudinous sensations and perceptions that adults possess – aggression may be an integral part of regressive defences as well as progressive orientations.

Finally, as stated at the outset of this chapter, a number of the mixed and functionally inappropriate motivations are in fact embodiments of the economic and societal paradoxes that constitute everyday life in and around education: Adult pupils, soldiers in nursing, men in women's jobs – are empirical evidence of contradictory demands of modernization, rationalization and labour market development. If they appear irrational, history is irrational, and a rational appropriation process will reflect it.

A REMARK ON THE METHODOLOGY

The general framework of my interpretation is that of a psychoanalytically oriented social psychology, that acknowledges preconscious and unconscious dimensions and dynamics in everyday life communication. It also appreciates participants' life history experience, the everyday life experience and the interplay between these subjective reservoirs.

In contrast to the well known clinical psychoanalysis, this approach is concerned with general cultural patterns of subjectivity, where a potential of politics of repression as well as of liberation is stored. Of course collective subjectivity is constituted by the interaction of individuals, and by the collusion of individual drives and dispositions. It might, for example, be productive to see the aggression of the men in the hospital as collectively re-iterated scenes of primary socialization, where identifications with mother and father respectively comprised not only "becoming like", but also counter-positioning, fights and ambivalent possession. For the men are under regressive pressure, they are infantilised and denied their status (and identity) as men. It is likewise interesting to consider the discriminating and rigid appropriation of "right" by the club pedagogues as an identification with a mighty if abstract aggressor – in momentary need of more specific, tangible and realistic ideals. Such deepening of the current analysis is indeed possible, but the procedure might create the impression that I was aiming at a redefinition of the educational setting into a form of collective therapy.

Although I am sure that educational settings are often the arenas of subjective liberation, including liberation from inner compulsions, the therapeutic fallacy (Alheit, 1994) is not mine. The primary socialization of participants is only relevant in this context insofar as it is activated and becomes decisive in the interaction, in the production of the meaning of everyday culture – including that of education. In that context the energies and search processes of participants must be respected – indeed they cannot be substantially changed without counterproductive effects. They must find their own – devious – ways (cf. Weber, 1995).

Learning and socialization is always a progressive-regressive process, and it always activates the inner resources of the learner. So the focus of the educationally relevant analysis is on the interaction with reality and on how it is voiced.

So a social psychology that draws on the tradition of psychoanalysis faces the theoretical challenge of understanding subjective energies not as natural instincts or fateful drives, but as energies organizing reality. This is the ambition of the German social psychologist Alfred Lorenzer, who defines drives with a view to societal and interactional logics meeting with the individual in primary and secondary socialization, shaping subjectivity but also being changed by the specific ways in which the logics are appropriated (Lorenzer, 1970, 1972). The concepts of ambivalence as defined by the Hungarian psychoanalyst Sandor Ferenczi: inner ambivalence stems from the contradictory qualities of reality, not from the confrontation of libido and thanatos (Ferenczi, 1972), as well as the whole tradition of object relations theory (e.g. Winnicott, 1987) point to the same concern for the outside world. With Lorenzer, however, it is an explicit point that unconscious processes themselves are not just products of individual repression, but societally produced ones. Life history is thus an ongoing process of socialization, not just an adaptation of individuals to reality, but a dynamic continuation of society and culture as such: Subjectivity is society in a specific historical and social mediation of individual sensation – bodily, emotional, cognitive perceptions – with language as the primary medium. The approach has been succesfully developed into a psychoanalytically oriented understanding of culture in general, comprising not only literature and media analyses, but also understandings of architecture, physical space in general, etc. (Lorenzer, 1986). Theorizing everyday life is a well established tradition in cultural studies and sociology, and the very concepts of every day life is developed into a theory of late modern consciousness by Thomas Leithäuser, who sees the different sections of everyday life as arenas of experience, adapting to necessities, repressing socially illegitimate sensations and reactions as well as developing wishes and ambitions. Leithäuser's concept of consciousness of everyday life point to the fact that attitudes and opinions may be-understood as pragmatic and situated – individual or collective – subjectivity, thus questioning the established concept of identity, as well as indeed the validity of any positivist registration of attitudes. Together with Birgit Volmerg and the Institute of Psychology and Social Research in Bremen the approach has produced a number of empirical studies, comprising workplace experience and experience in public space (Volmerg et al., 1986, 1994, Leithäuser, 1999).

Integrating a Marxian analysis of society – the separation of private and public sphere and the logics of production and reproduction – with psychoanalytical social psychology, Regina Becker-Schmidt et al. have produced a number of analyses of women's experience in work and family life. Becker-Schmidt applies the Ferencian concept of ambivalence as well as concepts of identification processes to the field of girls' and women's lives, and she contributes substantially to a gender-specific and historically sensitive understanding of socialization (e.g. 1995, 1998; see also Chapter 4, this volume).

The brief account of the approaches hardly do them justice, but they each served as inspiration to the analysis presented above. The theorizing of learning settings gains by a societal dimension that can see actions and attitudes, not as individual fallacies or shortcomings, but as valid reactions to complex and partly invisible logics. Before concluding this chapter I shall elaborate somewhat the underlying understanding of our media of communication – language.

LANGUAGE GAMES AND INTERACTION-FORMS

Language as an integral dimension of interaction and bodily experience has been theorized by Alfred Lorenzer, who sees the dynamics of subjectivity – of inner nature – and societal structure as authentically experienced bodily interactions, established as interaction-forms. They constitute the basic socialization, and they are progressively differentiated and refined as language is introduced. Only language also serves to render some interaction-forms acceptable, while others remain as bodily perceptions, pre-verbal – but none the less psychologically active. The basic epitome of the interaction-form is the mother and child, the dyad – not only because this stage in socialization holds importance, but also because it serves to illustrate the dialectic of refinement and deprivation that socialization is about. No verbalization, no establishment of symbolic interaction, takes place without leaving something behind, organizing perceptions, leaving some out and "forgetting" them systematically. Pre-verbal interaction forms melt into the symbolic ones as interaction-forms and language relate. Lorenzer ses this process as a potential for later reflected experiments (in the psychoanalytic sense: Probehandlungen) of action and expression.

Lorenzer's ambition is to theorize language, interaction and bodily experience in the context of their mutual societal settings and functions. The concept of language game, which stems originally from Wittgenstein, situates language practically and societally. The language game is a complex unity of the actual use of language, its practical functions and the general understanding of its life world. It mediates subjective and objective structures, and its genesis is indeed the constitution of the relation between individual and society. Language and consciousness are integral parts of societal praxis, and language games are accordingly the medium of subjective structuring of reality. In this sense individual subjectivity is societal from the outset.

In an intact language game the agents share pre-verbal interaction-forms as well as its specific verbalization, in language becoming a symbolic interaction-form – in short: that agents understand each other and empathically share explicit and implicit meanings.

Lorenzer introduces the concept of disturbed language to understand the process of the "re-division" of language games. Once accomplished competencies of symbolization – putting subjective structures to language – may, in specific situations, that recalls and activates inner conflict, cease to work. The capacity of expressing subjective experience is lost facing the confrontation of contradictory and irreconcilable interaction-forms. Pre-verbal interaction forms that have never been integrated into the language games at all may well be part of such conflict, although they are systematically left over to the unconscious. In such cases language is unfounded in experience, the words stand stripped of authentic meaning. Lorenzer uses the concept of sign about this language with no foundation in interaction-forms. Accomplished symbolic interactions may also be broken up for psychodynamic and/or societal reasons, the word stripped of its symbolic meaning, but still representing dynamic inner scenes – which, in their turn, may be activated without access to relevant means of communication.

Language games will not only echo interest and power relations in the social situation, they will also develop meanings of their own, register and comprise factual as well as implicit cultural and psychological meaning. They are dialectical unities of the use of language, everyday life as it is in fact lived practically, and the attitudes, opinions and ideologies it develops and makes use of. In the research situation we have "only" the words, but if we look at the communications in terms of a language game we have also a symbolic life world.

In the language game subjective structures are mediated with reality, with social and societal structures. When the appropriation of reality demands emotional or cognitive accommodation the language becomes vague, which gives the communication of everyday life its well known specific quality of implicit congeniality, of indefinite allusions that comprise a variety os different sensations and recollections. To each individual words and concepts possess an aura of implicit meanings founded in earlier experience, and in interaction and communication these meanings are sorted out and established as new collective formulations, that merge with the general cultural reservoir – confirming and changing culture. In this process factual information and authentic experience may find words – become symbolized – but as we have seen they may also be censored, withdrawn, only to sink back into the pre-verbal consciousness of individuals and institutions.

The club pedagogues certainly go through a process of negotiating and sorting out the relevant phrases before their implicit aggressions are finally focussed on the "danger" and dubious morals of the rehabilitating colleagues, whereas the men in the psychiatric hospital immediately share both a vocabulary and a cultural image of femininity. The former are bringing together vague anxieties stemming from number of different settings, whereas the latter have recently faced much the same challenges, which they can therefore readily communicate. Maybe the common gendered experience contributes to the immediate collusion in the male group. The cultural cliche of "cunt prat" actually brings together the subjects of the women's talk with the otherwise tabooed sexual connotations – not only implicit in the men's perception, but certainly in the workplace culture as well as in society in general.

On this background we may look at the text as a frozen version of specific interaction. We may look at the referential level, which is immediately understood because words refer to recognizable objects and situations, and where the cultural connotations are shared. As I have shown even this level raises a number of questions: the texts each possess a referential value that is unknown to the interviewer or discussion leader, and which he, in his turn, tries to come to terms with – as Steen, who does not personally share the emotional content of the communication, translating into the more general concepts of workplace culture. Of course the interviewer may simply get new information, but in the texts above, we are given to wonder, because the information we get does not agree with our existing knowledge of the field: We are cognitively as well as emotionally aroused. We think we know, for instance, that the administrators of the club education are not reckless – and we are disturbed by the prospect of alcoholics in social work. We react on behalf of the general cultural framework: this cannot or should not be so.[20]

So we move on to other potential sources of information in the text, to the communicative dimension and to be empathic on the communicative level as well: How does the mode of communication add or detract from the phrases, and which figures of rhetoric are employed?

By confronting these levels of reading, answering the research question: How do they talk about what? In this process new structures of subjective meaning, embracing implicit meanings as well as explicit ones, are formed, and we approach a motivational and perhaps an experiential, perceptual understanding.

Such understanding might inspire adult education to some abstaining from directing the learning processes towards specific curricular goals, and to a critical reflection of the relation between teaching and learning in general. People learn what they want to learn – and their rich ambitions of being recognized themselves as well as changing the world for the better are much easier developed if they are allowed to – and supported in – sorting out their ambiguities and reflecting on them.

NOTES

1 The evaluations were designed as theory based and qualitative, and the empirical material produced within the research context of the "Life History Project", a long term project on the subjective interplay between adult education, every day life and life history (Weber, 1997c, 1999b; Andersen,

2000; Salling Olesen, 2000a, 2000b). The Danish evaluation reports are Nielsen and Weber (1997), Weber (1997a), Lund and Weber (2000), as well as Weber (1997b) and presentations of analyses in English are Weber (1996, 1998, 1999a).

2 Besides myself: Research assistant cand.mag. Steen Baagøe Nielsen (now associated professor at Roskilde University), and research assistant cand.pæd. Uffe Lund, presently an education officer at the pedagogues′ union in Denmark.

3 The evaluations were financed by the County of Western Seeland and by the Ministry of Social and Health. Each in their way they were characteristic measures of the current transformation of the public sector in Denmark, that aims to change the traditional welfare state into an so-called "responsive state" – in this case in the sense that the public labour force must be (made) flexible. This theoretical and political discourse falls without the scope of this chapter, see, however, Weber (2001a).

4 The concept of "research subjects" referring to the population of informants and participants stem from Hollway and Jefferson (2000). It signals the dynamic and autonomous status of the people involved as opposed to the status of objects under positivist scrutiny.

5 The methodological implications of this double bind is a research field in itself. Likewise the different modes of text production, the informing group interview (cf. e.g. Kvale, 1996) and the thematized group discussion (cf. Cohn, 1976; Mangold, 1960; Leithäuser & Volmerg, 1985) represent separate fields of interest. In the present context, however, only the fact that the texts are group produced, and the fact that they comprise culturally significant outbursts of aggression, are looked into.

6 The group discussion leader is Steen Baagøe Nielsen, and the passage is translated from the evaluation report (see above, pp. 139–140).

7 Direct translations of the Danish "kussepladder" and "agurkesnak", both original and striking verbal innovations of a highly derogatory nature – from other group discussions of the men in the project.

8 This is actually changing in Denmark. The medical profession presently recruits a majority of women, but firstly this has not yet changed the work-places, and secondly it is still true that executive positions are held mainly by men. I.e. a horizontal gender barrier has been moved, but a vertical one remains.

9 The interviewer is Uffe Lund, and the passage stems from the background material of chapter 5 of the evaluation report (see above, p. 57 ff.).

10 The verifications of these facts with the administrative authorities of the college is solid. The identification of factual faults or inconsistencies in the communication is not motivated by any drive to "correct" things, but is a means to identify the energy and motivations present in the group. Of course evaluators and researchers should not communicate gossip and rumour as such, but in this approach gossip and rumour communicates something important besides their factual irregularities. So we take it on face value, we test it against the reality that we know something of, but which we may also learn about.

11 This is due to the educational policies of the liberal government in the 80'es, which restricted access to human service training and education considerably.

12 In fact some of the texts in this project could support the opposite thesis: A number of the rehabilitating colleagues appear lively, intelligent and well motivated participants with a realistic attitude to their handicap. Whereas some of the university drop outs could be said to signal problems of self esteem, and some of the skilled workers to manage the shift from production to social work less than well. But these are mere assumptions, associations in the research team, who have obviously been severely provoked by the group's unanimous problem identification. In it inherent in our approach not to censor such associations, but to register them, and to confront them with the text. You can say that at first we serve as a screen on to which the allegations of the group are projected. And next we react, and serve as a complementary mirror. Neither the construction of the group nor the associations of the research team are "true" in the literal sense, but they each constitute possible perceptions and dimensions of experience.

13 Not even the professional educations of 3½ or 4 years' duration – such as those of pedagogue, nurse or school teacher – can claim proper professional identity in the strict sociological sense, and when they try current modernization quickly get the better of them with further demands of flexibility and employability (Weber, 2001a; Salling Olesen, 2000b).

14 The life history of the group was not focussed on in the interviews. But we know what they are doing: Anna's task in the leisure centre is in the kitchen, where she bakes with the school children every afternoon; Kenneth dropped out of technical college and has made a career of working in the national organization of youth clubs, thus so far making further education unnecessary; Des is an immigrant with ten years of unskilled social work behind him, specialising in computer games and music; Peter is young and has no education or labour market experience other than that in the social project he is employed in; Val has an education as a teacher of textile work, i.e. she is working beneath her status, but indeed she does run the sewing workshop in her workplace.

15 Thus traditional profiling school-teachers-pedagogues, pedagogues-unskilled staff, unskilled staff-unemployed, etc. are well known. Of course they have their objective foundation in different status of the societal tasks, of income and status, but they are often voiced with more vigour than the objective differences would vouch.

16 This is not a question of statistical reliability, although by age and labour market position the populations may well mirror their social strata. Within the context of the club education the groups have been composed with a view to comprising the most characteristic empirical profiles – gender-wise and by educational background. The men in the hospital are simply those allocated from the local unemployment authorities, and so they represent the profile of qualifications demand in Western Seeland. Both populations are plausible examples of unskilled adults in education. For a discussion of validity in qualitative research see Kvale (1991) and Altheide and Johnson (1998).

17 At an individual level, with each adult man or woman it is of course much more complex. Some adults actually want the training, but not the job. Class and gender form different foundations for handling the dilemma. But in a strategy of theorizing the motivational conflicts one has to simplify, in this case by stating a common structural dilemma.

18 The underlying references here are the tradition from Pollock onwards, the group therapy (Foulkes) and communication in groups (Bion).

19 The analysis might at this point be extended in terms of exposing institutionalised defence mechanisms, cf. e.g. Menzies-Lyth.

20 Of course the individual characteristics of the researcher come into this process, both in the face to face interaction and in the interpretation. So we should reflect our idiosyncrasies and, our loyalties as well as our theoretical perspective in terms of transference and counter-transference. For a discussion see e.g. Hunt (1989) and Andersen (2001).

REFERENCES

Alheit, P. (1994). The biographical question as a challenge to adult education. *International Review of Education, 40*, 283–298.

Altheide, D. L., & Johnson, J. M. (1998). Criteria for assessing interpretive validity in qualitative research. In K. D. Norman & S. L. Yvonna (Eds.), *Collecting and interpreting qualitative materials*. London: Sage Publications.

Andersen, A. S., Andersen, L. , Dybbroe, B., Hutters, C., & Weber, K. (Eds.). (2001). *Bøjelighed og Tilbøjelighed. Livshistoriske perspektiver på læring og uddannelse* (3rd Report from the Life History Project). Roskilde: Roskilde University Press.

Andersen, L. (2000). *Telling modernization: Three voices. life history, gender and the discourse of modernization* (Paper No. 8). Roskilde: Life History Project, Roskilde University. Adult Education Research Group.

Andersen, L. (2003). When the unconscious joins the game: A psychoanalytic perspective on modernization and change. *Forum for Qualitative Social Research, 4*(3), Article 26.

Becker-Schmidt, R. (1995). Von Jungen, die keine Mädchen, und Mädchen, die gerne Jungen sein wollten. Geschlechterspezifische Umwege auf der Suche nach Identität. In R. Becker-Schmidt & G.-A. Knapp (Eds.), *Das Geschlechterverhältnis als Gegenstand der Sozialwissenschaften*. Frankfurt: Campus.

Becker-Schmidt, R. (1998). Trennung, Verknüpfung, Vermittlung: Zum femnistischen Umgang mit Dichotomien. In G.-A. Knapp (Ed.), *Kurskorrekturen. Feminismus zwischen Kritischer Theorie und Postmoderne*. Frankfurt: Campus.

Cohn, R. (1976). *Von der Psychoanalyse zur themenzentrierte Interaktion.* Stuttgart: Klett-Cotta.
Ferenczi, S. (1972/1926). *Das Problem der Unlustbejahung. In Schriften zur Psychoanalyse.* Frankfurt am Main: Fischer.
Hollway, W., & Jefferson, T. (2000). *Doing qualitative research differently. Free association, narrative and the interview method.* London: Sage Publications.
Hunt, J. (1989). *Psychoanalytical aspects of fieldwork. Qualitative research method series, No. 18.* London: Sage Publications.
Kvale, S. (1991). *Issues of validity in qualitative research.* Lund: Studentlitteratur.
Kvale, S. (1996). *Interviews. An introduction to qualitative research interviewing.* London: Sage Publications.
Leithäuser, T. (1977). *Formen des Alltagsbewusstseins.* Frankfurt: Campus.
Leithäuser, T. (Ed.). (1999). *Sicherheit im öffentlichen Raum. Alltägliche Gewalterfahrungen im Stadtteil. Sonderheft Arbeit und Politik.* Bremen: Akademie für Arbeit und Politik.
Leithäuser, T., & Volmerg, B. (1985). *Psychoanalyse in der Sozialforschung. Eine Einführung am Beispiel einer Sozialpsychologie der Arbeit.* Opladen: Westdeutscher Verlag.
Lorenzer, A. (1970). *Sprachzerstörung und Rekonstruktion. Vorarbeiten zu einer Metatheorie der Psychoanalyse.* Frankfurt: Suhrkamp.
Lorenzer, A. (1972). *Zur Begründung einer materialistischen Sozialisationstheorie.* Frankfurt: Suhrkamp.
Lorenzer, A. (1986). *Kulturanalysen. Psychoanalytische Studien zur Kultur.* Frankfurt: Fischer.
Lund, U., & Weber, K. (2000). *Kort og godt? Læring, kvalificering og effekt i klubuddannelse og klubarbejde.* Adult Education Research Group, Roskilde University.
Mangold, W. (1960). *Gegenstand und Methode des Gruppendiskussionsverfahrens.* Frankfurt: Europïsche Verlagsanstalt.
Nielsen, S. B., & Weber, K. (1997). *Jagten på den mandlige omsorgskompetence.* Adult Education Research Group, Roskilde University.
Salling Olesen, H. (Ed.). (1995). *Adult education and the labour market II.* Papers from the 2nd Seminar of the ESREA research network, Strobl, Adult Education Research Group, Roskilde University & Bundesinstitut für Erwachsenenbildung St. Wolfgang, Austria.
Salling Olesen, H. (Ed.). (1998). *Adult education and the labour market IV.* Papers from the 4th Seminar of the ESREA network on adult education and the labour market, Dubrovnik, Adult Education Research Group, Roskilde University.
Salling Olesen, H. (2000a). *Experience and life history life history project* (Paper No. 9). Adult Education Research Group, Roskilde University.
Salling Olesen, H. (2000b). Professional identity as learning processes in life histories. *Journal of Workplace Learning, 13*(7–8), 290–298.
Salling Olesen, H., & Forrester, K. (Eds.). (1999). *Adult education and the labour market V.* Papers from the 5th Seminar of the ESREA research network, Dubrovnik, Roskilde University Press, Roskilde.
Salling Olesen, H., & Rasmussen, P. (Eds.). (1996) *Theoretical issues in adult education. Danish research and experience.* Roskilde: Roskilde University Press.
Volmerg, B., Senghass-Knobloch, E., & Leithäuser, T. (1986). *Betriebliche Lebenswelt. Einer Sozialpsychologie industrieller Arbeitsverhältnisse.* Opladen: Westdeutscher Verlag.
Volmerg, B., Leithäuser, T., Neuberger, O., Ortmann, G., & Sievers, B. (1994). *Nach alle Regeln der Kunst.Macht und Geschlecht in Organisationen.* Frankfurt: Kore.
Weber, K. (1995). Learning processes in trade union education. What do unskilled women actually learn? In H. Salling Olesen (Ed.), *Adult education and the labour market II.* Adult Education Research Group, Roskilde University & Bundesinstitut für Erwachsenenbildung St. Wolfgang, Austria.
Weber, K. (1996). Experiencing gender – And a case of masculinity and social work. In H. Salling Olesen & P. Rasmussen (Eds.), *Theoretical issues in adult education. Danish research and experience.* Roskilde: Roskilde University Press.
Weber, K. (1997a). *SSA – mand!* [Social and health assistant – Man!]. Adult Education Research Group, Roskilde University.
Weber, K. (1997b). Køn, klasse og subjektivitet. Om erfaringsbegrebet i uddannelsesforskningen. [Gender, class and subjectivity. On the concept of experience in educational research]. In K. Weber

(Ed.), *SSA – mand!* [Social and health assistant – Man!]. Adult Education Research Group, Roskilde University.

Weber, K. (Ed.). (1997c). *Life history, gender and experience. theoretical approaches to adult life and learning* (1st report of the Life History Project). Roskilde University, Adult Education Research Group.

Weber, K. (1998). The hunt for the masculine competence for care. Qualification between labour market integration and feminization? In H. Salling Olesen (Ed.), *Adult education and the labour market IV*. Roskilde: Adult Education Research Group, Roskilde University.

Weber, K. (1999a). Insights into necessities … In H. Salling Olesen & K. Forrester (Eds.), *Adult education and the labour market V*. Roskilde: Roskilde University Press.

Weber, K. (1999b). *Concepts of life history and biography: Understanding lifelong learning?* (Paper No. 4)., Life History Project). Roskilde University, Adult Education Research Group.

Weber, K. (Ed.). (2001a). *Experience and discourse* (2nd report from the Life History Project). Roskilde University Press.

Weber, K. (2001b). Brok, brok, brok – om hverdagsliv, livshistorie og ambivalens i læreprocesser [Nag, nag, nag – On everyday life, life history and ambivalence in learning processes]. In A. S. Andersen (Ed.), *Bøjelighed og Tilbøjelighed. Livshistoriske perspektiver på læring og uddannelse* (3rd Report from the Life History Project). Roskilde: Roskilde University Press.

Weber, K., Nielsen, B. S., & Salling Olesen, H. (Eds.). (1997). *Modet til fremtiden. Inspirationen fra Oskar Negt* [Courage for the future. The inspiration from Oskar Negt]. Roskilde: Roskilde University Press.

Winnicott, D. W. (1965/1987). *The maturational process and the facilitating environment*. London: Hogarth.

KARSTEN MELLON

5. THE MILK LADY

A Nurturing Identification Object

This chapter presents results from the research project conducted as part of my PhD dissertation. Divided into two parts, the chapter begins with a contextualisation of the research project, which concerns students who use an alternative channel to enrol in a profession-specific education as a social pedagogue. The concept of non-traditional adult student is also defined. For readers unfamiliar with the Danish system, a brief description is provided of the profession of social pedagogue as well as the Danish practice of Validation of Prior Learning (VPL). Next, there is a short, introductory presentation of the life history research approach.

The second part of the chapter involves an analysis of a student enrolled in a professional bachelor degree programme. The case focuses on a non-traditional adult student who changed careers. Her name is Hanna and she was accepted into the programme on the basis of VPL, and is studying to be a social pedagogue. The analysis examines how Hanna while contributing to and benefitting from the study environment acquires a new professional identity as a social pedagogue. She emphasises her relationship with her mother as important to her choice of education. The way she paints her future, the role as a professional she anticipates and her experience of the degree programme appear to expose some contradictory aspects, which call for an interpretation of her relationship with her mother, who worked as the milk lady at Hanna's school when she was growing up.

NON-TRADITIONAL ADULT STUDENTS

The notion of the non-traditional student originates from the Anglo-Saxon term non-traditional adult student (Alheit, 2017) and is currently defined in multiple ways, though there appears to be a general European consensus on a common understanding of the term. Crosling et al.'s (2008) international study Improving Student Retention in Higher Education points out five categories used regularly in international access and retention studies to identify non-traditional students: (1) low socioeconomic status, (2) disabilities, (3) first in family to participate in higher education, (4) mature age and (5) minorities and refugees, which is also a recognised definition in the European Union (Meyers, Conte, & Rubenson, 2014). The term non-traditional adult student, however, must be used with caution as it is imprecise and defining it with precision is not possible since various students are considered

© KONINKLIJKE BRILL NV, LEIDEN, 2020 | DOI: 10.1163/9789004420274_006

traditional by some but non-traditional by others. The VPL students under study in this chapter are primarily mature-age students, including Hanna, studying to be a social pedagogue. In the Danish context, these students most often have a vocational educational background. In recent decades, policymakers in Denmark emphasised prior informal and non-formal learning in the effort to provide additional educational opportunities for non-traditional adult students (Aagaard & Dahler, 2010).

THE PATH TO ENROLMENT IN A SOCIAL PEDAGOGUE PROGRAMME

Since the end of the twentieth century lifelong learning has developed into a global political agenda (CEDEFOP, 2016). Despite consensus concerning the potential of lifelong learning on, for example, overall joint interests and visions, the group of stakeholders are far from clear-cut (Field, 2008). In general, lifelong learning is a field of political processes in constant motion (Salling Olesen, 2002, p. 4), influenced by business interests, concern for individuals' personal development and also local interests of e.g. education institutions. Learning opportunities in working life and education are central to lifelong learning and are based on a constant review of one's current skills and the acquisition of new ones (Merrill & Hill, 2003). The key interests for our study are the learning potential, capacity and adaptability of individuals to become competent while simultaneously increasing their self-awareness and sense of dignity as a responsible citizen (Singh & Duvekot, 2013, p. 16). Salling Olesen (2017, p. 37) points out that lifelong learning as an imperative can be viewed as a response to the overriding pressure put on people concerning plasticity and readjustment that stems from capitalistic functionality.

VPL in adult education has a strong tradition in Denmark and the other Nordic countries, though approaches vary regarding policy development, systems, solutions and practical implementation. In 2007, a crucial year for the acknowledgment and development of adult education in the context of lifelong learning, adults in Denmark became entitled to have their prior learning, i.e. what they know and can do, recognised and validated (Aagaard & Dahler, 2010). A new law about lifelong upgrading of education and skills (Danish Ministry of Education, 2007) obliged providers of adult and continuing education to offer people an assessment of their real competences in relation to the objectives of one or more of the subjects or modules in the education or its admission requirements (Nistrup & Lund, 2010, p. 10).

The 2011 an Executive Order on Professional Education replaces the term assessment of real competencies with a more individualised approach, individual competence assessment (IKV). It requires institutions to consider whether an applicant has professional qualifications comparable to what the admission requirements stipulate. The educational institution undertakes an individual assessment based on information about the applicant's overall knowledge, skills and qualifications, regardless of where they were acquired. If the applicant is deemed to have professional qualifications equivalent to those specified in the admission requirements and the institution in question considers the applicant capable of completing its programme, then the applicant must be considered on an equal footing with other applicants who fulfil the standard admission requirement, which is an A-level examination.

These developments and current conditions involving VPL mean that non-traditional students like Hanna now have a greater chance of applying for and being accepted to university college degree programmes as a social pedagogue.

THE PROFESSION OF SOCIAL PEDAGOGUE IN DENMARK

The social pedagogue profession is specific to Denmark and a few other countries but to some extent analogous to pre-school teachers in a large number of other countries. Comparable positions in out-of-school care include social workers, educators, play workers and recreation instructors. The pedagogue degree programme provides professional qualifications for people to work with the development and care of children and young people in e.g.: day nurseries, day care centres, pre-school classes, recreation centres, school-based leisure time facilities, after-school clubs and in 24-hour service institutions); in institutions for children, young people and adults with reduced psychological or physical capacities; and in family centres and child and youth psychiatric hospitals for adults with social problems (homelessness, substance abuse and mental disorders (Bupl, 2016).

A PSYCHOSOCIETAL APPROACH TO LIFE HISTORY

To gain insight into the career changes of students who undergo an individual skills assessment and acquire a new career, I apply a life history research approach. Using life history makes it possible to examine the individual subject – experienced from the lived life, contemporary experiences and future perspectives – and how they co-constitute the acquisition of the new profession. The specific research approach of psychosocietal interpretation does not involve a causal understanding of career development but seeks to interpret the complex, dialectically subjective processes that unfold and lead to the educational situation.

Across Europe, recent decades have witnessed a considerable expansion of biographical and life history research (Hallqvist, 2013) on non-traditional learners in higher and adult education (EU, 2011). Non-traditional students' stories are seen as a relevant way to gain knowledge regarding the formation and transformation of identity in education (Bron & Thunborg, 2016). The focus on biographical and life history research is part of a more general trend across the social sciences. The biographical approach has become an increasingly recognised tool for examining how learning takes place in relation to people's life transitions (Hallqvist, Ellström, & Hydén, 2012, p. 70). This flourishing research trend on non-traditional learners is partly fuelled by dissatisfaction with surveys and other traditional research methods, which tend to marginalise the individual perspectives and subjective experiences of learners (West et al., 2007; EU, 2011).

In Denmark, especially at Roskilde University, various approaches to life history have been developed, inspired by experience with biographical research in education, sociology and other disciplines (Salling Olesen, 2016, p. 11), as well as a general inspiration from critical theory, which is also known as the Frankfurt School. One of the leading Danish contributions to the field of life history research is the psychosocietal approach, a neologistic term, which is a combined theoretical and methodological approach that Henning Salling Olesen and his colleagues developed (2007, 2012, 2013a) and which is applied in this chapter. Salling Olesen (2016) states that: "The term 'approach' indicates the intrinsic connection between the theory, the empirical research process and the epistemic subject […] Paradigmatically this is a mediation or synthesis of critical theory of society and the symbol interpretational focus in psychoanalysis".

The theory of subjective experiences conceptualises individual psychological development as the interactional experience of societal relations. These experiences and encounters with the external sphere produce an inner psychodynamic as a conscious and unconscious individual resource (ibid.). The psychosocietal approach embraces the life history perspective, where biography is used not to understand the specific individual but to learn about individual subjectivity and its psychological and societal dimensions by integrating a theory of subjectivity and a hermeneutic interpretative methodology to explore the lived life experiences. The psycho-societal approach is interdisciplinary, emphasising the dynamic interaction between the individual and the environment, thus integrating the psychological and social dimensions of experience.

To avoid reductive constraints in the interpretation, three levels of awareness are maintained, as illustrated in Figure 5.1, which shows what we are attempting to identify, i.e. learning processes, the subjective analysis of experience and the identity process in a specific profession. This heuristic research approach was developed to examine the experience of professionals and professional development. In my research it was however used as inspiration on a more general level.

The triangle in the centre illustrates the research areas of relevance for this chapter. The three circles in the model represent relatively independent dynamics that are mediated in the specific learning and identity building of individuals. The items listed in the circles, but outside the triangle, are beyond the scope of this chapter but will be touched upon briefly as they are pertinent to my research field but can also be understood as widespread structures in society that must be recognised and described on their own terms (Salling Olesen, 2006).

Individual life history, placed in the top circle, represents the individual or non-traditional student's unique life history, which comprises, for instance, childhood memories, school experiences, relationships and work. Life history is not the focus in and of itself but is used as an aspect of interpretation to reveal the complexity of subjective processes. As the items not in a circle in the centre of the triangle illustrate, individual subjectivity is formed by and as an interplay between the individual (and his or her life history) and social and societal (historic) factors in the broadest sense.

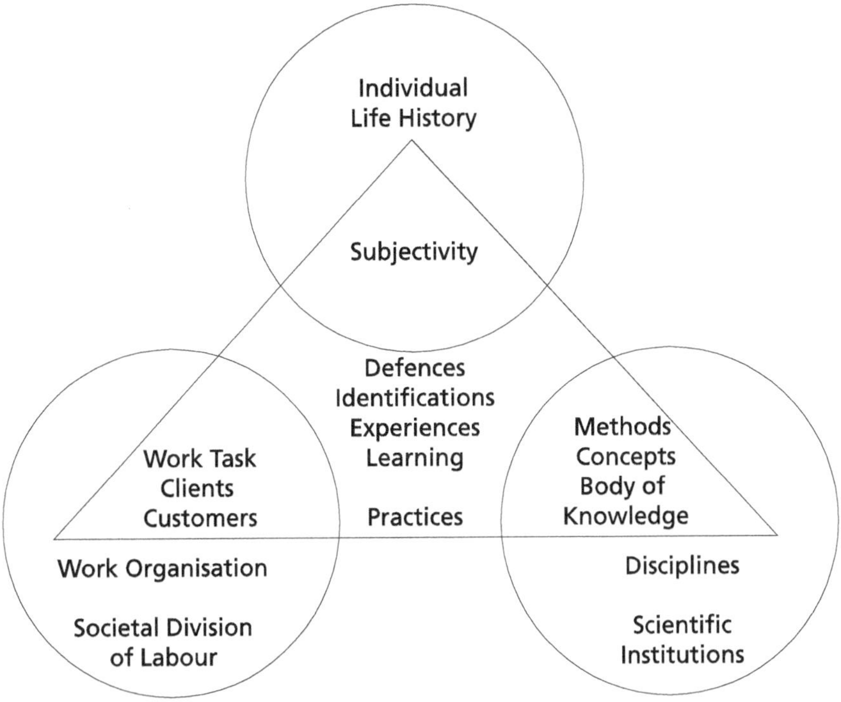

Figure 5.1. Heuristic research model (from Salling Olesen, 2007)

The circle on the left involves the societal division of labour, which consists of the educational institution, tasks involved in being a student, fellow students and the teachers. The circle on the right represents scientific institutions or the theory base of the professional field, and the wider cultural framework of thinking around it.

In order to understand the interviewee's experiences and how they are brought to the surface and revitalised through new (mainly study) experiences, I employed a semi-structured interview approach focusing on narration (Kvale & Brinkmann, 2009, p. 173) inspired by various life history approaches (West et al., 2007; Salling Olesen, 2013a, 2013b) and structured by an infinite number of themes but also left open to allow spontaneity and free association (Hollway & Jefferson, 2007: 36–39). I draw on the interpretation approach developed in connection with the International Research Group for Psychosocietal Analysis (see Introduction in this volume). The group works with concrete empirical material among others inspired by the hermeneutic (interpretational) understanding that is used in psychoanalytical therapeutic practice, converted into "scenic understanding" (Salling Olesen & Weber, 2012). The particular value of these ideas mainly becomes evident in reflecting a research practice that involves subjectively engaging in the interpretation and tracing aspects of social relations that are not immediately visible and that may not even be conscious ones for the actors in question. Salling Olesen (2017, p. 35) suggests that the most critical aspect of the method is its ability "to lift out societally repressed meanings and point to their potential as radical imaginations of alternative realities". Although the theoretical complexities will not be delved into further, I shall just describe the specific analytical procedure used in this study (Gripsrud & Mellon, 2017). The various stages involved in reading a text draw on various aspects of experience, including: common sense understanding; immediate physical reactions of comfort or discomfort; and the sensuous and dramatic patterns of group dynamics. The following three questions are used to explore the empirical interview data from the case study on Hanna in this chapter:

- What is said? In other words, what is the text about?
- How is it said?
- Why is it said in this particular way?

These questions relate to different levels of understanding people's speech and communication. What is said corresponds to the propositional meaning; how it is said corresponds to both the meta-communicative meaning and the pragmatic meaning, while why it is said in a particular way can be differentiated into the manifest intentions and the hidden, excluded intentions. The manifest intentions might be obvious, but it is possible that the interviewee may employ an unconscious strategy that can only be understood when we, as researchers, are aware of our own feelings, such as irritation, confusion and shock (Urwin, 2012), but also of the transference and countertransference of our own reactions (Hollway & Froggett, 2012). The responses of the interviewee and the researchers represent a mirror of the unconscious (scene) (Hollway & Volmerg, 2010; Weber, 2001).

An important point in terms of how to act as a participant in the interpretation process as Weber (1995, p. 132) mentions, is that the researcher is not outside the process; on the contrary, the participant, i.e. the researcher, is also a significant factor in the process, which is why spontaneous reactions should not to be suppressed as an unprofessional disruption but rather seen as a source of critical reflection. Awareness of these aspects in the interpretation process is necessary and acknowledging them is crucial because they can influence the outcome.

ANALYSIS OF ONE SPECIFIC NON-TRADITIONAL STUDENT, HANNA

As presented in the introduction, my focus is on how a non-traditional adult student, Hanna, who began as an VPL student enrolled based on an individual skills assessment in a professional bachelor degree programme, acquires a new profession as a social pedagogue. The key area of interest is investigating how she acquires a new professional identity, for example, how she contributes to the study environment that she is part of and what future perspectives she sees as a social pedagogue. First, I present a summary of the portraits derived from a content analysis of the interview (narrative segments), which is followed by an analysis and short discussion.

VIGNETTE OF HANNA

At the time of the interview, Hanna, married with two children aged 11 and 16, was 49 years old. She had been in the bachelor degree programme for social pedagogues for almost one year before participating in the interview. Until early adolescence she grew up in one of Denmark's larger cities with her parents and two younger siblings, a brother and a sister. Her childhood home, which was located close to a cemetery, is described only briefly. Stories about her school, however, are highlighted. From first to tenth grade, she attended a primary school located at the city's harbour. A quiet, clever and well-liked child who also received praise from her teachers, she remembers going to school as enjoyable. Despite describing school as pleasant, she also mentions being teased and bullied because there were "some things" that were difficult in relation to her classmates. Her father, for example, worked at the cemetery and her mother was an unskilled worker. Her descriptions of her father are very modest, often stated in a neutral or critical manner. Her mother, in contrast, is described frequently throughout the interview as a central figure. She worked multiple places, for instance, in a nursing home and in various kitchens, until ending as a milk lady at a school. While still young, Hanna trained to be a relaxation therapist and initially got a job as a day care helper but was fired because she was not a professionally trained child minder. She later worked at a care home at a time when no skilled physical therapists were available but was later dismissed because she did not have the right professional certification. Next, she worked in a day care centre as an assistant, hired due to her background as a trained relaxation therapist, even though this was not a specific job category at the day care centre.

THE MILK LADY

As the portrait of Hanna shows, and as is evident in the interview, going to school was a topic she talked about a great deal, but the associated thoughts and feelings also occupied her. Her time at school is described in contradictory terms, with school viewed as a good place, where she learned something, but is also simultaneously seen as a source of discomfort, where bullying took place and where she did not learn very much. This ambivalence presents itself both as the desire and lack of desire to go to school. Another significant topic involving dynamic psychosocial processes in relation to her school years concerns her mother and an immediate, clear idealisation of her as well as "otherwiseness", or what could be called "cracks", in the narration, which helps to clarify more complex (and contradictory) aspects in the empirical material.

Hanna presents her mother in a positive light, for example when she talks about how her mother gave birth to a child at a very young age that she had to give away but nonetheless managed to care for through life. She also mentions the courage her mother showed in resisting the wishes and expectations of her family. For instance, at one point she chose to move in with a man at the other end of the country, which required moving from a rural to an urban setting. Hanna also describes how her mother was a good mother. For example, she and her mother made an effort to rein in her sister when she was smoking too much hash. When her parents divorced, Hanna's mother was strong and generous, inviting Hanna's father to attend holiday events.

A closer examination of Hanna's story shows some cracks, for example, when her mother began working at Hanna's school, where she was very popular, when Hanna was in ninth grade. Hanna's initial description is favourable:

> […] and there she was, the milk lady, in her final working years. And she somewhat turned into an institution for many of the youngsters. They often came down to have a chat with her. She had a sort of a little house there, just like this, with milk and … a small shop. They came down to chat with her. They really liked her.

This quote describes how Hanna experienced life at school when her mother was the milk lady and had responsibility for not only distributing the milk but also served as a likeable hub, around whom the school's children gathered daily. In the following quote Hanna describes her feelings towards her classmates, from whom she dissociates herself by calling them 'the other youngsters", and the envy she experienced: "I remember that sometimes I became a bit envious of the other youngsters, that they experienced her in a way that I didn't quite get to". This story about her mother's relationship with her classmates challenges the idealistic description Hanna presents by also portraying the resentment she felt toward her mother's nurturing behaviour, which she felt did not extend to her. As mentioned previously in this chapter, there is a dialectic dynamic at play in these processes. This includes the mother's role as the milk lady, where she nurtures the students and gives them approval, even the ones who, at least according to Hanna, were part of the reason that she experienced unpleasant situations at school.

Hanna's idealised narrative about her mother as being kind and well-liked in her role as the milk lady, but not toward Hanna, raises some questions. Hanna also mentions her disappointment concerning the attention her mother bestowed on the other pupils. Her narrative describing how popular her mother was may be a bit of an exaggeration and an idealisation of what happened.

This reduction can be understood as a 'security principle', where opportunities for change are pushed to the side or avoided, cf. Leithäuser's (2012a, 2012b) theory of everyday consciousness, which involves many types of defence mechanisms. Hanna's idealisation of her mother must be seen in light of the social conditions that Hanna grew up with: an absent father, who apparently had alcohol problems, and a mother who worked a great deal and took care of practical tasks in the household.

In the following statement Hanna describes the attention, or lack thereof, that she received from her parents:

> They were very, well … everything is going well, that's great … they had no ambitions on my behalf in any way, that's … that's actually something that I missed sometimes, that they … I wasn't able to talk seriously with them about what I wanted to do and what I was good at. They just thought … that's great … that's what you want – just do that. And you know … we never talked about what I was truly good at … "I actually think that you're really good at this or something like that" – that wasn't on their minds. We didn't talk to each other like that.

Hanna uses the pronoun 'they' to discuss her parents and does not call them mom and dad. This passage and other statements indicate that it is easier for Hanna to mention her mother's more negative roll and actions by using the more distant 'they' – though there are only a few examples of this. Hanna desired greater participation from her parents when she was a child, wishing that they had taken the time to discuss with her and show an interest in her and her activities. She felt that they did not acknowledge what she did and that they did not have any ideas or show any interest in speaking with her about what she should do. Now an adult, Hanna imagines, however, that they perhaps spoke nicely and in positive terms about her to their friends. This positive desire can be interpreted as another attempt *not* to break with her idealistic perception of events, or to break with what Leithaüser calls "subjective barriers to liberation" (2012b). This example, in connection with the previous examples, perhaps indicates that the difficulty or difficulties Hanna experienced as a child created barriers that make it hard to develop new understandings of her own experiences. There are subjective circumstances that contribute to solidifying the idea or feeling that "everything is okay", i.e. that there is nothing to worry about, but that also leads to directing or projecting the problem(s) elsewhere, for example, toward the classmates or herself.

This is an example of the anomalies or "cracks" that the analysis points out in relation to the mother's role and which allow new understandings to occur. Hanna mentions that at one point her class teacher, a woman, became her friend. Unlike with her mother, she does not describe the teacher as having a wealth of outstanding abilities, but in terms of the positive influence the relationship had on her. The teacher, who was childless, also plays a role later in Hanna's life. She also wanted to talk to Hanna, for instance about the problems that later occurred in the family. The teacher's interest in Hanna, which is described as caring, is thus put into perspective in contrast to her parents' alleged role. Hanna explains that the teacher's kindness was important during a rough patch in her life.

Some of the familial challenges Hanna later faced transpired due to the harsh circumstances that arose some years after her parents' divorce. Her mother's financial situation was apparently poor and the family was abruptly evicted from their home during Hanna's final year in school, an information that Hanna suddenly mentioned, without providing the details, while talking about her time in school:

> [...] You mean where I went to school? In ninth, tenth grade, yes, in fact something terrible happened in my family, because ... we were thrown out of our home, evicted. A really traumatic experience. At that time we moved from Valby to Nørrebro and later on to Vesterbro, where my mum got a flat. And that's ...

This story, which came as a surprise at the end of the interview, is an indication that the mother was not the perpetually nurturing milk lady; in other words, she was unable to provide for her family. This experience was presumably, in Hanna's words, a highly distressing experience, one that, in a classical sense, Hanna is unable to adequately process and where her response is defensive.

Hanna breaks away from the predominantly positive narrative about her mother as the happy, encouraging milk lady who has time for everyone, with a few, brief stories. In this way, the aforementioned everyday consciousness also contains a sense of hope due to the ambiguity present because it is possible to avoid habitual behaviour and put new themes in motion. New sides of Hanna appear.

The interpretation of Hanna's childhood, youth and school years, in addition to her experience, appears to influence the way she perceives studying to be a social pedagogue and perhaps also her choice of degree programme.

BECOMING A PEDAGOGUE – AND A NURTURING MILK LADY

When Hanna originally applied to the social pedagogue programme via the individual skills assessment channel she wanted to avoid receiving any credits that exempted her from any teaching and internships because she wanted to experience everything the programme had to offer. She had various reasons for choosing the social pedagogue programme. On the one hand, she already had a job in an after-school programme and collaborated with primary schools, but not as a trained pedagogue. In order to protect herself against being fired due to a lack of formal education, she explains that the reason for her choice of programme was to be able to document her abilities – and what she wanted to learn. Her desire to get a degree and thus obtain formal credentials was also possible due to a school reform implemented in Denmark that involves the increased presence of trained pedagogues. Hanna's stories also communicate her interest in learning something new, for example, new theories and novel perspectives on teaching, and via her new knowledge, the ability to challenge the practices that she thinks are so familiar.

Hanna describes the teaching in the social pedagogue programme as academic and extremely difficult, but also explains that she is happy with her choice and that the programme has become easier along the way. This is especially true because she works in a disciplined way, which she says she does more now than when she was young.

Hanna's study group sees her as well-functioning when they work together, even though it can be a bit of a puzzle to organise everything. She sees herself as the participant with the most experience. While working on their various mandatory assignments, it is important to her to produce quality work. If the other members of her study group do not do their best or do not have the required professional skills, she accepts that but expects herself to do her best.

Her career change, from relaxation therapist, to studying to be a pedagogue, does not immediately appear to be a big one. However, even though Hanna has insight into what being a pedagogue requires, she has no experience or knowledge concerning the degree programme and is thus in the process of acquiring a new professional identity. Hanna's future work prospects are to head a preschool at some point. In other words, she would like to work as a pedagogue at an elementary school and head up the first graders (comparable to kindergarten). Hanna combines her previous training with the new, which is a recurring topic among most VPL students (Mellon, 2016). In addition she is pleased to be in a role where the children perceive her as doing a good job and where she feels she is a success. During her internship Hanna also experiences new ways of approaching education.

> [about the internship] I did a programme like that. It was so much fun. And I also spend a great deal of time … doing massages with the children and that's … a big hit, [the children] enjoy it immensely and really like it. So I spend a good deal of time on exercise and massage in a variety of ways. Well, I actually spend a large amount of time on well-being, the well-being of the class.

One of Hanna's driving forces is to be recognised and loved by the children. Hanna idealises the role of the pedagogue and consequently herself, through the nurturing role that is required when working with well-being. The pedagogue programme and the internship have led to new reflections on what an educator's role is, initiated by the experiences Hanna brought with her, the new ones she is acquiring but also the new discussions arising due to the new role of pedagogues in elementary schools. The prospect of one day becoming the head of a kindergarten is also appealing.

On the one hand, there seems to be an attraction to the "milk lady" phenomenon, where Hanna's mother had the role of being a popular figure who all the children adored. Apparently Hanna would like to be popular just as her mother was, as Hanna saw it at any rate. A recurring topic, on the other hand, which was also mentioned in her description of her childhood, is the importance of talking to one another, for example, in the form of the emotional and attentive relationship that Hanna had with her own class teacher. The issue of relationships appears both in connection with the pedagogue degree programme and during adolescence, where she talks about her upbringing, the divorce, being evicted and her mother meeting another man.

> [on changes in her family life] I think that it's more the life experiences you bring with you that play a role when you work with people – that you have personal, first-hand experiences. Because I have, in fact, been interested how people interact and how people talk to each other and that kind of things […]

Hanna mentions how life experiences, i.e. her own experiences, significantly affected her own awareness of what a lack of conversation and care means. What today would be described as negligence in certain pedagogical contexts, or at least detrimental from a mental health perspective (National Board of Social Services, 2017), has left its mark and is a part of her reflections on her educational choices and goals. Hanna's interest in conversing, talking and having a caring relationship with children has apparently not changed since she began to study, but her degree programme appears to have helped fulfil a desire originating at both a professional and a personal level that involves her professional identity and the continuing struggle to define herself, as evidenced by the above quotation.

CONCLUSIONS

This analysis focuses on a single case in a multi-case study with a non-traditional adult student, who made a career change. She was admitted via an alternative VPL channel. The overall analysis of Hanna centres on two main themes: (1) her relationship with her mother and (2) issues related to studying and acquiring a professional identity as a pedagogue. The analysis demonstrates how Hanna interprets her life story in light of her present choice of education and being a professional pedagogue. Part of Hanna's idealised narrative about her mother contains what I term "cracks", which seem to indicate that Hanna has been affected by the lack of care and concern in her childhood. This affected her choice of education and her acquisition of a profession – a professional identity – but also a dialectical shaping of the question "who am I?", i.e. what we call personal identity. Hanna's ideas about the future, which Leithäuser (2012b) calls "desirable ideas", likewise contribute to the process that she is in as an VPL student acquiring a professional identity.

The two main themes that emerge during Hanna's interview, i.e. Hanna's mother as the milk lady and Hanna's experiences and reflections as a student, indicate that Hanna also wants to be a nurturing milk lady. This interpretation shows that the desire to repeat the positive story about being a good mother – regardless of whether her mother actually was a good mother or not – plays a role in Hanna's choice of profession: being like the milk lady, nurturing and making everyone happy. Another aspect concerns being a competent, professional pedagogue, someone the children look up to. The mother's norms involving doing something for others appear to represent a form of socialisation that I would define as normative pressure that cannot simply be managed cognitively and reflectively. Leithäuser (2012b, p. 605) points out various aspects of everyday life that intrude upon and permeate the *entire* layout of one's psyche. What we perceive as conscious and (mostly) reasonable choices also contain an unconscious dimension filled with ambiguities and revisions, which the analysis also examined. In other words the norms that influence people's actions and that are rewarded and praised by one's self if they are exercised will have this type of invisible power and a hidden dimension that can be difficult to grasp and hold onto. According to Leithäuser's (1976, 2012b) theory of everyday consciousness,

Hanna's life stories and experiences serve as a projection screen where the mother and the milk lady become a guide for Hanna's current endeavours. It also represents, however, the challenge of recognising and accepting the projections, of developing a more realistic and ambiguous professional identity.

In conclusion, I would like to point out one issue that concerns a specific aspect of my analysis. While interviewing Hanna, hearing about the family's eviction came quite unexpectedly and I chose not to follow up on her statement. Why did I refrain from doing so? Was it due to a sense of modesty, an overwhelming feeling of empathy and the matter of confidentiality, causing me to doubt whether I could morally continue, or was it the need to maintain the positive atmosphere? This issue caused me to reflect on my subjectivity as a researcher but will not be delved into further in this chapter, though it is pertinent to mention Weber's (1995) perspective on the research results. According to Weber, a prerequisite for the research process is that subjective and objective idiosyncrasies clash and manifest themselves as new meanings. The interpretive findings cannot be isolated from the interpretation process, and should not be, but must be understood in tandem with it. As a result, according to Weber's (1995, p. 136) perspective, the researcher is inextricably interwoven into and coloured in various ways by the interpretation of the material and the findings. The analytical results in this chapter are therefore based on a psychosocietal approach and the method of interpretation previously described was developed through interpretation processes that coloured my professional subjectivity as a researcher. The dialogues and interpretation processes in the collective field of research, for example, in the Dubrovnik method, have nonetheless contributed to refining the task of interpretation and are one perspective from among the wealth of knowledge that the individual informant's empirical data contribute.

REFERENCES

Aagaard, K., & Dahler, K. M. (2011). *Anerkendelse af realkompetencer: En antologi.* Aarhus: VIA Systime.

Alheit, P. (2017). De uønskede studerende. Lukketheden i det tyske universitetssystem [The unwanted students: Closure tendencies of the new German university system]. In K. Mellon (Ed.), *Læring eller ikke-læring?* (pp. 145–164). Frederikshavn: Dafolo.

Andersen, L. L. (2003). When the unconscious joins the game: A psychoanalytic perspective on modernization and change. *Forum: Qualitative Social Research, 4*(3), Article 26. Retrieved from http://nbn-resolving.de/urn:nbn:de:0114-fqs0303261

Andersen, L. L. (2006). Det indre og ydre liv på arbejde – en kritisk introduktion til Tavistock og den psykoanalytiske socialpsykologi. *Tidsskrift for Arbejdsliv, 8*(3).

Andersen, L. L. (2012). Inner and outer life at work: The toots and horizon of psychoanalytically informed work life research. *Forum: Qualitative Social Research, 13*(3), Article 26.

Bron, A., & Thunborg, C. (2016). Theorising biographical work from non-traditional students' stories in higher education. *Terazniejszosc – Czlowiek – Edukacja, 19*(3), 139–153.

Bubl. (2016). *Pædagogen.* Retrieved January 21, 2016, from http://www.bupl.dk/english/pedagogy_in_dk

Crosling, G., Thomas, L., & Heagney, M. (2008). *Improving student retention in higher education: The role of teaching and learning.* London: Routledge.

Danish Ministry for Children, Education and Gender Equality. (2008). *Realkompetencevurdering inden for voksen- og efteruddannelse: en håndbog. Undervisningsministeriets håndbogsserie no. 3.* Retrieved March 2016, from http://pub.uvm.dk/2008/rkvivoksen/hel.html

European Lifelong Learning Project 2008–2010. (2011). *Access and retention: Experiences of non-traditional learners in HE. Literature review: Final extended version.* Retrieved September 9, 2015, from http://www.dsw.edu.pl/fileadmin/www-ranlhe/files/Literature_Review_upd.pdf

Gripsrud, B. H., & Mellon, K. (2018). Dubrovnik-metoden – et analytisk værktøj til undersøgelse og forståelse af læreprocesser. In K. Mellon (Ed.), *Læring eller ikke-læring?* (pp. 71–82). Frederikshavn: Dafolo.

Hallqvist, A. (2013). Biographical learning: Two decades of research and discussion. *Educational Review*, 1–17.

Hallqvist, A., Elleström, P., & Hydén, L. (2012). The many faces of biographical learning. *Studies in the Education of Adults, 44*(1), 70–84.

Hollway, W., & Froggett, L. (2012). Researching in-between subjective experience and reality. *Forum: Qualitative Social Research, 13*(3), 17.

Hollway, W., & Jefferson, T. (2007). *Doing qualitative research differently: Free association, narrative and the interview method.* London: Sage Publications.

Hollway, W., & Volmerg, B. (2010). *Interpretation group method in the Dubrovnik tradition.* Retrieved from http://oro.open.ac.uk/34374/

Kvale, S., & Brinkmann, S. (2009). *Interview: Introduktion til et håndværk.* Copenhagen: Hans Reitzel Publishers.

Leithäuser, T. (1976). *Formen des Alltagsbewusstseins.* Frankfurt/M: Campus.

Leithäuser, T. (2012a). Psychoanalysis, socialization and society: The psychoanalytical thought and interpretation of Alfred Lorenzer. *Forum: Qualitative Social Research, 13*(3), 17.

Leithäuser, T. (2012b). Teorien om hverdagsbevidstheden i dag' [Formen des Alltagsbewusstsein]. In K. Illeris (Ed.), *49 tekster om læring.* Frederiksberg: Samfundslitteratur.

Salling Olesen, H. (2006). Discourse and experience: Examples from the medical profession. *Nordisk Pedagogik, 26*, 358–371.

Salling Olesen, H. (2007). Theorizing learning in life history: A psycho-societal approach. *Studies in the Education of Adults, 1*, 38–53.

Salling Olesen, H. (2012). The societal nature of subjectivity: An interdisciplinary methodological challenge. *Forum: Qualitative Social Research, 13*(3), 4.

Salling Olesen, H. (2013a). The societal nature of subjectivity: An interdisciplinary methodological challenge. *Historical Social Research, 144*(38).

Salling Olesen, H. (2013b). Beyond the current political economy of competence development. *European Journal for Research on the Education and Learning of Adults, 4*(2), 153–170.

Salling Olesen, H. (2016). Learning and experience: A psycho-societal approach. In M. Milan et al. (Eds.), *Handbook of adult and lifelong education and learning.* London: Palgrave Macmillan Ltd.

Salling Olesen, H. (2017). Læringsbarrierer, læringsmodstand og læringsforsvar –prismer for en historisk konfliktudfoldelse. In K. Mellon (Ed.), *Læring eller ikke-læring?* (pp. 23–38). Frederikshavn: Dafolo.

Salling Olesen, H., & Weber, K. (2012). Socialization, language, and scenic understanding: Alfred Lorenzer's contribution to a psycho-societal methodology [73 paragraphs]. *Forum: Qualitative Social Research, 13*(3), Article 22. Retrieved from http://nbn-resolving.de/urn:nbn:de:0114-fqs1203229

Singh, M., & Duvekot, R. (Eds.). (2013). *Linking recognition practices and national qualifications frameworks.* Hamburg: UNESCO Institute for Lifelong Learning.

Urwin, C. (2012). Using surprise in observing cultural experience. In C. Urwin & J. Sternberg (Eds.), Infant observation and research: Emotional processes in everyday lives (pp. 93–103). London: Karnac.

Weber, K. (1995). *Ambivalens og erfaring: mod et kønsdifferentieret laeringsbegreb: en analyse af kvinders læreprocesser i fagbevægelsens interne uddannelsessystem* (PhD dissertation). Roskilde University.

Weber, K. (2001). *Aggression, recognition and qualification: On the social psychology of everyday life in adult education.* Frederiksberg: Roskilde University Press.

West, L., Alheit, P., Andersen, A. S., & Merrill, B. (2007). *Using biographical and life history approaches in the study of adult and lifelong learning: European perspectives.* Frankfurt: Peter Lang.

SISSEL FINHOLT-PEDERSEN

6. WHAT DOES IT MEAN TO BECOME A CHURCH MINISTER?

Life History and Imaginations of Future

INTRODUCTION

In the following, I will show how the psychosocietal approach has contributed to the interpretations of the qualitative interviews in my PhD dissertation A lifelong and life-wide perspective on students of theology and their constructions of themselves as ministers (Finholt-Pedersen, 2018). Halfway through my PhD, I became familiar with the psychosocietal approach and the lifelong learning project at Roskilde University with its theoretical approach to understanding learning and professional identity; this eventually became the main theoretical perspective in the analysis and interpretation of the data in my dissertation (Salling Olesen, 2006, 2017; Laursen, Moos, Salling Olesen, & Weber, 2012).

The psychosocietal approach theorizes professional identity development and learning as a process where new learning is always based on previous life experiences. Drawing on psychoanalytic interpretation of subjective experiences and cultural phenomena, where psychological dynamics are seen as produced by societal relations and representing an inner psychological modality of culture, the psychosocietal approach understands learning as taking place through the patterns of interpretations already established in the learning subject. In this perspective, learning is understood to be both biographically situated and taking place within the specific context of the learning subject (Salling Olesen, 2007).

In the following, I will show how this theoretical approach contributes to a multi-layered interpretation of two of the interviewees in the dissertation, Aksel and Ingrid, and particularly how their constructions of themselves as church ministers may be interpreted in a life history perspective, understood as their subjective processing of cultural meaning and social conditions.

The starting point and focus of the interpretations was therefore the students' life-historical experiences, understood as their specific individual mediation of their social conditions and historical circumstances, generating the individual's subjectivity that unfolds itself in consciousness and engagement later in life (Salling Olesen, 2007). In order to achieve this, I carried out hermeneutic interpretations of the students' life history narratives, guided by the conceptual framework of psychoanalysis and knowledge of the societal, historical and cultural contexts of these students.

© KONINKLIJKE BRILL NV, LEIDEN, 2020 | DOI: 10.1163/9789004420274_007

The aim of this chapter is to demonstrate how the psychosocietal approach to interpreting students' subjectivity, both on an individual and a societal level, enhances understanding of their learning development (Salling Olesen, 2007).

BACKGROUND TO THE PROJECT

Initially this PhD was planned as an inter-disciplinary project involving psychology and professional ethics. I was particularly interested in studying how the development of virtues for working life takes place in students of law and theology during their education. Twelve students of theology were interviewed three times over a period of about 15 months. The students of theology were students in the three schools educating Lutheran ministers in Norway: the Norwegian School of Theology in Oslo, the Faculty of Theology at the University of Oslo and VID Specialized University, which has incorporated the School of Mission and Theology in Stavanger. Fifteen law students were interviewed, but due to the huge amount of data, these interviews were omitted from the study.

The theology students certainly addressed many ethical topics regarding their future work in the interviews, but it was not their development of virtues that caught my attention as I started to analyse the interviews. The observations that struck me most were the students' reflections about their future ministry as a subjective conflict. The students were reflecting on themselves as future ministers in a life-historical perspective, addressing their future identity as a continuation of past experiences at home, at school, and in other contexts.

Another observation of note was that the students, in spite of their different life-historical experiences and backgrounds, articulated themselves in similar ways and within a specific theological discourse.

I also observed many inconsistencies in the students' articulations about themselves. These contradictions appeared far too significant to be ignored and I therefore wished to include them in the analysis and interpretation. I searched for new theoretical perspectives that could embrace them, instead of ignoring them. Individual interpretations and the virtue perspective seemed insufficient, and I started to use the psychosocietal approach as the main theoretical foundation for my analysis and interpretation of the data. The research question was reconstructed to include the different aspects of the students' socialization and subjectivity:

> In which ways do life-historical processes of socialization play a part in theology students' development of a professional identity as a minister?

AKSEL'S PERCEPTION OF BECOMING A MINISTER IN A LIFE-HISTORICAL PERSPECTIVE

I will demonstrate how the students' individual mediation of their social conditions and historical circumstances generated their individual subjectivity by presenting one of the main topics in the interviews with Aksel and my interpretations of it. A strong ambivalence and insecurity unfolds when Aksel reflects on himself as a future minister. On a referential level, Aksel discusses the role of a minister in the context of the historical role and the general conceptions of the role in Norwegian society; however, my attention is focused on how Aksel's ambivalence and insecurity regarding the role of a minister may be interpreted in a life-historical perspective.

Aksel was raised in a religious family; his father is a Lutheran minister and he himself took part in church activities for children and young people. Aksel is not able to articulate clearly why he has decided to become a minister. When asked about his choice of career, he explains that what he now says about becoming a minister at the end of his studies must be understood as a rationalization of his reasons when he was 18. Another explanation is that as long as he, as the son of a minister, sees no need to distance himself from the Christian faith, joining the clergy is an obvious choice. Aksel has known many ministers since his childhood, many of his friends are ministers, he is happy to study theology and he has met several ministers during the practical component of his theology course; however, in spite of all this, his conceptions of being a minister are strikingly ambivalent and he appears to be deeply insecure about the role of a minister.

One of the conspicuous observations in the interviews with Aksel is his theoretical way of speaking about himself. He describes and explains himself through a theological discourse, positioning himself as a liberal theologian as opposed to "the pietists". In this discourse, pietists are constructed as abusing power and are associated with feelings and experiences. Liberal theologians such as Aksel are perceived as intellectual and as preaching about a loving and life-giving God. This polarization between pietists and Aksel himself as a liberal theologian is found in all the three interviews with Aksel.

Aksel's ambivalence and insecurity about the role of the clergy is expressed in his description of what he himself calls "the caricatured pastor", a pietistic pastor who abuses his professional power to present his own thoughts as God's thoughts. Aksel's description of the caricature of the pastor is contradictory. He describes a strongly problematic role as a member of the clergy, representing both the historical role and current conceptions of the role in Norway. At the same time, he affirms that this role does not really exist in today's society. Following this, when Aksel has firmly distanced himself from the caricatured pastoral role, he explores the pietistic pastor in more detail:

> The pastor who has a suppressed sexual life and wants to tell the congregation how things should be, but he himself, inside he feels insecure and so on, and breaks down.

This pastor is described with distance and contempt. But more broadly, Aksel attributes to the clergy a huge responsibility for the people they meet, involving both their religious development and a general psychological foundation for life. He sees these demands as almost impossible to meet without hurting others. In spite of these perceptions of the role of a the clergy and its unrealistic demands, he also emphasizes that many people do have great trust in ministers on an individual level, which does not correspond to the general negative cultural conceptions of the clergy.

This ambivalent and insecure image of the clergy is related to Aksel's descriptions of himself as a minister; he is deeply concerned with the importance of being himself as a minister, but is not really able to convey what this means to him. Instead he expresses himself on a theoretical level, searching for theoretical concepts to settle this concern, but without success. At first, Aksel's concern about being himself as a minister appears to be general and obvious, but in a life-historical perspective on the interviews with him, it appears to have a deeper personal meaning.

Aksel's concern circles around the fear that his family will experience a split between his person as a minister and his person as a family member. He deals with this question in the framework of his wish to go to the pub; this has been one of Aksel's great concerns for years, which he discussed in all three interviews, and is also part of the polarization between pietists and liberals. As a young man in his home church youth group, Aksel wanted to go to the pub, but the pietists in the group argued that this would not be acceptable according to good Christian leadership standards. Now, years later, living in another city and not having the same group leadership responsibilities, Aksel could go to the pub. But still he does not "because that would make me feel like I was hiding away". In all three interviews with Aksel, he dwells upon this topic, but does not sort out if he can go to the pub or not, and expresses this as the fundamental question of whether he can be himself as a minister or whether he has to submit to the pietists' opinions about how he should live his life.

The liberal theologians' view of God, in contrast to that of the pietists, is also striking when Aksel speaks about his parents.

> Well, er, the image of God, er, many researchers believe this is related to how your upbringing has been, and I had a great, nice upbringing with nice parents, and that, in a way, has given me security, and given me a good image of God, … er, intellectually I like to think that it has to do with role models in the Faculty of Theology who have shown me an inclusive and loving God.

In Aksel's narrative, pietists are associated with feelings and experiences, unlike the intellectual liberal theologians. Being a liberal theologian, he does not make decisions based on experiences or strong feelings. As an intellectual, he reflects and makes decisions based on well thought out rational considerations. Further, pietists are associated with the abuse of power and an image of God as controlling, in contrast to the liberal view of an inclusive and loving God. Against this background, I found it notable that Aksel speaks about his meeting with the inclusive and loving God at the Faculty of Theology as a new experience compared to his childhood, while he also emphasizes that he received a good image of God at that time.

Aksel's description of his childhood gives the impression that he has not reflected much about it, and may be interpreted as containing an emotional simplification, expressed in the formulation nice and secure childhood. Aksel's descriptions of his childhood and of his experiences in the Faculty of Theology represent a break, not a continuation, in his narrative. First he assures me his childhood was nice and secure, and gave him a good image of God, but then he goes on to explain that it was in the Faculty of Theology he met the inclusive and loving God. This apparent lack of continuity between his childhood and his time in the Faculty of Theology seems to contradict his statement about his childhood as only nice and secure.

Considering Aksel's insecurity and ambivalence reflecting on the role of a minister in a life-historical perspective, the dichotomy between the pietists and the liberal theologians in Aksel's narrative seems to represent more than just different Christian traditions in Norwegian society. One possible interpretation is that this dichotomy can function as a defence system, giving him a language to handle difficult experiences. Pietists could then represent earlier experiences of power abuse now being articulated in Aksel's doubt as to whether he can be a minister or not. This theological discourse interpreted as a defence system could then represent his own personal insecurity, still unconscious to him but now expressing itself in a desire to tell others how to live, as the caricature of the pastor does, in order to protect himself from his own painful feelings of insecurity.

INGRID'S PERCEPTIONS OF BECOMING A MINISTER IN A LIFE-HISTORICAL PERSPECTIVE

Let me now turn to some of my observations in the interviews with Ingrid and her constructions of herself as a minister, interpreted in a life-historical perspective. Ingrid is well familiar with church life and many of her friends are also studying theology. As a future minister, Ingrid hopes to give people an experience of being valuable and loved by God. When Ingrid states her decision to become a minister, it appears to be the most obvious choice. However, when the interviews are examined more closely, her choice of becoming a minister seems both ambivalent and contradictory – and not so obvious after all.

When Ingrid talks about her decision to become a minister, I am struck by how haphazard her decision to study theology appears. She speaks as if she ended up studying theology by accident. Ingrid tells me about her original plans to spend a year as a volunteer in a Christian organization in northern Norway and then to take a master's degree in leadership studies. However, things did not work out as she had planned. She was unhappy in the North and after some difficult months, she decided to give it all up and leave the volunteer job. She describes this as a fundamental experience since this was her first time ever to give up on something. She had nowhere to stay, no job and had not been accepted for any courses that semester. Her friends told her she could still be enrolled in the School of Theology and she decided to do the first year of a bachelor's degree in theology and then move on to leadership studies.

On a referential level, it seems to be almost by accident that Ingrid is to become a minister, but in a life-historical perspective, some observations in the interviews point in another direction. From early childhood, Ingrid was conscious of becoming a minister and stated this at the age of eight. She used to play being a minister and when she went to church with her parents, she paid careful attention to the minister, imagining how she would like to perform the tasks herself. Some of those ministers appeared very boring to her; she used to think it was important to have creative ministers, and as she liked to draw, she had the idea of incorporating drawing into her work as a minister.

Ambivalence also occurs as a striking theme in the case of Ingrid, when her decision to become a minister is examined more closely. In spite of her awareness about becoming a minister as a child, as a young adult, she is remarkably uncertain. She describes her insecurity about becoming a minister as a struggle between feelings and rationality. Her rationality tells her she does not like studying theology, but her feelings tell her theology is exciting and that she should continue studying the subject. Ingrid had difficulty in deciding whether to continue to do theology and become a minister and it was not until her father gave her his support that she decided to do so.

Ingrid's ambivalence about becoming a minister is articulated in terms of two significant themes in the interviews. As a minister, she imagines she will be able to express her feminine traits, to be a woman and to become a calm and peaceful person, not always the one who fights for what she believes is right, as she describes herself in the interviews. From an early age, Ingrid has paid attention to women ministers and she says that the fact that these women are ministers touched her in a special way. One of these female ministers is a friend of her parents she has known all her life. Even though this friend lived elsewhere and they did not go to her services, the fact that this woman was a minister, she tells me, was of great importance to her from an early age. Talking about the female ministers she has met as a young adult, Ingrid emphasizes these women's expression of their feminine traits as crucially important to her.

> It's very much like, they have, that someone have given me the feedback, and that has meant a lot, er, yes, (silence) yes, about style, that you're dressed nicely, that's actually been very important to me, (laughter) that you're not like dressed in a rubbish bag, just because you're a girl and a minister, and don't have to cut off your hair, like, be tough and so on, I find that very nice, and it's meant a lot to me, "wow, you had that nice skirt" "yes, isn't that nice" "and that jewellery" that it may be fashionable and stylish and so on, I think it's fun, that you don't have to be a grey mouse, or, or, become masculine to be a minister, one of them I met, she was wearing black shoes and had a black skirt just above, right above the knees and nice tights, and a nice black top, her hair all over, and a lot of make-up, she was about 60, and in high heels, and a real lady, I think it was really great that someone really had the guts to be a real, a real woman, but that's maybe, not, more those kinds of things than theology or I think "you must do this and that" but it's more like, yes, yes,

> more the everyday life or obvious stuff maybe, mm, … yes (silence) I think it's legitimiz- legitimizing my choice in a way, that I can be myself, and I can be a minister …

The expression of her femininity and her desire to be a real woman is one of the main dynamics in Ingrid's reflections about her future as a minister. Furthermore, this is also a significant theme in her life history that she mentions as having to do with integrating her thoughts and emotions. It is through counselling sessions offered by the student chaplain at her school that Ingrid has become aware of this. As a young student of theology, she faced difficult existential questions like: who am I, why am I here and how have I become the person I am today, and therefore decided to start counselling sessions. Dealing with these questions, she has become aware of past experiences, particularly an experience of being harassed by one of her school teachers. Ingrid says she was an active and engaged child, but was told by the teacher: You must restrain yourself, and she considers this to be another fundamental experience with regard to her further development. She understands this experience to be the reason why she became cognitively strong and a person who stands up and fights for what she believes is right, at the expense of relating to her feelings.

In defending herself against the teacher's harassment, Ingrid took on a tomboy role to express strength and did not allow herself to show weakness or insecurity. In retrospect, she thinks being a tomboy appeared to be an easy solution to the situation she faced back then, giving her the opportunity to express her masculine qualities, but not the totality of the person she was. In this way, the tomboy role also shielded her from figuring out how she, as a girl, could integrate her feminine and masculine qualities. Now, as a young adult, Ingrid finds the tomboy role too limited. At the time of the interviews, she is searching for a way to integrate her femininity into a new role where she can both be a woman and express her abilities. In this life-historical perspective, Ingrid's constructions of herself as a minister appear to be a way of expanding the tomboy role that has now become too small for her.

GENDER SUBJECTIVITY AND BECOMING A MINISTER

The life history approach seeks to bridge the gap between the individual life course, the societal context of the individual's life that determines his/her experiences and the discourses framing that life and narrated by the individual (Salling Olesen, 2007). Ingrid's struggle can obviously be interpreted in the light of gender stereotypes and a social environment not allowing a girl to be autonomous and assertive. The tomboy is a temporary compromise, which must be resolved in a new way in the understanding of the role of a female minister. The psychoanalytic interpretation of cultural phenomena sees psychological dynamics as produced by societal relations and representing an inner psychological modality of culture, i.e. society plays a role on the inside, not only from the outside, of students' subjectivity (Salling Olesen, 2006). In this perspective on cultural phenomena, emotional and cognitive processes are seen as closely interwoven and as aspects of the subjective processing of cultural meaning and societal conditions. This can also be revealed in a close examination of male students' constructions of themselves as ministers in light of the social and implicit meanings associated with the role of a minister.

THE SOCIAL AND IMPLICIT MEANINGS ASSOCIATED WITH THE ROLE OF A MINISTER

The role of a minister exists within a socio-cultural context and is deeply involved in societal processes and structures. Historically, the clergy belonged to the aristocracy and the vocation is still associated with a male role. The relationship between the historical and present roles is not a linear process; the historical role was associated with formal and informal power, whereas in modern society, ministers are left without any kind of power. Some of the topics standing out in the interviews with the male students are related to their representations of the historical powerful clergy; the power they themselves will possess as ministers is an important issue for them. They express intense insecurity and ambivalence when thinking about themselves as powerful ministers.

The male students articulate an omnipotent role; as ministers they imagine that they will literally become almighty. They are fascinated by and fear the idea of being a minister. They position themselves in relation to the power associated with the role and seem to be trained to reflect on the powerful minister, being well aware of the illegitimacy in professional power abuse in today's society. I am struck by their understanding of power of the clergy as mainly negative, abused to repress others.

An important issue for them in connection with these concerns is the historical role of the clergy and the formal power and authority involved, especially the pietistic pastoral role, as represented by the caricature mentioned by Aksel. This pastor, according to Aksel, told others how to live, especially in the sexual domain, as a cover for his own insecurity. Furthermore, the male students speak about how the very role of the clergy may lead its members to harm others.

These perceptions of the power associated with the clergy may also be understood as articulations of the social meaning associated with the vocation, expressing something that transcends the actual role (Salling Olesen & Weber, 2012, section 62). The meaning exists in the connection between the individual dynamics and the socially shared meaning. To identify this relationship in the context of the clergy, I feel that Aksel's caricature of a pastor serves as a good example.

The caricature of the pastor as a person with double standards presenting himself as a good moral person, telling others how to live to compensate for his own insecurity, and abusing his professional power to fulfil his personal needs, makes intuitive sense. Although we believe that this does not represent the truth about most pastors, the caricature may still exemplify a meaningful articulation of implicit and subtle meanings in our cultural perception of the role of the clergy – which the students also have.

In the analysis and interpretation of the interviews with Aksel, I interpreted his uncertainty about the role of a minister as a misinterpretation of his personal insecurity expressed in his mention of the problem of the historical role of the pietist pastor. Interpreting the male students' uncertainty in light of the social and implicit meanings associated with the role of the clergy, understood as part of a cultural discourse, contributes to and expands the life-historical interpretation of their individual constructions of themselves as ministers. In the discourse in which these students understand themselves, the role of the pietistic pastor figures as a social representation of the authoritarian clergy. In this perspective, the social and implicit meanings associated with the role of the clergy may be interpreted to represent the male students' unconscious wishes and personal need for power, to compensate for their personal insecurity, producing intense ambivalence and possibly affecting their agency. Their role as ministers becomes important to them, as something they fear but also need, and it contains their unconscious wishes and needs.

THE FEMALE STUDENTS OF THEOLOGY AND THEIR GENDER SUBJECTIVITY

Reading the interviews with these theology students reveals a striking difference between male and female students in how they articulate their subjectivity in relation to their future vocation. The female students express their thoughts and experiences of the role of a minister as women, and in relation to how they have been perceived as girls in their childhood and as young women. The male students, by contrast, do not articulate their subjectivity in relation to their maleness. The topic of power is absent from the interviews with the women, but notably present in the interviews with the men. Based on these differences, it is interesting to reflect on Ingrid's constructions of herself as a minister, not only in her individual life perspective, but also in the way in which a societal perspective may expand and supplement the interpretations previously made in the life experience perspective.

Ingrid was brought up in a society where the perception of women's equality is well established. In Norwegian society, gender equality is considered an important value and women's possibility to become ministers may be seen as a contemporary expression of this. The first female minister, Ingrid Bjerkås, was ordained in 1961, and today there are many women in the clergy. In 2016, 406 of the 1273 ministers in the Norwegian Church were women. Of the 202 ministers under the age of 40, 92 are women (Ragna Dalen, adviser in the Norwegian Church Council, e-mail 08/11/2017). However, the role of a minister is still perceived by many as a male role and Ingrid has made a challenging professional choice even today. In this broader societal perspective where ministers are associated with a male role while women are perceived as equal, I will reflect on how Ingrid's constructions of herself as a minister might be understood as an expression of her struggle to come out of the tomboy role.

In a material perspective, Ingrid's construction of herself as a minister may be considered an expression of a step out of female subordination. An approach that considers women equal to men takes for granted that women have been freed from subordination and have the opportunity to construct themselves as men do. In spite of the fact that Ingrid will take on a traditionally male role as a minister, her experiences and emotional conflicts bring into question the perception of gender equality in the society in which she was brought up.

From an early age, the female and male students are socialized differently, as I explored in the analysis of the interviews with the male students, who are socialized in perceptions of the powerful minister. Ingrid's ambivalence between being a woman and autonomous can be interpreted as an expression of women's socialization to subordination, articulated as a discourse where women are perceived as little, a child, dependent, quiet, passive and sweet. Girls' socialization to subordination has been strong in childhood and should be understood as part of their upbringing and repeated in their educational environment. Due to these cultural differences in girls' and boys' socialization, the female and male students' constructions of themselves as ministers are not comparable.

I mentioned above how Ingrid was expected by the teacher to restrain herself. This might be interpreted as an expression of the girl child's socialization to subordination as sweet, quiet and passive. As a girl, Ingrid had to give up her autonomy, and she took on a tomboy role to survive as a different girl. In a life-historical perspective, this was interpreted as a way of restraining her from expressing herself as a girl.

At the time of the interviews, Ingrid interprets the emotional conflicts she is struggling with as her private conflicts, articulating them within a life-historical framework. She understands the solution as lying in her ability to connect her feelings and thoughts and to come out of the tomboy role. This puts her in a state of mental conflict and she continues to struggle in the tomboy role that has become too small for her, while searching for a new role where she can integrate and embrace all her feelings, thoughts and qualities, and be a woman at the same time. It is within this societal situatedness that Ingrid as a young woman is trying to come out of the tomboy role and find a new role where she can be autonomous. In this societal perspective, Ingrid's constructions of herself as a minister might be interpreted as her search for a new role; taking on a male role associated with power may be seen as a search for a role where she can integrate being a woman and being autonomous. In this way, she is attempting to produce a new gender profile (Salling Olesen, 2005).

Ingrid struggles to grasp what it means to her to be an autonomous woman. She constructs herself as autonomous by taking on the role of a minister, but is left with no language to articulate what this means, other than talking about female ministers who appear as sweet, dressing in a feminine way and wearing make-up. She thus seems to remain in the ambivalence between being a woman and being autonomous.

Ingrid's way out of subordination appears to be more complex than taking on a male role. Ingrid's construction of herself as a minister may in a societal perspective be understood as a continuation of the existing structures of subordination of her childhood. Furthermore, she seems to be trying to come out of women's subordination within the structures of subordination. This places Ingrid in a psychodynamic sphere and in a societal contradiction: the perception of women's equality coupled with her socialization to subordination. She seeks autonomy within the social order she is socialized into, trying to construct herself as autonomous in a male role associated with autonomy.

CONCLUSION

These examples have shed light on how the psychosocietal approach provides an in-depth interpretation of the socialization of theology students, examining how one may theorize the dialectic relationship between the subject and the society in which the subject is constituted. This perspective reveals the complexity of learning processes, as well as possible barriers to learning and processes involved in the development of an identity as a minister. Based on the concepts of life history, subjectivity and experience, the psychosocietal approach offers an in-depth understanding of the processes of identity construction in students of theology. The life-historical perspective explores how one can theoretically connect individual students' integration of their previous experiences and orientations with the theological perspectives and understandings of their future profession they meet in their educational institutions. Theological education is placed within a lifelong perspective and studied in light of the opportunities it provides in all aspects of life, not just the clergy profession.

The life-historical socialization processes active in the development and establishment of a professional identity as a minister can be understood as different forces producing a dialectic result consisting of a particular historical subject in a particular social situation. These forces, which are active in individuals' constructions of themselves as ministers, are partly related to the individual life experience, which is socially constituted, and partly related to the specific situation in which the subject is active. This gives rise to a wide range of contradictory notions among the students about the role of the clergy and their ideas for the future, which are important for their orientation horizon and thus their development of life strategies.

The concept of life history derives from a critical theoretical tradition and opens up the interpretation of the data in light of how the socialization of theology students into the clergy is embedded in broader societal processes, such as the modernization of Norwegian society and the development of gender equality. An example of this is how female subordination should not be limited to an isolated challenge for theological schools or the Church, but must be understood in the wider societal context where these schools and the Church are situated. In this way, the psychosocietal approach provides insight into the subjective learning process as not limited to the institutional sphere of education, but also understood in the broader social context of theology students and theological institutions.

This critical perspective particularly illustrates the ways in which the educational programme promotes or constrains opportunities for the individual theology student to develop a professional identity as a future minister in modern Norwegian society.

An example of this is the theological discourse where the positioning between pietists and liberals functions as a psychological defence reaction to the students' insecurity and fear of the role of the clergy and hinders them in expressing themselves in a new role as a minister.

REFERENCES

Finholt-Pedersen, S. M. (2018a). *Hva er det å bli prest? Teologistudenter og subjektivitet – en kvalitativ analyse* (PhD dissertation). Roskilde University.

Finholt-Pedersen, S. M. (2018b). *Hva er det å bli prest? Teologistudenter og subjektivitet.* Retrieved from https://video.ruc.dk/media/t/0_fmyll2no

Laursen, P. F., Moos, L., Salling Olesen, H., & Weber, K. (2012). *Professionalisering: en grundbog.* Frederiksberg: Roskilde Universitetsforlag.

Salling Olesen, H. (2005). Work related learning, identity and culture. New work – new genders? New genders – new work? In A. Bron, E. Kurantowicz, H. Salling Olesen, & L. West (Eds.), *"Old" and "new" worlds of adult learning* (pp. 25–39). Wagonowa: Wydawnictwo Naukowe.

Salling Olesen, H. (2006). Diskurs og erfaring. Eksempler fra lægeprofessionen. *Nordisk Pedagogik, 26*, 358–371.

Salling Olesen, H. (2007). Theorizing learning in life history: A psycho-societal approach. *Studies in the Education of Adults, 39*(1), 38–53.

Salling Olesen, H. (2017). Learning and experience: A psycho-societal approach. In M. Milan, S. Webb, J. Holford, R. Waller, & P. Jarvis (Eds.), *The Palgrave international handbook on adult and lifelong education and learning* (pp. 169–185). London: Palgrave Macmillan.

Salling Olesen, H., & Weber, K. (2012). Socialization, language, and scenic understanding. Alfred Lorenzer's contribution to a psycho-societal methodology. *Forum: Qualitative Social Research, 13*(3). http://dx.doi.org/10.17169/fqs-13.3.1906

PART 3

UNDERSTANDING INTERACTION AND LEARNING IN ORGANIZATIONS AND INSTITUTIONS

ÅSE HØGSBROE LADING

7. A PSYCHOSOCIAL STUDY OF COLLEGIAL RELATIONS AMONG SECONDARY SCHOOL TEACHERS IN TIMES OF REFORM

INTRODUCTION

The following chapter is based on two consecutive qualitative studies. The focus is on teachers' collegial relations at a Danish upper secondary school in the context of a major educational reform.[1] My interest is centered on the minority among the teachers who were critical of the reform and the repercussions their opposition had for the traditionally unified collegiate group.

BACKGROUND

Since the 1990s the educational sector in Denmark has been in a process of modernization with the object of transforming the school system both organizationally and pedagogically. In this, there was a move away from a traditional view of the *general gymnasium* as center of *Bildung* where the aims of the education were defined in terms of enlightenment and personal development to an orientation towards the competitive demands of the labour market and economic productivity (Korsgaard, 1999). Along with this development, New Public Management was introduced with an emphasis on leadership to create clear strategies, efficiency and control in the educational system (Greve, 2002; Jacobsen & Buch, 2016). A small minority of teachers was being promoted to take up the newly established positions in the enlarged school management team. However, there was still a substantial number of teachers working at the same level, about 70 or 100 at most *gymnasier*. In terms of psychosocial organizational theory, they form a well-defined *group* in an institutional context where they share a primary task, meet regularly face-to-face and form emotional bonds which, however, are rarely put into words (Bion, 1961; Lading, 2006, 2010; Visholm, 2004). The group is further inscribed in a profession that provides it and the individual members with an identity, which, ideally, builds up a sense of social legitimacy and personal self-esteem. A reform has both new professional and personal meanings and exposes the fact that there is not just one professional identity, but several identities (Day et al., 2006).

THE RESEARCH PROJECT

The first piece of my research was undertaken in 2002–2003 at a time when the Ministry of Education offered selected schools a possibility of testing reactions in the schools to the educational reform before it was to be implemented in the *gymnasie* system as a whole. Whether these schools would accept or reject becoming test schools was put to the vote in the teachers' council, which is an advisory organ where both teachers and management are members and attendance compulsory. Central in the reform was that teachers had to work part of their time in interdisciplinary teams. The teams had two overriding aims: one was pedagogical. Across their different disciplines teachers were to organize interdisciplinary projects for students, focusing on their active exploration of real-world problems. The other was making teachers cooperate around their classes. The reform contained other changes, but it was the obligation to form interdisciplinary teams, which created the biggest controversies among the teachers, and this is the theme I am concerned with here.

The Ministry of Education and the school managements presented teams and the new project pedagogy as 'progressive' in journals on education. Inspiration came from influential thinkers in modern educational theory, and among them especially Oskar Negt (1964), John Dewey (1938) and Henning Salling Olesen (Olesen & Andersen, 2015; Salling Olesen, 1971). In primary schools and at the young universities at Roskilde and Aalborg the theories had been successfully implemented, and professionals in the ministry found that the turn had now come to the *gymnasie* schools (Lading, 2006). In the media, university teachers praised the ideas of the reform, but more traditionally minded educational researchers objected that they had little to do with the learning realities in the *gymnasie* schools. They claimed that students and pupils should learn the basics of the individual disciplines before they could embark on interdisciplinary project work (Iversen, 2002; Schmidt, 1999; Nicoll & Olesen, 2013).

Empirical Investigation

My research project was carried out at three test schools. As I was aware that different opinions of the reform among all parties in the process, I also expected that at the individual *gymnasier,* teachers would disagree about its perspectives and about the prospects of becoming a test school. I also imagined that some, perhaps many, teachers would be concerned that the reform would interfere with teachers' traditional individualistic professionalism which was based on identification with one teacher, one subject, one class, in one room and with much freedom in both the choice of teaching methods and professional focus. Differences in views would, I assumed, affect the collegial relations and the group dynamics in the relatively close-knit professional group. I was particularly interested in the experience of teachers who were critical of implementing obligatory professional team and project work in the *gymnasie* system. They represented a deviance from the dominating political discourses on progressive pedagogy, and I wondered how their points of view were represented in discussions about the reform. In the following, I shall refer to these teachers as 'critics' and those in favour of the reform, as 'reformers'.

There were many similarities in the teachers' reactions at the three *gymnasier* I visited, but at Stjerneborg *gymnasium,* the reform created the biggest conflicts. For this chapter, I have therefore chosen the dynamics of this collegial group as an extreme exemplary case (Flyvbjerg, 2006).

Seven years after I had concluded my first study, I had the opportunity to explore how teachers in the same schools saw their collegiate relations after the reform had been introduced in 2005. In the second part of this chapter, I am presenting an analysis of Stjerneborg *gymnasium* as a follow-up to my first piece of research.

Recontextualization

Modernization has subjective and contextual sides to it, which are dealt with by the people involved in the process. It takes place in the everyday lives where interpersonal relations constitute a complex mixture of planned and unplanned incidents which take on different meanings dependent on persons, groups, time and place (Lading, 2004, 2006). In order to understand the specific teachers' reception of the educational modernization process, it should be emphasized that educational ideas and strategies are mainly produced in institutions outside the schools, in pedagogical and business universities and in governmental research units. These institutions have their own agendas, which are negotiated with governmental educational policymakers. They are then introduced to the *gymnasie* system where the aims are expected to be turned into professional routines in the day-to-day work, but this process takes place in the very different cultural and practical context of schooling (Bourne, 2003). The official educational discourse as stated in government policy documents is confronted with the schools' traditional institutional forms and cultures and implies a process where the 'outside' educational ideas are recontextualized by the 'inside' with *their* spoken and unspoken agendas. The process of recontextualization as such not only interferes with pedagogical practice, but with teachers' sense of the meaning in what they do and affect their experience of their value for students and in a wider perspective, for society at large.

In the first part of my chapter, I am focusing on a specific moment in the recontextualization process where a teachers' council has to decide for or against testing key elements in the educational reform. As most teachers have limited experience with what team and project work may imply, their vote is based on what they *imagine* will be the outcomes. They exist in what I, with a reference to David Armstrong (2005), shall call their *reform-in-the-mind.* When I visited the school again, teachers have had experiences with the teams, and 'the-reform-in-the-mind' had been confronted in their everyday lives with 'the-reform-in-practice'. How the teachers as a group deal with their potential differences of opinion in this respect is part of the recontextualizing process in the ongoing practice in the school. In the following, I shall be looking into this process through the lenses of psychoanalytically informed psychosocial thinking.

Psychosocial Thinking

Psychoanalytically informed 'psychosocial' research is a reference to studies where concepts of the psychic, the social and societal are deeply interconnected. The ambition is to situate the microanalytic studies in analyses of societal courses of events. A key point is that conscious as well as unconscious emotions and affects are seen as contextual and not only experienced individually, but embodied in groups, organizations and cultures (Jaques, 1951; Menzies Lyth, 1961; Dawson, 1994). Inspirations are critical theory, open systems theory and object relational theories mainly drawn from the tradition of the Tavistock Institute of Human relations (Miller & Rice, 1967, Visholm 2004), and more recently, from the University of the West of England (Clarke & Hoggett, 2012). For the present chapter, I rely on studies by Graham Dawson (1994), Wilfred Bion (1961) and Isabella Menzies Lyth (1961). In different ways, they include the concept of social defense against anxiety in their analyses: Dawson traces it in the overall regulation of our everyday lives, Bion in small groups and Menzies Lyth in organizations.

The Everyday Regulation of Peoples' Lives

Graham Dawson is an English cultural analyst with a background in the Birmingham school of cultural studies. He follows a tradition begun by Henri Lefebre's (1968) phenomological analyses of everyday life which were later elaborated by Thomas Leithäuser (1979) from a Marxist perspective. In his studies, Dawson includes narrative and psychoanalytic theories. He focuses on how people try to reach 'relative psychic comfort' when dealing with their everyday tasks in a *cultural praxis.* He describes how there is

> […] deeply embedded in everyday life, a creative activity in which everyone engages. Even the most mundane of narratives is an active composition, created through formal arrangements into a whole. In composing a story of the day's events, for example, a complex process of selection, ordering and highlighting gives prominence to some events over others and interprets their significance, thereby making sense of an objective world. At the same time, the telling also creates a perspective for the self within which it endeavours to make sense of the day so that its troubling, disturbing aspects may be "managed", worked through, contained, repressed. (Dawson, 1994, p. 22)

Dawson points out that the meaning made of anxiety-provoking experience relies on culturally accepted narratives or discourses in the context. When interpreting their significance, unconscious processes such as defensive activity are activated, but also possibilities of confronting the difficulties. However, in his analysis Dawson disregards the importance of group dynamics for the ways in which individuals manage to create "a story of the day's events". Bion (1961) has shown how people become emotionally dependent on the group and that they under pressure develop a 'group mentality'. Group members form a set of shared assumptions of themselves and the world, thus defining correct behavior, status structures, accepted rituals etc. It is created by "the unanimous expression of the will of the group, contributed to by the individual in ways of which he is unaware, influencing him disagreeably whenever he thinks or behaves in a manner at variance with the basic assumptions" (1961, p. 65) and this prevents what he defines as 'containment' (Bion, 1962, 1963). The concept refers to the more positive aspect of group functioning where the group forms a 'container' for 'troubling, disturbing aspects' of living that Dawson mentions. Ideally, they can be contained, that is reinterpreted, sorted out and given new perspectives in the group. Still, there will often be inner and outer threats against the group's containing capacity. If the threats are experienced as overwhelming, the group may defend itself against its dissolution by regressing to more primitive states of mind. Bion distinguished between group functioning as a *work group* and a *basic assumption group* while stressing that groups alternate between these states. In the first case, the group deals with the complex realities surrounding its tasks, in the second it is dominated by regressive feelings whose psychic rationality is creating unity through excluding individualities and loosing contact with reality.

Contrary to Bion, Menzies Lyth is oriented towards organizational and institutional analysis. Her most famous case dates back to the 1950s when she was consultant to a hospital where there were dissatisfaction and a big turnover among the nurse trainees. It illustrates ways in which difficult emotions were experienced or avoided, managed or denied, kept in or passed on in the organization. In her analytical process, Menzies Lyth first considered the overt problem as the 'presenting symptom' and reserved her analysis to after she had diagnosed it in the first place. The immediate symptom was the nurse trainees' irrational ways of dealing with patients. Looking into what this practice could be a symptom *of*, she found that that the young nurses' *primary task* included close contact with illness and death, and it activated feelings of helplessness, sorrow and fear of dying. The unconscious defenses against these anxious feelings were part of the organizational life, and in agreement with Bion, Menzies Lyth pointed out that the defense mechanisms did in fact not alleviate the feelings that were the undercurrents of the defensive activity.

The Teachers' Tasks

Secondary schools and hospitals are clearly different, but my point here is that they share challenges in their daily face-to-face contact with people, which activate many feelings that are hard to cope with (Hoggett, 2014; Lading, 2004). In the teachers' case, authority is a key issue. Teachers must act in roles of authority when teaching, evaluating and examining students (Lading, 2007), but in relation to the school management their authority is destabilized by the more hierarchical New Public

Management system in the organization. At the same time, traditional authority structures in society are losing their legitimacy. Students' respect for their teachers are based not on their position, but on the way they present themselves as persons (Ziehe, 2001; Lading, 2006, 2007).Whether the individual teacher succeeds in making herself popular or not, she can never be sure of how her interaction with the students will turn out in the long run. The personalized relationship causes everybody to be at risk and as such, it is a shared condition. Defenses against the anxiety that the precarious position activates are unconsciously built into the professional culture, and is further enhanced by the changes introduced in the reform. Menzies Lyth argues that

> [c]hange is inevitably, to some extent, an excursion into the unknown. It implies a commitment to future events that are not entirely predictable and to their consequences, and inevitably provokes doubt and anxiety. Any significant change within a social system implies change in existing social relationships and in social structure. It follows that any significant social change implies a change in the operation of the social system as a defence system. While this change is proceeding, i.e. while social defences are being re-structured, anxiety is likely to be more open and intense. (1993, p. 22)

At the psychosocial level, the traditional individualized system in the schools served as defenses against colleagues' and leaders' potentially critical eyes. In teams, each person is out in the open and has to negotiate her ideas with her colleagues. Although most of the teachers at Stjerneborg voted for the reform, it could still be felt as an anxiety-provoking challenge whose specific outcome could not be predicted and therefore imbued with both positive expectations and fears.

Following Menzies Lyth's process of investigation, I was first looking out for data showing signs of what was going on in the collegial group at Stjerneborg. In accordance with classic psychoanalytical clinical methodology, I chose to work with qualitative methods, which limit interactional censorship and encourage free-floating attention both in the research objects and in myself (Hollway & Jefferson, 2000). Analytically, my focus in the first place was on what seemed incongruous or irrational in the light of organizational aims and interests. This I saw as the overt 'presenting symptoms' of the psychological state of mind in the collegial group. At the level of interpretation, I followed three steps (Salling Olesen & Weber, 2012, Raae, 2018): First, I situated the empirical scenes, actions and sayings in time and context. Then I attempted to open my mind to free associations concerning what people were saying and doing and how it was enacted while simultaneously writing my associations down. I was specially looking out for what surprised me, for lack of logical cohesion, paradoxes, and emotionally charged statements (Rosendahl et al., 2017; Hollway & Jefferson, 2000). The last analytical step was critically examining my immediate responses and ordering my material thematically as well as finding theoretical concepts that could add meaning to what I had before me (cf. Salling Olesen & Weber, 2012; Hollway & Jefferson, 2000). In accordance with the hermeneutic and psychoanalytical stance inscribed in the methodology, I went back and forth between these levels and incorporated references to them in the interpretation process centered on what happened and why.

TEACHERS' COUNCIL MEETING AT STJERNEBORG GYMNASIUM

My empirical observations began with my presence at the teachers' council meeting at Stjerneborg *gymnasium.* It was to be unstructured and as unobtrusive as possible (Bernard, 1998). Being a former *gymnasie* teacher, I felt that my presence did not attract much attention. I immediately felt at home when I entered the common room with its modern design furniture and people dressed very much like me. I knew the unwritten rules for participation in the council meetings. In order to make the most of some often boring hours, one talks in a low voice with others, correct students' exercises, read a paper or jot down doodles on a piece a paper, listening halfheartedly to what is going on. But this meeting was different as the question of becoming a test school was going to be put to the vote. When it came up, the whole room seemed to stiffen. Teachers stopped whispering to their neighbours or correcting students' essays and looked up. Two teachers in a row took the floor and gave arguments for becoming a test school. The first one was chairman of the council. He argued that by accepting to become a test school, "we" would be in the front when in a few years the reforms were to be introduced to all *gymnasier*. He added that interdisciplinary teams and project work are methods that "the newest and most advanced Danish schools and universities had already integrated in their studies and "we" should do what students are supposed to do: work together and create projects where the complexity of things can be dealt with. Only in this way could "we" prepare students for their future studies and careers. Then another teacher stood up, presented the particularities in the test process and added that there was an economic incentive behind it all as the government had promised extra financial resources.

While the teachers were speaking for the test school, I noticed several in the audience looking resignedly at others across the tables. One of them got up and in an annoyed tone asked if 'we' really had the time and energy to spend time on a reform that was inevitable and could not be much altered. "It is fake democracy", she almost shouted. Another one added in an ironic voice, "it seems as if there are people among us who are not entertained by sticking to their own subjects and are ready to give them up to interdisciplinary projects and team work". The last one to present a comment added that somehow entertainment would be the guiding principle in the future and the end of the *gymnasium* as an academic institution. Students would start working with projects before they even knew the basics of the individual disciplines. With no other interventions, the meeting ended before the interval by a show of hands. There were 48 for, 22 against and 8 pass, so the proposal was carried through. During the interval, there was a celebration of a teacher's 50s' birthday with snacks and wine. A colleague made a very amusing and learned talk, and people were chatting and laughing loudly. I did not hear anyone referring to the vote.

In my notebook afterwards, I wrote that at the meeting, teachers opened up to what could have developed into a professional and nuanced discussion of the opportunities and negative aspects of the reform, but the discussion petered out. The two reformers seemed sure of their victory, the critics that they were losers in the game. Overall, it was remarkable that only five out of about 70 teachers – who are used to argumentation and speaking up in the classrooms – came forward with their opinion. It was significant, too, that in spite of the formally defined aims of New Public Management, not anyone from the management presented their views on the subject.

Group Interviews

I had put a note up in the common room, asking people who were either in doubt or against the decision to become a test school to contact me in order to participate in two group interviews. Ten volunteered and for practical reasons I ended up with six who met for the first time five days after the council meeting. I followed Hollway and Jeffersons' recommendations for open interviews (2000, 2008) and started out by asking" Can you tell me about recent organizational and pedagogical debates at the school?" thus assuming that the interviewees would come up with what was first on their minds. However, I had to be more explicit in some of my further questions as the openness seemed to be confusing and even seen as a way of hiding what I really wanted to hear.

The first person to speak voiced his dislike of a pedagogical method being forced upon the school from the outside:

> […] all our work is focused on nuancing the learners' knowledge about and experience of the world, and if our work is standardized, the everyday life at the school is impoverished. All these concepts, team building etc. which really are not Danish, press us into specific forms […] we feel that it is a devaluation of the school that we feel belongs to us ….

There is a strong emotional content in what this teacher saw as a split between 'them' from the outside and 'us' who by tradition and practice "own" the school. School is 'impoverished' and so is his job. Although he referred to 'us' and 'we', he also commented on colleagues who are in "conspiracy" with the Ministry of Education to ruin the *gymnasie* school. For him the professional autonomy was the key issue, but the others in the group quickly turned to the communication in the collegiate. They referred to alliances between 'certain' teachers and the management. There was especially one person the interviewees saw as in a secret alignment with the headmaster and who was referred to as the *alpha male*. He was described as an informal leader in the collegiate group, and one who silenced nuanced discussions of the reforms. Most exchanges, the teachers said, about what was going on therefore took place in private conversations among equally minded persons. One male teacher elaborated on his views and stressed that people

> [...] dare not say what they think. They vote for experiments they do not want, they ... I say this on behalf of new teachers, for I have been here so long, I can manage – but the young ones have considered leaving because they do not want to be called 'reactionary'.

According to this teacher, colleagues refrained from voting against becoming a test school out of fear. The double communication – voting for something that one does not believe in – created an even more ominous atmosphere in the collegiate. He described the reformers' methods as "terrorist" and referred to a feeling that the reformers indirectly used threats of social exclusion to intimidate others to further their own position. Teachers feared being excluded from influence and sociality if they were positioned as against so-called progress. In the situation, the crucial theme was the power to define one's own professional, political and personal identity. The critics felt humiliated as they were looked upon as 'old school', as 'reactionaries' and thus inferior. Anger was personalized and the 'alpha male' and those who were seen as his allies were blamed for the changed collegial relations.

As a contrast to these views of the state of affairs, I recalled my experience of togetherness at the personal celebration at the council meeting. It seemed then as if teachers, in spite of their differences, identified themselves with each other and wanted to keep up good contact. Therefore, it surprised me to listen to the critics' experiences only five days later. I took into account that the teachers, who volunteered to be interviewed, were the ones who would be expected to feel most mortified by the process. Still, when speaking informally to other people in the staff room, I got the impression that the antagonisms among the teachers were indeed very heavy.

Symptoms and Interpretations

The diagnosis of the collegial tension in the *gymnasium* based on my empirical investigations is *the lack of public debates* on the complexities of the coming reform and reasons for different points of view. Moreover, a further symptom was the ostracizing of individual teachers' personal identity resulting in fear of exclusion of the collegiate group. To overcome the frustrating reality, teachers split up into subgroups where they each created simple oppositions between good and bad pedagogical and organizational development. Instead of a mutual exchange of criticism, difficulties, apprehensions and doubts, the situation encouraged personalization and splitting, the projection of all the bad parts onto the opposite subgroup while keeping the good ones for one's own. Everybody knew that the management was for the new reform and saw becoming a test school as a possibility of being noticed by the ministry. As one teacher said, he would like to hear them (i.e. the leaders) say so. But the management blended into the collegiate group and according to the critics, used hidden strategies, which were parallel to the teachers'.

The suppression of disagreements and lack of responsiveness can paradoxically be interpreted as attempts at keeping a favoured group together. Out of fear of losing the common 'we', the teachers held their silence publicly and talked about *the others* privately. As it was, each part was cornered by the group dynamics where organizational and pedagogical issues turned into personal conflicts. The collegiate group became a basic assumption group. The opposing subgroup was used in defensive splitting as the vehicles for projections, and the possibility of a full awareness of the actual issues was overridden by strategies for the management of psychic conflict (Dawson, 1994, p. 37).

STJERNEBORG *GYMNASIUM* REVISITED IN 2009

In 2009 I had the possibility of going back to Stjerneborg *gymnasium*. Although seven years do not count as much in a working life perspective, the societal context had changed considerably during this time. In the first years after the millennium, the Danish economy was booming and there was generally an optimism regarding economic growth in the future and the rate of employment was high. However, signs of a financial crisis showed in 2007 and escalated in 2008 and in the following years, the job market became unstable and there was a general sense of insecurity in the work force.

In 2005 the reform was passed in Parliament and became the juridical foundation for all *gymnasie* schools. It had become part of the everyday working lives and I was curious to see how the group had developed. Were there traces of what Hargreaves called 'Balcanized relations'? Could one still talk about an oppositional minority? Had former antagonisms been passed on?

This time I was observing activities in the staff room over one week. I placed myself at different tables and fumbled with my papers while observing what was going on around me. Later I made two group interviews with five former critics as well as two newly appointed teachers. The group interview was repeated twice although the teachers found it hard to find the time for it. I started out with an open question: "how would you describe the collegial atmosphere at Stjerneborg today?" People were more ready to elaborate on their experiences of their daily lives compared to last time, and I just added a few direct questions at the end of the interviews.

Thirteen new teachers had been appointed and seven had retired since I was at Stjerneborg. This in itself made the staff room appear different, but it was not only because of the mixed age group. Teachers as a whole were busier, coming into the staff room with their computers and papers and leaving it quickly afterwards. Groups had meetings in the sofa arrangements and only a few sat down to rest with a cup of coffee. At lunch people talked loudly to one another, but often they left the table quickly, taking a half-eaten sandwich with them. The room looked like a busy railway station hall, and the atmosphere seemed to be full of nervous energy.

This impression was reinforced when the teachers discussed their working life in the group interviews.

The two young interviewees told me that they had heard about collegial conflicts "way back", but seemed not very interested in hearing more about them. They agreed that while some were "of course" closer to specific colleagues than others were, they did not feel people were on unfriendly terms. One said that as a newcomer, she was welcomed by her professional subgroup, but she had only got to know the other teachers "a little bit" after a couple of years. If there were one split, both of the newcomers said, it would be between new and old teachers. But the important problem for especially the young ones, was the workload:

> I have small kids, sometimes they cannot fall asleep early, and then I have not enough time to prepare my lessons, or I must work longer than I want to. I need more sleep, but how is it possible? My husband is a teacher, too, and we try hard to be efficient, to organize things so that our two little boys do not feel that they are in the way, but sometimes we have to tell them that we cannot do this and that together because one of us has to work even at weekends.

Here the young teacher describes problems with the life-work balance in her job. However, the others in the group insisted that it was not just the young ones who were unable to finish their tasks within "reasonable working hours". There were more lessons to prepare, papers to correct, and informally, students demanded much individual attention because of personal and educational difficulties. However, teachers also stressed that they liked the time together with colleagues. Overall, there was a positive view of the atmosphere in the collegiate group, and the older ones among the teachers said that they could partly thank the newcomers for that. One mentioned that it made a difference that 'the alpha male' had left the school for a job elsewhere, and the others did not contradict him. To my surprise the critics were not altogether against the teams, but one said

> I used to – as you know – to be fed up with all these team and project ideas, but now the reform has become part of our normal working obligations, I am still not satisfied with it, but somehow you get used to it.

As a group, the interviewees commented on teachers in the teams who were less cooperative. One said

> Some colleagues are more ready to follow up on what we have decided than others, but we are disciplined, most of us. We have to. I like people to be reliable because in the teams we are dependent on each other.

In the same vein, a critic remarked:

> Efficiency is 'in' (laughing), it really is. Count me out if someone has not done what she was supposed to do […] I do what I am paid to do and I won't be set back by people who don't care to organize themselves.

The critics insisted that they were ready to work with colleagues outside their own circles, and the main criterion for being a 'good colleague' was reliability, not ideological correspondence. They agreed that there was more work to do compared to the beginning of the century and that they had learned from their young colleagues to closely observe the formal regulations and be paid for extra work. Back in the 1990s a new collective agreement had been introduced in the schools which implied that if teachers took up tasks which they were not formally required to do, they would be paid individually for them. However, it seemed that it was not until much later that it was internalized in teachers' ways about their job, and it certainly played a role in 2009.

At the end of the group interview, I asked the teachers directly if people felt hesitant about speaking up at the council meetings about especially the workload, interactions in the teams and what could be done about the personal problems among the students. They told me that the school had special councilors who helped individual students, and thus transferred responsibility for the well-being of students to specific teachers, but still they worried about how they could help their troubled students. Three critics were convinced that speaking publicly about working relations and the increased strains in the job would be of no consequence as these things affected people differently and had no common long-term solutions. They added that they did not want to end up in a situation as the one in the past, but the young teachers and two other critics were sure that this would not happen today. One of the young teachers summarized the common outlook when he said, "we have a lot to do and won't argue". Time, not fear, set the limit to discussions. The idea that people were so stressed that they did not want to "to argue" or go into pedagogical discussions indicated that the young as well as the senior generation had resigned themselves to the existing state of affairs even though they did not think the demands were fair.

The group as a whole seemed more regulated, more individualized and more oriented towards getting their financial dues. Questions regarding being reactionary or progressive did not crop up, neither did specific pedagogical issues. So the-reform-in-practice was not evaluated in the collegiate group, but each had her own experiences of how things were working out. The atmosphere in the collegial group was, as I have shown, explicitly described as 'friendly' and old animosities were put aside. Nevertheless, there were indications that there were certain disagreements in the group, and that the description of a very harmonious group was an idealization of the state of affairs. The focus on people who were not 'reliable' or unprepared indicated problems in some of the teams. When one critic said he had resigned himself to the team structure, but that he was not "satisfied" with it, his views were not contradicted. The young teachers also suggested that there was "a split" between the old and the young members of the collegiate group, and this did not receive any comments either. I was surprised that the critics did not come up with more details about their relations in the group, and about how there former status as a minority – and one that was overridden by the reform – had affected their views of their work.

I noticed that they were quick to leave the questions of collegiality – which was my opening question – in order to speak negatively about the workload, which appeared to be something that everybody could agree on.

SUMMARY

Many of the teachers I had met in 2002 had started their careers in the 1970s and early 1980s where in society as such there were hopes for improving conditions for the diverse mass of students coming into the *gymnasier.* The job was associated with political and pedagogical perspectives and the traditional organization of the schools did not stand in the way for individual group experiments. The demands that all teachers were to work together and around similar projects changed that. Conceived as ways of making use of different competences and professional perspectives in the collegiate whole group, it did change the everyday lives of the teachers and students. But the reform also opened up to individual dominance and splitting into subgroups, leading to mutual suspicion and fears. As a professional group with a common primary task, teachers were unable openly to discuss the complexities of their job and the substance of the future reform. The changes in the organization of the school and its pedagogical outlook involved further top-down regulation from both the Ministry of Education and the school management as well as collegial negotiations in the teams. The contrast between the teachers' explicit and implicit views of the collegiate group suggests that in order to achieve 'relative psychic comfort' there were negative feelings about how things had developed, that the teachers did not want to talk about or get into contact with. Imbedded in the collegiate culture, I saw their silence as a paradoxical defensive activity against the anxiety that the attack on teachers' autonomy and the divisions in the group created. On the one hand, public silence represented a wish that conflicts, if they are not voiced, will disappear and the group become a safe haven, on the other hand, public silence encouraged hidden communication and distrust. In the present case, colleagues formed a basic assumption group where fighting each other became the central activity in an attempt to ban individuality and evade the intricate realities.

The collegial relations in the organization, I revisited, had improved. Old struggles seemed to have evaporated. The critics were determined that collegial conflicts should not again arise, and the young ones thought of conflicts as belonging to the past and the more fussy older generation. However, new conflicts loomed under the surface and discussions on this and other relevant themes were not on the public agenda. A culture of silence was passed on to the collegiate group at Stjerneborg *gymnasium* from earlier times, but as a form of unconscious social defense it had taken on a different meaning. In 2002, people were personally taken up with the principles governing the future of the school, whereas in 2009 teachers appeared less interested in the ideological aspects of it and at the same time, they put more emphasis on their identity as wage earners.

The teachers' focus on having a peaceful everyday contact with each other suggest that again they found differences were a hazard to collegial harmony. Good working relations meant being able to rely on each other's support in the effective exercise of one's duties, but not having discussions on the overall perspectives in what teachers were doing. The everyday challenges of communicating with the students as well as coming to terms with colleagues in the teams in a stressed environment made the immediate concerns more imperative.

Central in the very first reactions to the reform were questions concerning its pedagogical perspectives: would it contribute positively to learning and teaching in the institution? Underneath was also the question of personal meaning: would I be doing a good job under the new circumstances? In this way, the original conflicts incorporated both professional *and* personal identity issues, and this was why they turned into personalized attacks. The intensification of the teachers' work had later led to more individualistic strategies for survival. The collective financial agreements, intensification of the professional demands, and possibly also a more precarious labour market were reasons for the young generation to introduce a different attitude to being a *gymnasie* teacher, which disseminated to the group at large. My resumed empirical investigations thus showed that the culture of achieving relative psychic comfort through collegial silence in the public room had remained an element of the collegiate group mentality. Although collegial peace was won, the situation seemed to me to be more alarming. It indicated that what teachers wanted to be silent about was the threat of loss of meaning in their work.

It was not possible in my studies to explore what would have happened if teachers and management had in fact spoken up about their views of the reform and the intensification of their job as well as their feelings about each other. I am not blind to the fact that this could have created many difficulties, too. However, openness has to be learned, and dealing with it also has to be learned and inscribed in the cultural practices in the schools. How such a situation could come about, will have to be researched in a future project.

NOTE

1 Here I shall refer to the Danish upper secondary school by its Danish designation: i.e. as *gymnasie* in the singular and *gymnasier* in the plural. I am here dealing with the general *gymnasie* which in contrast to technical and commercial *gymnasier* is aimed at providing general education and study competences in the humanities and the natural and social sciences with a view to being able to go through college, university and other schools of further education. It takes three years to complete. It provides a number of compulsory subjects, but part of the instruction is implemented as multi-subject courses. It is the most popular post-compulsory education for young people in Denmark. The *gymnasie* schools have become self-governing and the principle of pay-per-graduated person made the schools encourage an even bigger intake of youngsters. The teachers all have master degrees from a university in two subjects. In addition, they have to have completed a one-year course in theoretical and practical pedagogics before becoming full time teachers.

REFERENCES

Armstrong, D. (2005). *Organization in the mind*. London: Karnac Books.

Bernard, H. R. (Ed.). (1998). *Handbook of methods in cultural anthropology*. Walnut Creek, CA: AltaMira Press.

Bion, W. R. (1961/2000). *Experiences in groups and other papers*. London: Routledge.

Bion, W. R. (1962). *Learning from experience*. London: Heinemann.

Bourne, J. (2003). Vertical discourse: The role of the teacher in the transmission and acquisition of decontextualised language. *The European Educational Research Journal (EERJ), 2*(4), 496–521.

Clarke, C., & Hoggett, P. (Eds.). (2009). *Researching beneath the Surface*. New York, NY: Karnac.

Dawson, G. (1994). *Soldier heroes. British adventure, empire and the imagining of masculinities*. London & New York, NY: Routledge.

Day, C., Kington, A., Stopart, G., & Sammons, P. (2006). The personal and professional selves of teachers: Stable and unstable identities. *British Educational Journal, 32*(4), 601–616.

Dewey, J. (1938). *Experience and education*. New York, NY: MacMillan.

Flyvbjerg, B. (2006). Five misunderstandings about case-study research. *Qualitative Inquiry, 12*(2), 219–245.

Frank, K. (2010). Job-embedded professional development: Reducing teacher isolation by enacting social change. *Dissertation Abstracts International Section A: Humanities and Social Sciences, 70*.

Fullan, M. (2001). *Leading in a culture of change*. Indianapolis, IN: Jossey-Bass Wiley.

Greve, C. (2002). New public management – en kort oversigt over begrebets anvendelse og udvikling. *Nordisk Administrativt Tidsskrift, 83*(1).

Hargreaves, A. (1994). *Changing teachers, changing times: Teachers' work and culture in the postmodern age*. Toronto: University of Toronto Press.

Hjort, K. (2012). *Det affektive arbejde*. København: Samfundslitteratur.

Hollway, W. (2008). The importance of relational thinking in the practice of psychosocial research: Ontology, epistemology, methodology, and ethics. In S. Clarke et al. (Eds.), *Object relations and social relations. The implications of the relational turn in psychoanalysis*. London & New York, NY: Karnac.

Iversen, J. (2002). Kernefaglighed – et dynamisk begreb. *Uddannelse, 3*.

Jacobsen, A. J., &. Anders, B. (2016). Primus inter pares – paradokser, deadlocks og omveje i gymnasieledelse. *Tidsskrift for arbejdsliv, 3*.

Korsgaard, O. (1999). *Kundskabskapløbet – uddannelse i videnssamfundet*. Gyldendal.

Krantz, J. (2006). Dilemmas of organizational change: A systems psychodynamic perspective. In L. Gould, L. F. Stapley, & M. Stein (Eds.), *The systems psychodynamics of organizations: Integrating the group relations approach, psychoanalytic, and open systems perspectives*. London: Karnac Books.

Lading, Å. (2004). I forbindelse med team skal der nødigt være kærlighed« – om de personlige dimensioner i gymnasielærernes formaliserede samarbejde. In K. Borgnakke (Ed.), *Et analytisk blik på senmodernitetens gymnasium* (Gymnasiepædagogik, Nr. 47). Institut for Kulturvidenskaber, Syddansk Universitet.

Lading, Å. (2006). *"Vi er jo kolleger, ikke konkurrenter ... " – en analyse af moderniserede gymnasielæreres strategier i gruppe*. Odense: Syddansk Universitet.

Lading, Å. H. (2007). Gymnasielærerprofessionens sorte boks. *Dansk pædagogisk tidsskrift, 4*.

Lading, Å. H. (2010), Bions gruppe. In Å. H. Lading & B. A. Jørgensen (Eds.), *Grupper*. Frederiksberg: Frydenlund.

Lefebre, H. (1968). *La vie quotidienne dans le monde modern*. Paris: Gallimard, Collection Idées.

Leithäuser, T. (1976). *Formen des Alltagsbewusstseins* [Forms of everyday life consciousness]. Frankfurt/M: Campus.

Lerche Nielsen, J., & Webb, T. (1999). *Project work at the new reform University of Roskilde – Different interpretations?* Roskilde: Roskilde University Press.

Menzies Lyth, I. (1960). A case-study in the functioning of social systems as a defense against anxiety. In A. D. Coleman & W. Bexton (Eds.), Group *relations reader 1*. A. K. Rice Institute. London: Tavistock Publications.

Menzies Lyth, I. (1988). *Containing anxiety in institutions. Selected essays* (Vol. 1). Oxford: Free Association Books.

Miller, E. J., & Rice, K. A. (1967/1975). Selections from: Systems of organization. In A. D. Colman & H. Bexton (Eds.), *Group relations reader 1* (A.K. Rice Institute Series). London: Tavistock Publications.

Negt, O. (1964). *Soziologische Phantasie und exemplarisches Lernen.* Frankfurt: Europäische Verlagsanstalt.

Nicoll, K., & Olesen, H. S. (2013). Editorial: What's new in a new competence regime? *European Journal for Research on the Education and Learning of Adults, 4,* 103–109.

Obholzer, A., & Zagier Roberts, V. (1994). *The unconscious at work: Individual & organizational stress in the human services.* London: Routledge.

Raae, P. H. (2004). *Træghedens rationalitet.* (PhD Thesis). Syddansk Universitet.

Salling Olesen, H. (1971). Politisering eller strømlinet modernisering? Om basisuddannelse og humaniora. *Kritik, 20.*

Salling Olesen, H., & Andersen, A. S. (2015). *The Roskilde model and the challenges for universities in the future. The Roskilde model: Problem-oriented learning and project work.* https://doi.org/10.1007/978-3-319-09716-9_17

Salling Olesen, H. (2014). The invention of a new language of competence – A necessary tool for a lifelong learning policy. In R. C. Duvekot, D. Joong Kang, & A. Murray (Eds.), *Linkages of VPL: Validation of Prior Learning as a multi-targeted approach for maximising learning opportunities for all* (pp. 37–44). Rotterdam: Vught: EC-VPL.

Salling Olesen, H., & Weber, K. (2012). Socialization, language, and scenic understanding. alfred Lorenzer's contribution to a psycho-social methodology. In H. Salling Olesen (Ed.), *Cultural analysis and in-depth hermeneutics. Forum for Qualitative Social Research, 13*(3).

Schmidt, L. H. (1999). *Diagnosis III. Pædagogiske forhold.* Copenhagen: Danmarks Pædagogiske Universitet.

Thomsen, M., Rosendahl, K. L., Horne, M. L., Ringgaard, D., Rösing, L., & Munk, S. P. (Eds.). (2017). *Literature. An introduction to theory and analysis.* London: Bloomsbury Academic.

Thompson, S., & Hoggett, P. (Eds.). (2012). *Politics and the emotions.* London: Continuum.

Visholm, S. (2004). Organisationspsykologi og psykodynamisk systemteori. In T. Heinskov & S. Visholm (Eds.), *Psykodynamisk organisationspsykologi I.* Copenhagen: Reitzels forlag.

Ziehe, T. (2001). *The dominance of personal life worlds'. Uddannelse 10,* Copenhagen: Undervisningsministeriet.

PETER HENRIK RAAE

8. EFFECTIVE LEADERSHIP?

A Case Study in Work Psychodynamics

INTRODUCTION

Based on a psychodynamic analysis of a leadership interview, the chapter discusses how public modernisation initiatives have put educational leaders on terms where they handle their leadership roles by drawing on special forms of defence. It is asked if the demands for 'effectivity of leadership' can trigger defensive patterns of interaction that are counterproductive rather than effective – at least if effectivity means the ability of the leader and the employee to handle the increasing complexity caused by modernisation.

In recent decades, Denmark and the other Scandinavian countries have been characterised by ever more frequent political and administrative initiatives taken in the public sector that are meant to improve efficiency. In the field of education, the measures range from actual educational reforms to initiatives on finding new ways to harness existing resources. A recurrent theme has been the issue of leaders and leadership, which has increasingly come to the fore – how do educational leaders run schools and how do they manage to implement initiatives effectively?

The context in which these leaders find themselves is marked by both decentralisation and recentralisation. On the one hand, leaders have had a greater influence on, and responsibility for, school finances and the recruitment of students in connection with parents' (partial) right to choose schools freely. On the other hand, the relative autonomy and the teachers' freedom to choose their own teaching methods have been challenged by standardised state-wide tests, and both national and municipal governments, parents, the press and competing schools have been allowed to monitor how schools perform by data from a Data Warehouse, where the Ministry keeps records of each school's graduation grades, ability to balance social differences, student well-being and so on (Møller, Iversen, & Andersen, 2016). Both trends of de- and recentralisation may be regarded as an extension of New Public Management – the dominant management trend in welfare areas of recent years.

It is not hard to believe that this new situation engenders a complex kind of pressure, which forces leaders and employees to account for many different, but not necessarily convergent, considerations. It causes an increased pressure for learning for all in the staff. A number of studies have emerged over time, which investigated whether management actually functions properly and how leaders handle pressure

© KONINKLIJKE BRILL NV, LEIDEN, 2020 | DOI: 10.1163/9789004420274_009

(Hansen & Boje, 2016; Møller, Iversen, & Andersen, 2016; Wiedemann 2016; Kaspersen & Knudsen 2016; Hjort, Qvortrup, & Raae, 2012), but studies on the subjective behaviour of leaders and how the leader facilitates necessary organisational learning are under-represented. This behaviour is the focus of this chapter.

Based on a case analysis, I describe an ambitious leader's attempt to deal with demands for greater efficiency. Rather than just an increased workload this demands for efficiency derived from increasing work intensity: While the leader is expected to meet a range of different expectations of various interests, pulling him in different directions, he must create a unifying focus for the staff.

Against this backdrop, I ask how the leader in question attempts to overcome the situation he is put in by his management work. Out of interest in psychodynamics, I go on to ask whether the leader's attempt to handle the contradictory circumstances of reality ends up exacerbating the contradictory nature of the situation. Is the leader, in his efforts to act as an effective leader, going to counteract the development of the reflexivity enabling the organisation to handle the new conditions?

The chapter thus relates to the tradition of studying leaders and organisations that are already established in the field of psychodynamic theory. References are often made in this regard to Kernberg and Kets de Vries. Kernberg describes how inadequate leadership can stem from certain personality traits or a lack of competence, which he believes can bring out paranoid traits in organisations that should otherwise perform well (Kernberg, 1980). Moreover, according to Kets de Vries, leadership personality has far-reaching consequences for an organisation's efficiency, as personality affects the fantasies of organisation members (Kets de Vries & Miller, 1984). Kets de Vries mentions that conversely, however, some situations can bring out certain personality traits in the leader (Kets de Vries, 1992).

I do not take my point of departure as the leader's personality, but instead address how the management-induced conditions might add to *certain work psychodynamics,* which are part of the particular patterns in the leader's interactions with others. Although the chapter's focus is on the leader's situation and leadership work psychodynamics, it also takes an interest in the dynamics of the interaction between the investigated and the researcher(s). This project called for special methodological requirements, which meant that the methodology section was afforded a relatively significant amount of space.

THEORY AND METHODS

My interest in the dynamics between leaders' particular work situations and their subjective behaviour meant that I applied a particular perspective to the psychoanalytic tradition. The leader's behaviour is not seen in the light of recollections of one's life story or traumatic experiences, as is common in classical psychoanalytic studies. Instead, the task is to understand a particular *form* of interaction between the individual and the world around them, while focusing on how the *employment situation in an interplay with the individual life history mobilises or actualises subjectivity in a particular way* (Wolf-Ridgway, 2012).

The case works off of an interview, while therefore also incorporating the process that occurred in the interpretation of the interview, i.e. the initial interaction that took place between the interviewee and the interviewer, as well as later on between the case and the analysts. The actual interview which the case takes as its starting point is a qualitatively oriented, semi-structured research interview (Kvale, 1994), where the primary and immediate interest is generally in what knowledge the researcher can obtain about and via the interviewee in connection with a given phenomenon. The interview analysis is different in this case, however, because the methodology also aims to acquire knowledge of the further interaction between the interviewee and the interpreter(s) of the interview. The basic psychoanalytic-inspired assumption at play here, is that the interaction does not reproduce intentionally misleading patterns in the interviewee's behaviour towards his world and his professional life. For this part of the interpretation, I refer to the psychoanalytic-therapeutic discussion on transference and countertransference, and it should be noted that I did not subscribe to any therapeutic intent (Casement, 1985). I will elaborate on this later.

Communication and Interaction

The assumption is that the interviewee not only communicated intentionally and consciously on the facts of the case but also sought to organise his story in a way that influenced his listener to take on his version of reality. This is a well-established phenomenon in the field of narrative theory (Bruner, 1990), but it is also a matter that is discussed in psychoanalysis as a kind of quiet manipulation or an unconscious situation where the patient subtly tries to get the therapist to display a particular behaviour in order to relieve the patient's anxiety (Sandler, 1976). Freud terms the phenomenon '*transference*' – the process in therapy where unconscious desires and fantasies, which originate in other situations, are brought before the therapist. Freud found that transference also affects the analyst's fantasies of, and attitudes towards, the person being analysed, which he termed *countertransference* (Freud, 1992).

Projection is included as a mechanism in both transference and countertransference. Projection essentially stems from the desire to break down a threatening part of the self by projecting it on another person. The projection mechanism, however, rarely appears on its own. The concept of *projective identification* describes an extension of the concept. The mechanism is discussed by Ogden, among others, in a series of steps that begins with the subconscious fantasy of getting another person to have or bear certain feelings on behalf of oneself. The sender of the projection puts pressure on the other person in their interaction to get him or her to think, feel and act as an extension of the motive behind the projection. Provided the other person gives in to this pressure, the sender is then relieved of the projection once he or she is able to identify the threatening feelings in the other person (Ogden, 1982; Visholm, 1993). In the slightly longer term, however, the process entails limited interaction, as it takes place on the special premise which is the reason for the projection: to create a *form* of interaction as a type of defence against certain threatening feelings.

Although the ensuing interaction can be traced back to the original projection, it is not a one-to-one relationship between the original projection and the result because the projection that is sent is enveloped in the receiver's feelings and fantasies, and thereby becomes a part of that person's countertransference. These dynamics are of key interest to the analysis conducted here.

Transference and countertransference have been the subject of further therapeutic-methodological discussions, which are of significance here. Freud considered countertransference mainly to be a disturbance to therapeutic work that ought to be eliminated, but later approaches to the issue relativised this and found that one must, in part, regard countertransference as an inevitable aspect of the overall communication between patient and therapist, and partly – and of key importance in this context – as information that provides deeper insight into the motives belying the process (Heimann, 1950; Casement, 1985; Igra, 1989).

From Interaction to Interpretation

The transference and countertransference phenomenon also occurs in the interview situation and must also, consequently, in a situation such as this be seen as a path to more deeply understanding what is at stake for both the sender and the recipient: in this case, the interviewee and interviewer (Hollway & Jefferson, 2000). Detecting these processes, however, requires distance for interpretation, which in turn imposes certain requirements for the methodology.

A methodological framework that supports this distance references Alfred Lorenzer's work and was developed by the International Research Group for Psychosocietal Analysis (Salling Olesen & Weber 2012; Hollway & Volmerg, 2010). The method is, for instance, put into practice in a model that works at three levels: *what is said*, i.e. the immediate content of the level of expression, *how is it said*, i.e. a level that focuses on the pragmatic level of the interview, and finally *why is it said that way*? At this third and final level, one looks for the unconscious strategy which directs the two previous levels – the depth-hermeneutic understanding of what is at stake in the interview. The method adds a significant element regarding the organisation of the process, in which the same empirical data is met by several individual reactions. Hence projective processes can be reproduced in the group setting and a be an object of renewed interpretation. For a further review of the method see Salling Olesen and Weber (2012).

INTERVIEW WITH AN EDUCATIONAL LEADER

To begin, one might ask what knowledge you can acquire about a leader's practices through an interview, or what story a leader tells about his or her practices. Here, one can argue that leadership today is, to a significant extent, communication. Linda

Smircich and Gareth Morgan discuss management as a social process in which the leader succeeds in defining reality for those being led in ways that seem trustworthy to them (Smirchich & Morgan, 1982) – management of organisations is just specially institutionalised forms of this generally described process. The interest in so-called narrative leadership, or leading by telling stories of leadership motivations and intentions, can be read as an expression of the same (e.g., Boje, 2001; Downing, 1997; Charniawska, 1997).

The task of this case analysis is thus to shed light on another layer of communication, namely the unconscious, affective interaction that is part of communication and that has the intention of persuading the listener about a particular perspective on reality. The purpose is to examine whether there are special motives or intentions related to the communication which limit or restrict the receiver's learning, apart from what I mention with Smircich and Morgan. Here, the communication is between the interview and the analysts, that is to say, the analysis group and me, and the interest is not centred as much on the leader's perspective on reality as it is on the form of the interaction. Against this background, I assert that there is a significant relationship in the psychodynamics between subjectivity and work-related requirements for the interviewed educational leader. For the same reason, the analysis will focus on the ambivalent fantasies that the requirements arouse and the form of defence that the ego establishes against (anxiety about) failure and powerlessness in this connection.

The interviewee has been the leader of a medium-sized primary and lower secondary school for some years. Recently, however, his job has expanded to where he now has yet another school to manage. I have asked him to talk about the school and the development tasks he envisions.

What Is Said?

Below is a very brief description of the educational leader's response to my questions about school and his development tasks.

He notices that the increased workload forces him to work as a more generalised or strategic leader – to lead through leaders, he says emphatically. He talks about time constraints because the department heads at the 'new' school have to get to know him and learn how he thinks. For example, they need to know that he is very careful with the school's finances, to build up some room to manoeuvre – something that people at the 'new' school apparently are not used to. However, it is not just the school and its department heads that must adjust to him. He will have to get used to the fact that parents and students at the new school do not know him as well as those at his old school, and this – he stresses – requires that he consistently communicate much more and more extensively.

He describes the new school for which he is responsible as well-run – stresses that it is well-run! – but there have been some cases of protracted sick leave that he attributes to some 'strong teachers' having left the school and some – possibly more vulnerable – teachers having stayed behind. As a countermeasure, it is therefore urgent to promote what he calls a robust environment. He explains that the school has struggled with bad figures (grade point average, statistics of student well-being and absences and socioeconomic reference[1]) and attributes it to disadvantaged students that come from stressful environments in that part of the city. He adds that to be fair, they managed to improve some figures before he stepped in – and he emphasises that it is a school characterised by the kind of cooperation between teachers that goes beyond that normally seen. On the challenging side, it should be mentioned that student enrolment has been declining, and this development appeared at the same time as he was appointed, giving rise to speculations among teachers and parents of there being a secret plan to merge the school with his old school. Is it possible to keep the school and one of the parents' highly valued primary school departments? These reactions put him in a difficult position because his personal opinion is that the school, out of consideration for employee resources, would gain from a merger.

Whether an actual merger with his 'old school' will happen depends not least on local applications for enrolment. He is, in fact, in an odd situation. On the one side, he must work to build a reputation for his new school that can stabilise the in-flow of applications and save it. At the same time, he is met with suspicion among teachers and parents that his real interest is bringing the school under the old school he has led for a longer amount of time, with the financial and staff resource gains that could be an issue in the longer term!

How Is It Said?

The analysis in this section applies to the interview's pragmatic and meta-communicative level. This section is divided into three parts. The first is my initial analysis of the interview, the next section covers my response when re-listening to the interview, and the last is the analysis group's response.

I observe that the educational leader speaks energetically and emphatically. There are not many breaks in his speech, and I notice that I often have to interrupt him for clarification, because the information is apparently too succinct for me. Especially when I re-listen og re-read the interview I feel it is overloaded with information – much is said within a short span of time, and the educational leader often switches focus: between individuals, locations, tasks and conditions. He has just spoken of himself, and then he has moved on to the new school's department heads, and before you know it, he is talking about the vulnerable or strong teachers and then on to the parents. The same applies when making mention of the two different geographical locations where he acts as leader. He describes his work in several organisational fields, each with its own tasks, rapidly moving between these responsibilities. He briefly mentions the challenge of changing from the job's hands-on level to a more generalised, strategic level. He briefly talks about the different organisational conditions for the two schools and briefly about the special architectural conditions' practical importance for the teachers' cooperation. I notice that many current buzzwords from both national and local leadership discourse find their way into the interview: from generic leadership discourse, commonly used expressions, such as *to lead through leaders*, to be *conscious of one's communication task*, the need for *close economic follow-up*, to *maintain some room for manoeuvres*, and to work for *organisational resilience*. However, the newer leadership or management discourse in the education field also leaves its mark here: *generating data, performing at student welfare, a keen focus on 'the school's figures'*. As something consistent, I observe that he clearly strives to be nuanced, so that the ratings appear to be the results of analyses of both the 'pros and cons' of situations or conditions: The school he now manages is a well-run school, *but* there are some cases of long-term sick leave. He acknowledges that there are a great many educational developments that have been started *but* some of the teachers may not be strong enough to follow up on the developments. The local department heads at the new school are already referred to as 'we', *but* to become a fully-fledged 'we', they must learn to understand the leader's thinking so that they can lead more independently. It is not only a school with poor figures. He acknowledges that the school has struggled with poor figures and disadvantaged students and, therefore, has learned much *but* on the other hand, it is still challenged if it is to survive as an independent entity.

His nuanced style gives one the impression of a leader with an analytical view who identifies an important task but also demonstrates having the surplus energy to acknowledge working with any weaknesses. Thus, with this style, he is portrayed as both a competent and significant person in the world in which he takes action: At the school where he has now been assigned, he can recognise it as a school that is making good progress *but*, on the other hand, one that needs to be better equipped for a world that has become more demanding. He must, therefore, challenge the new school in an appropriate manner so that it can meet these requirements, and he is clearly someone who has the ambition and insight into how to succeed in doing so. *Therefore*, he will teach the department heads better financial monitoring, *therefore* he will teach his management team and teachers that he has the strategic vision and role, and *therefore* he must enable them to handle the job that by and large he performed before: *He* must show the school and himself that people can lead and be led through communication. Thus, in each instance where doubts are expressed, such doubts are not disqualifying. On the contrary: the doubts make one notice his analytical thinking.

The many words and concepts drawn from both the current generic leadership discourse (economy, organisational structure and leadership), the current national educational management discourse (data, 'the school's figures') and the local, municipal school discourse (utilisation of resources, school mergers) portray him as well-informed on more recent leadership discourses, and his succinct flow of information gives the impression of efficiency.

All in all, the interview discourse fits nicely into the popular image of a competent, effective leader, cf. for example, the Agency for the Modernisation of Public Administration's brochure entitled *Good Employer Behaviour* (phrases as clear strategy, efficient staff resources, focus on results, trust-based management; Moderniseringsstyrelsen, 2015).

My reaction when re-listening to the interview and the work using the transcript was significant. It struck me when re-listening to the interview that I evidently go out of my way to support the leader. My replies seem to be *very* obliging and supportive and not neutral or investigative: I make a point of emphasising that I understand (and even sometimes firmly), giving affirmation throughout and signalling complicity. I do, for example, interrupt by making an inside joke, referring to a matter in local politics. When I ask for clarification about a potentially critical matter, I apologetically stress my ignorance of his field. A third example is a sequence where the leader mentions some cases of long-term sick leave, where I almost apologetically on his behalf say that long-term sick leave is hardly a question of leadership. When re-listening to the interview, the question occurred to me: What was it that made me abandon a neutral, investigative role?

The analysis group's immediate reaction was just as significant but appeared at first to be quite different. My notes show that the group evidently found it difficult to follow the content of the interview. A few of the group members broke the rules of method – that I should remain silent – by trying to have me elaborate on the logistical and organisational patterns at the school (even though they appeared in the preface to the transcript). The person who played the role of interviewer during the reading audibly sighed several times while reading his part. At one point, the group began to respond in an openly critical manner, even hostile, towards the interviewee. One of the group participants wondered continually – even almost indulgently mused – over the exchange of words about sick leave, which, as I mentioned above, it is, of course, a matter for management to address cases of long-term sick leave! Another participant reacted critically to the leader's idea that the department heads must learn to think like he does so that they can lead independently (!) on the basis of his ideas – apparently without him explaining what he specifically wants?

It was relatively clear that these were emotionally charged reactions, but the verbalisations point in many directions and the group found it difficult to conclude the phase 'what is said'. Nonetheless, the phase ended abruptly with a remark from one of the group members, who pointed out that a less negative and more empathetic approach to the analysis work, where one empathises more with the interviewed leader's problem, *was indeed also* an option!

Why Is It Said That Way?

The interview and subsequent responses to it pose a series of questions about how the interview played out: How can we understand the form of interaction that occurs in the group? Like any other observation, one can view the interview as an example of attempts at impression management (Goffman, 1959). Here, however, the impression management seems to have an ambiguous effect on the surroundings.

I have described how the interviewed leader envisions himself facing a new and challenging task. You can understand if the task is met with ambivalent feelings – on the one hand, a fear of helplessness, powerlessness and total or partial failure, and on the other hand, the desire to overcome the challenge, a fantasy of omnipotence. Ambivalent feelings are well documented reactions when confronted with the duties in one's role – Zaleznik describes them as fundamental to a leader's experience of reality, not least because the expectation from his followers is that he exudes an ability to overcome the challenges (Zaleznik, 1966). In Goffman's words, one might imagine that the pressure on a leader about facework is considerable (see also Wolf-Ridgway, 2012).

In an extension of this argument, it makes sense to examine the interaction using the concepts of transference and countertransference and the psychoanalytic-inspired perspective on unconscious influence via projective identification.

The Ambiguous Response

I previously mentioned that each recipient's response to the same projection differs since the projection is enveloped in each recipient's fantasies. It is still crucial that responses can be traced analytically back to the same projection. The following sets out to examine the interviewer's and the analysis group's responses, respectively, in this light.

The interaction established *between the interview and the interviewer* can readily be described as a reaction against the backdrop of one of my perceived fears of potential helplessness and failure. In this way, my supportive manner is understandable, where I 'help' the leader, so to speak, not to feel powerless by almost putting words in his mouth ('that's not a matter for management, though', see above). I withdrew from my neutral investigative role since a more or less unconscious interaction was being established, a collusion where I try to compensate for a threatening sense of helplessness (Willi, 1975; Jakobsen & Visholm, 1988). Thus, the collusive relationship results in a kind of mutual seduction – it shields the leader from experiencing a threatening reality but at the same time dislocates the interviewer's neutral investigative role.

In relation to the interpretation group, a different pattern appeared. Their response can be described in three sequences. First, there was some prevailing confusion. Questions such as 'we need to know some more about the logistical patterns, some more about the organisation' were raised. This may be quite a rational reaction, but the many attempts to break the rules – which the group was familiar with, regarding the framework for analysis – would seem to indicate that there was something more at stake: One could see the group's response as an unconscious guard against a feeling of powerlessness, which an immediate sympathy for the leader could evoke. Next was a phase where the group's irritation with the leader (or possibly with the leader's and my collusive relationship) became apparent. The next instance of aggressive irritation could be seen in response to the educational leader's way of dealing with the threatening reality, as he sought to protect his ambivalence by trying to appear all the more competent. One could notice the group's preoccupation with the sequence on long-term sick leave not being a problem for management: According to my notes, the wonder that was expressed was almost marked by indignation, directed just as much at me as it was at the leader. In this sequence, the group did not appear to serve as a neutral investigative interpretation group either but instead was characterised by what Bion calls a basic assumption group, where individuality is reduced according to a common, unconscious collective agreement (here a fight-flight group; Bion, 1961). The third sequence of the group's response contrasted markedly with this. It occurred as a group member went against the distinctly expressed emotion by urging participants to look at the leader's reaction as a response to a difficult task that could have been expected. Here, the interpretation group sought to restore a more distanced and neutral investigative stance.

Following Rosenbaum (2002), Sandor Ferenczi, who at an early stage in the development of psychoanalytic therapy was involved with countertransference, explains that countertransference often proceeds in the three phases described here. In the first phase, the analyst has some control over his emotions, but reacts with confusion to the material for transference; the second phase is often characterised by the analyst's loss of perspective, which leads to his dismissive and hostile responses to the patient. The third phase takes place when the analyst recognises his response precisely as countertransference.

Conclusion: Where, in his countertransference, the interviewer evidently immediately reacts in a helpful and supportive way and thereby reflects the pole of helplessness in the interviewee's ambivalence, the interpreting group responds in its shared transference as immediately hostile to the interviewer's pole of omnipotence (and the latent violence within an omnipotent feeling's intention of control and triumph). Here, the response is directed towards the power and dominance that are at stake. Through the concepts of transference and countertransference, one can see the widely varying manifestations of responses to the same basic feeling of (fear of) helplessness.

Manic Defence as Unconscious Action

It is important to emphasise that we are dealing with a person whose actions at first seem to meet the expectations of efficiency that others have of him. *At the same time,* the analysts' response suggests that interwoven with the verbal content of the level of expression, more about the leader's ambivalent relationship with his task is communicated than what can be observed in a simple content analysis. It is recorded by both myself and the interpretation group, and it appears as initially opposite responses. In understanding this conflict, I will introduce the concept of *manic defence.*

Manic defence refers to the Kleinian psychoanalytic tradition. From a psychogenic perspective, the manic defence is regarded as a defence against the sorrow that follows the individual's general maturation, a maturation that means we have to live with the risk of even the certainty of losing security. Manic defence is described in contrast to (constructive) resignation over one's limited abilities to restore (fantasised) security. Using the defence mechanism, one seeks to put off or banish sorrow and associated feelings of powerlessness – of course, with the risk that the defence mechanism will at some point break down. Klein specifies that manic defence fundamentally consists of ideations of omnipotence, denial and idealisation – omnipotence with a view to controlling and ruling over objects, but without caring for them on a deeper level, denial about wiping the mind clean of dependence on others and the idealisation of holding on to everything good in the world and oneself by refusing awareness of anything threatening (Klein, 1992; Akhtar, 2001). Segal, Jaques and Winnicot characterise the basic feelings of manic defence as control, triumph and contempt (Segal, 1973; Jaques, 1965; Khan, 1975). Jaques sees manic defence appear in situations where the realisation of one's own vulnerability asserts itself (and therefore describes it as often occurring in midlife crises). Control, triumph and devaluation of others become a special (albeit frail) way of confirming that one is alive.

I find Winnicot's warning against understanding manic defence based on generalised symptoms to be of particular importance. Instead, he argues that manic defence must be understood as a particular 'economy' or dynamic, a certain unconscious way of handling the outside world: Can one understand a particular way of dealing with the outside world as an attempt at keeping the experience of defeat, failure and chaos at bay (Winnicot in Khan, 1975)?

In my use of the term, I will not emphasise manic defence as pathology but view it as an extension of Winnicot's suggestion: as a particular way of dealing with the reality that occurs as a universal form of psychological emergency management, and which particular circumstances in a stressful world can induce. Put another way, the term can be defined as *a universal, subjective disposition that can be awakened in certain situations and which means that the individual is engaged in a particular form of interaction with his/her surroundings.*

In light of this understanding, the leader keeps the challenging and immanent threat of defeat and failure in his surrounding environment at bay by identifying with a particular leadership discourse and its expectations for leaders and management. Striving to that end, he orchestrates the world around him – he does it unconsciously to those involved with this project, whether it is to the party that helps and supports him or to the party that confirms his view that the world must be actively controlled. In this is the projective identification process. A psychodynamic is established, which is understood here as a subjective response to specific and distressing conditions. How this particular response is a natural form of interaction for management to seize upon 'under modernised circumstances' is the subject of the following section.

EXPERIENCING MODERNISED CONDITIONS: THE HEROIC LEADER?

Peter Gronn speaks in the same vein of the complexity that New Public Management-inspired modernisations generate, of particularly 'greedy' management work, and against the background of a particular character expected of the leader, which he describes as 'the heroic leader' – the person who must be able to overcome the greedy aspect of work. According to Gronn, schools, hospitals, local authorities etc. are facing a growing number of tasks, not least in relation to resource cuts (Gronn, 2003, p. 147 et seq.). Here, I will add an issue that accompanies the generally peaked political interest in education and the ever-increasing frequency of reforms, which is the result: In addition to work intensification resulting from cutbacks, frequently modified procedures and routines constitute a burden, but there is also the fact that the public organisation, for better or for worse, is open to voiced concerns from different groups that can demand to be heard. Partial free choice of school means, for example, that parents' comments are given new importance for the educational leader and the strategic management of the school. The same applies to 'the school's figures'. The school's figures will be a platform for monitoring for both state and municipal governments and groups of parents. The heightened interest in national and local political profiling means greater pressure on, and speed of, implementation, which may also call upon teachers to speak up. However, the interests that the voiced concerns represent may very well point in different directions and have different ideas of efficiency. Does efficiency mean complying with budgets, bringing up the school's grades or improving well-being? Not all of these voiced concerns will be new but the legitimacy, which the New Public Management-inspired decentralisation and recentralisation entails, means that their conflicting content will be intensified and fragmenting impact will be greater. Adding a new level of expectations for the educational leader. The educational leader must not only be able to create sufficient cognitive coherence for himself in this tangle of interests but must increasingly communicate such coherence. He must increasingly be able to *convince others that this coherence is a reality which is valid above all other possibilities.*

A consequence of this new level of expectations is pressure on the leader's subjectivity. One can imagine that it entails an aggravation of what, as a universally human phenomenon, Goffman terms facework and impression management – preoccupation with controlling the impression the individual leaves on others (Goffman, 1959). The different voiced concerns and the legitimacy with which they demand attention from the leader of the public organisation mean that the pressure on the leader's ability to be able to engage in interaction with them is greater. *The leader must increasingly be able to convince others that the coherence that the leader has formulated is that which is valid above all other possibilities* (see my previous citation from Smircich and Morgan). One must imagine that manic defence is a subjective response to this pressure – as a particular 'subjective economy' meant to keep the threat of failure at bay but, at the same time, designs the relation between leader and staff member in a particular way, a way that can even be seen as counterproductive from the point of view of the leader whose aim is to enhance an efficient approach to the new, surrounding conditions.

Probably, new voices, close to the core processes of the school, have gained legitimacy with the New Public Management-inspired modernisation. These voices call upon increased professional and organisational reflexivity. The emphasis on *developing organisational capacity, vigorousness and distribution of leadership* (also mentioned in the interview with the leader) is a sign of this: capacity, vigorousness and distribution of leadership refer to or presuppose organisational and professional competence, an ability to decode continuously and reconfigurate demands that are often discordant, but these voices propose, so they appear as manageable tasks.

However, the manic defence seems to counteract this learning process. Though the projective identification the interaction actively defines the employees as actors who position themselves in unreflected pro and con attitudes. Ironically this goes against the learning process that seems more and more necessary as an answer to the complexity of modernisation.

NOTE

1 *Socioeconomic reference* is an indicator for comparing a student's performance with statistic calculated expected performance referring to gender, age, ancestry and parents' education and income (Ministry for Children, Education and Gender Equality, 2016).

REFERENCES

Akhtar, S. (2001). The experiental world of maternally deprived individuals. In S. Akhtar (Ed.), *Three faces of mourning. Melancholia, manic defense and moving on.* Northvale: Jason Aronson Inc.

Bion, W. (1961). *Experiences in groups.* London: Tavistock Publications.

Boje, D. (2001). *Narrative methods for organizational and communication research.* London: Sage Publications.

Bruner, J. (1990). *Acts of meaning.* Cambridge, MA: Harvard University Press.

Casement, P. (1985). *On learning from the patient.* New York, NY: Tavistock Publications.

Charniawska, B. (1997). *Narrating the organization: Dramas of institutional identity.* Chicago, IL: University of Chicago Press.

Downing, S. (1997). Learning the plot. *Management Learning, 28*, 27–44.

Freud, S. (1968–1973 (1912)). *Zur Dynamik der Übertragung, Gesammelte Werke VIII.* Frankfurt: S. Fischer Verlag.

Goffman, E. (1959). *The presentation of self in everyday life.* Doubleday: Anchor Books.

Gronn, P. (2003). *The new work of educational leaders. Canging leadership practice in an era of school reform.* London: Paul Chapman Publishing/Sage Publications.

Hansen, D., & Boje, J. (Eds.). (2016). *Mellem ledere. Uddannelsesledelse som problem eller svar* [Between leaders. Leading education as at problem or as an answer]. Århus: Klim.

Heimann, P. (1950). On counter-transference. *International Journal of Psycho-Transference, 31.*

Hollway, W., & Jefferson, T. (2000). *Doing qualitative research differently.* London: Sage Publications.

Hollway, W., & Volmerg, B. (2010). *Interpretation group method in the dubrovnik tradition.* Unpublished Paper.

Igra, L. (1984). *Objektrelationer och psykoterapi* [Objectrelations and psychoterapi]. Stockholm: Natur og kultur.

Jakobsen, P., & Visholm, S. (1988). Projektiv identifikation/delegation/kollusion [Projective identification/ delegation/kolusion]. *Matrix.* Henning, information missing. Is this a journal, then please give volume nummer and pages.

Jaques, E. (1965). Death and midlife crisis. *International Journal of Psycho-Analysis, 4.*

Kaspersen, L. B., & Knudsen, J. N. (2016). *Ledelseskrise i konkurrencestaten* [Crisis of management in the competition state]. Copenhagen: Hans Reitzel.

Kernberg, O. (1980). *Internal world and external reality. Object relations theory applied.* New York, NY: Jason Aronson.

Kets de Vries, M. (1992). The CEO Who couldn't talk straight – and other tales from the boardroom. *European Management Journal, 10*(1), 39–48.

Kets de Vries, M., & Miller, D. (1984). *The neurotic organization: Diagnosing and changing counter-productive styles of management.* San Francisco, CA: Jossey-Bass.

Khan, M. (1975[1935]). The manic defence. In D. Winnicott (Ed.), *Through paddeatrics to psyco-analyses.* London: The Hogarth Press.

Klein, M. (1992[1935]). A contribution to the psychogenesis of manic-depressive states. In M. Klein (Ed.), *Love, guilt and reparation and other works.* New York, NY: Free Press.

Kvale, S. (1994). *Interwiew. En introduktion til det kvalitative forskningsinterview* [Interview. An introduction to the research interview]. Copenhagen: Hans Reitzel.

Moderniseringsstyrelsen. (2015). *God arbejdsgiveradfærd* [How to behave well as a empolyer]. Copenhagen: Moderniseringsstyrelsen. Retrieved from http://hr.modst.dk/~/media/God%20 arbejdsgiveradfard/Pjece%20om%20god%20arbejdsgiveradfaerd.ashx

Møller, M., Iversen, K., & Andersen, V. (2016). *Review af resultatbaseret styring. Resultatbaseret styring på grundskole-, beskæftigelses- og socialområdet* [Resultbased stearing review. Resultbased stearing on school, employment and social areas]. Copenhagen: KORA Det Nationale Institut for Kommuners og Regioners Analyse og Forskning.

Ogden, T. (1982). *Projektiv identifikation och psykoterapeutisk teknik* [Projective identification and psychotherapeutic technique]. Stockholm: Natur og Kultur.

Raae, P. (2012). Den nordiske uddannnelsesmodel og det danske gymnasium [The Nordic model of education and the Danish upper secondary school]. *Nordic Studies in Education, 3/4.*

Rosenbaum, B. (2002). Modoverføring [Countertranference]. In O. Olsen (Ed.), *Psykodynamisk Leksikon.* Copenhagen: Gyldendal.

Salling Olesen, H., & Weber, K. (2012). Socialization, language, and scenic understanding. Alfred Lorenzer's contribution to a psycho-social methodology. In H. Salling Olesen (Ed.), *Cultural analysis and in-depth hermeneutics. Forum Qualitative Social Research* (Vol. 13/3).

Sandler, J. (1976). Countertransference and role-responsiveness. *International Review of Psycho-Analysis, 3.* Retrieved from https://manhattanpsychoanalysis.com/wp-content/uploads/readings/ Green%20CPP%202013%20Uploads/Sandler,CountertransferenceandRole-Responsiveness.pdf

Segal, H. (1973). *Introduction to the work of melanie klein.* London: The Hogarth Press and The Institute of Psycho-Analysis.

Smirchich, L., & Morgan, G. (1982). Leadership: The management of meaing. *Journal of Applied Behavioural Science, 18*(3), 257–273.

Visholm, S. (1993). *Overflade og dybde. Om projektiv identifikation og det modernes psykologi.* [Surface and depth. About projective identification an the psychologi of the modern life]. Copenhagen: Politisk Revy.

Wiedemann, F. (2016). *Send mere ledelse. En analyse af Ledersamfundets konsekvenser* [Send for management. An analysis of the consequensces of the management society]. Odense: Odense Universitetsforlag.

Willi, J. (1975). *Die Zweierbeziehung.* Hamburg: Rowolt.

Winnicott, D. (1971). *Playing and reality.* London: Tavistock Publications.

Wolf-Ridgway, M. (2012). Application of work psychodynamics to the analysis of CEO's representation of the self: Resorting to an 'asture' clinical methodology. *Journal of Research Practice, 8*(2).

Zaleznik, A. (1966). *Human dilemmas of leadership.* New York, NY: Harper & Row.

LYNN FROGGETT

9. THE USES OF OBJECTS

Reflexive Learning in the Epistemic Museum

INTRODUCTION

Drawing on the author's own research in socially engaged museums and the spirit of Kirsten Weber's work this chapter echoes her interest in the societal role of the arts, and in the scenic and life historical dimension of adult learning. It considers the museum from a psychosocietal perspective as an epistemic space and site of object relating whose value lies in storing, conserving and presenting artifacts through which the museum visitor can realise a relationship to a shared culture. This chapter concerns education and learning in contemporary museums in its instructional, interactive and epistemic modes. It considers these alternatives in the light of the often unacknowledged role of the museum as a cultural repository where socially unconscious phenomena can find symbolic form through the man-made and natural objects with which the sensible world is populated. It suggests that the locus of reflexive knowledge produced in the epistemic museum is in the generative interaction between the museum visitors and museum contents and it is here that the societal contradictions in which the institution is enmeshed are disclosed.

In dedicating the chapter to Kirsten Weber I am referring to a conversation that developed over the years that I knew her in which we struggled to bring into dialogue British and Continental intellectual traditions. Key influences for Kirsten included the social psychology and theory of consciousness of the Frankfurt School – in particular as represented by Theodor Adorno; and feminism, especially through the work of Regina Becker Smith. On my part, the project of the Frankfurt School articulated with the British Kleinian and Object Relations tradition through C. Fred Alford's work; Anglophone psychoanalytically informed feminism was informed by different sources: on the one hand the Post-Freudianism of Juliet Mitchell, on the other, Relational School authors such as Jessica Benjamin concerned with intersubjectivity and recognition. For me, however, many of our most useful conversations were about Alfred Lorenzer and I have a vivid after-dinner image of the two of us by the bookshelves in her home, poring and puzzling over one of his particularly convoluted texts. With her knowledge of both German and English she was much better versed than I was in Lorenzer's writings and its subsequent developments (Salling Olesen & Weber, 2012; Weber, 2012).

© KONINKLIJKE BRILL NV, LEIDEN, 2020 | DOI: 10.1163/9789004420274_010

Kirsten was instrumental in founding the International Research Network for Psychosocietal Analysis, through which I first met her, in order to work intensively with alternative modes of hermeneutic interpretation. The network, that still meets annually in Dubrovnik is grounded in an interpretation group practice which was already well developed at the University of Roskilde where she worked, and that drew inspiration from Lorenzer's theory and method. The Dubrovnik interpretation groups have experimented and evolved over the years, and variations in the practice have been explored, enriching the encounter between these intellectual traditions and others, very much in the spirit of Kirsten Weber's own outlook and trajectory. I have taken what I have learnt from these groups into the field of research in the socially engaged arts and culture that now occupies much of my time. It has influenced the way I interpret visual and performative art and its practices, and the artefacts of material culture. It was Kirsten herself who presided over a session in which we interpreted photographs and in which I made my first move in this direction.

As a non-German speaker the network offered an 'apprenticeship' in this previously unfamiliar research practice and Kirsten generously provided the conversational context in which I came to understand it a little better. Her interests were wide, but converged with my own on matters of politics, learning, and 'high' and 'low' culture. In bringing these conversations to bear on how we can discern the socially unconscious aspects of a cultural institution and its contents – in this case through museum based learning – I am presenting ideas on a subject which I am certain would have engaged her, though I cannot pretend to know that she would have agreed with me.

MUSEUM BASED LEARNING AND CULTURAL (UN)CONSCIOUSNESS

What do we keep stuff for? In particular what lies behind the cultural inclination to select, collect, conserve and display objects and keep them expensively in museums for public benefit?[1] The regional Museum, known as The Harris, local to the university where I work in Preston in the North West of England, is home to a permanent collection and runs temporary exhibition programmes housed in a late 19th century building, resplendent with neo-classical portico and pediment of self-conscious grandeur. The building is raised above the main city square on what appears from the front aspect to be a massive plinth. In fact the portico is for the birds. A side entrance allows access to human visitors via a gloomy, atrium tucked away underneath. Once inside, the museum offers a monumental setting, with rotunda and grand staircase of four stories, rising 120 feet to the lantern that surmounts the roof; the walls are embellished with stucco friezes. It is as if the visitor must be chastened and over-awed, the better to abase her before the high culture she is about to receive.

Following Adorno (2002) we might consider that the import of the cultural institution lies less in its overt function than in what it reveals of societal contradictions by virtue of its own dynamic relation to the social and political context, and the public it ostensibly serves. This changes over time and in its current form The Harris has become a site of struggle between on the one hand the modernisers who want to put culture at the heart of local regeneration, so transforming the museum into a civic hub; on the other, the conservationists who hope to preserve an emblem of Victorian civic pride intact for the edification of future citizens. In the febrile political climate of Brexit, the museum is also enmeshed in tensions between cosmopolitanism and provincial retranchement, and between sentimental nostalgia and the manic optimism of populism.

There is much in museum curation and education, as well, as in the contents of institutions such as The Harris, that enables us to reflect on what we unconsciously value as a society, what we repudiate, and how these change through processes which at the time are themselves socially unconscious. I became interested in how cultural institutions relate to their publics, when it occurred to me that part of what they do is offer a space for the contemplation of what we might tacitly know, but have not yet conceived – or what we might call the 'unthought knowns' of cultural life (Bollas, 1987). The function of the museum is as much to hold the line against a collective forgetting through memorialization (Mack, 2003) as it is a repository for the evolving symbolic life of city, region or nation. Museum collections may literally 'hold' tacit or disavowed cultural knowledge until there is an interpretive community ready and willing to receive it. Such is arguably the case with historical records of slavery or the subjugation of aboriginal peoples. Over time, and in the particular quality of setting the museum can provide, we encounter objects that stimulate associations, thoughts and feelings whereby the unthought known can find symbolic form in material culture and be recognized. In this respect the educational function of the museum is not so much to inform us of culture as to hold up a mirror to it so that, as Winnicott (1971) would have put it, each generation discovers for themselves what is there to be found. As individuals when we visit a museum we encounter an array of objects into which we can project self-states and aspects of our habitual relations to people and things. They may become objects of identification and identity formation (Newman & McLean, 2006). They may also offer an aesthetic third (Froggett & Trustram, 2014) around which we can elaborate new symbolisations.

In this chapter, rather than approach the knowing and learning that takes place in museums from the field of museology, I take a psychosocietal perspective drawing on psychoanalytically informed traditions of thinking on culture from Britain and Continental Europe that converge on the problem of our relation to the sensible world. The question of interest here is how what is socially unconscious, or in the hinterland of consciousness, can be apprehended through the collections that a museum houses. Museology in general has been more concerned with what we can 'see' than with what is 'hidden', although the accent on visual display has begun to change as the 'post-museum' seeks out new opportunities for encounter and communication with its audiences (Barrett, 2011). This opens the door to a psychosocietal perspective that asks what emerges in the space of interaction between museum-going publics, museum contents (including its personnel), and the society on whose behalf this work is done. I shall give an example of the interpretive potentials of material objects followed by a brief overview of the educational function of the museum in its instructional and interactive modes. This will help to clarify its epistemic role (Born & Barry, 2010; Muller et al., 2006; Miettinen & Virkkunen, 2005) in enabling a public interaction with its objects that produces reflexive cultural knowledge.

INTERPRETING OBJECTS

In 2010 a series of radio programmes, fronted by the Director of the British Museum, Ian McGregor, captivated mass audiences by presenting a 'History of the World in 100 objects' selected from the museum's vast collections[2]. With an object per fifteen minute episode, and a web-site that recorded the text and enabled viewing of the selected artefacts on-line, it was a tour de force of museum pedagogy that enabled the public to encounter each object in terms of the cultural attributes that have made it meaningful over time. For example, a Victorian stoneware tea set, dating from the 1840's and partially overlaid with silver work, is understood not only through its materiality and its aesthetic, but through the layers of signification that expose the intricate mesh of social relations, military forces, geo-political administrative and legal powers, along with a household gender order and rituals of decorum, conviviality and probity enacted in the 19th century bourgeois parlour. Nor is this to forget the promotion of tea in the service of temperance to divert the labouring classes from their habitual alcoholic beverages, thereby enhancing the discipline of industrial capitalism's burgeoning workforce.

The success of the series lay in the artfulness with which it enabled the ordinary museum goer, without any specialist knowledge, to acquire the curiosity and method to 'read' each exhibit as a text, understanding it as embedded in social practices and historically produced. The tea set might once have been celebrated simply as an instance of expanding market production, which combined with the craftsmanship of its silver overlay, indicated a new compromise between utility and refined taste in an affluent and aspirant middle class. Nowadays it would just as likely be associated with the imperialism that required agriculture, trade and industry to submit to a British 19th century quest for global domination. In providing expert knowledge of the history and social relations that underlie tea drinking, McGregor offered 'instruction' in the importance of tea production, trade and consumption, which we can further elaborate, and also illustrated the scope of the curator's trans-discipinary repertoire. Audiences could consider a tea set as a domestic object that stood at an intersection of global geo-politics, so that within its symbolic presence in the household was an implicate class-based, gendered and racialized social and political order. By thinking in this way about a material object, resonant because it is a special instance of a commonplace piece of household equipment, we could, if we wished, make imaginative comparisons between 'then' and 'now' – bringing to attention the temporal compression of contemporary working lives that invades the home, so that the tea set as a focal point of interaction disappears, to be replaced by a box of mass produced bags and an electric kettle. The 'Fordist' erasure of ceremonial tea-making processes comes to light through this juxtaposition, and with it the distinctive performative idiom of the domestic tea time – or what in British workplaces once constituted the tea-break – a social interlude and point of contestation in labour relations.

We understand through these comparisons a politics of the workplace and the home which is entangled with a changing aesthetic of living in the sensible world, that finds expression in objects of mundane, as well as artistic creation. These are particles of the 'distribution of the sensible' that Ranciére (2004) describes as "a delimitation of spaces and times, of the visible and the invisible, of speech and noise, that simultaneously determines the place and the stakes of politics as a form of experience" (2004, p. 13). However, Ranciére's discussion remains at a metatheoretical level and describes broader epochal shifts between aesthetic 'regimes'. The contents of museums offer the opportunity to discern more localized and differentiated shifts in sensibility. This requires a view of how people have consciously interacted with the objects that they collect, conserve and present, and how we apprehend their unconscious uses as distillates of unacknowledged past and potential experience.

Besides the tea set's status as a manufactured item (the stoneware) we regard it as a crafted aesthetic object (the silver overlay) – in either case embodying the sensuous symbolic interaction forms that are materialized in process of moulding and making it, and in its ritualistic social uses (Lorenzer, 1972, p. 50).[3] In a domestic setting the set is evocative of intimacy and the relations, harmonious or fraught, that can typify patterns of habitual family interaction. In my own family there is a teapot surmounted with a little silver bird that was gifted to my daughter as a child by her grandmother. The pot was in use in the grandparental home, and for the small child was invested with a fantasy of continuity and stability in a household that was becoming increasingly disordered through dementia and frailty. It served as a transitional object (Winnicott, 1971) insofar as she chose it as a receptacle for her illusion of reliability, supported by the potential space[4] of the family teatime – an interlude of shared 'play' in afternoons that were otherwise fractious with inter-generational discontents. At the same time the teapot maintained a real existence of its own, durable but dented with the imprint of clumsy handling from more boisterous and carefree times.

"Without hallucinating the child puts out a sample of dream potential and lives with this sample in a chosen setting of fragments from external reality (Winnicott, 1971, p. 51).

Lorenzer and Orban – perceiving the close correspondence between transitional phenomena and the theory of interaction forms remark "… the transitional object is part of the scene, the realisation of one moment of the interaction form which is able to become independent and concrete, in the light of which the emergence of self and object can be elaborated and demonstrated" (Lorenzer & Orban, 1978, p. 478).

At stake here is a transformation of the object from its status as 'container' of sensual symbolic interaction forms that derive from its material nature to the biographically specific interaction forms that arise from personal uses of a cultural artfact – thereby composing a familial 'scene' in which a relationship to the cultural field is enacted. Similarly, the potential spaces of the museum gallery offer an array of 'evocative objects' (Bollas, 2009) in which this transformation can occur so that the possibilities of symbolization are multiplied – or rather, the galleries can create the conditions – spaces of containment[5] – under which objects become evocative for the people who attend to them, so that they can be creatively used and transformed (Froggett & Trustram, 2014).

There are a number of ways of conceiving the educational function of the museum. It can offer an authoritative, didactic space imparting a cross-disciplinary knowledge of cultural forms through the cognitive processes of museum interpretation; or, if we acknowledge the museum's socially unconscious functions, it can be a site of scenic experience (Lorenzer, 1986) for the visitor who becomes reflexively enmeshed in a matrix of interaction forms with objects that are available for symbolization[6]; or it can be a potential space where material objects become the containers of unconscious phantasy (object relating), and the museum itself functions as an institutional container that allows unconscious cultural material to find symbolic form. In this mode it can offer resilient and evocative objects (Bollas, 2009) that we endow with vitality, selecting, using and 'releasing' them so that they act back on us by virtue of their intrinsic properties (Winnicott, 1971). I shall return to these questions later in this chapter.

THE SYSTEMATIC AND INSTRUCTIONAL MUSEUM

The radio series, probably one of the most successful the BBC has ever produced, was not only instructive, it was also interactive insofar as it was accompanied by on-line pedagogic resources for schools and adult education. In a move designed to intensify public engagement, individuals and local and regional institutions were invited to upload objects of their choice. All of this activity potentially offered rich data to anyone with an interest in material culture, whilst the selection and display of objects revealed preferences and prejudices in curatorial practice, and by extension those of the society on whose behalf the museum exhibits.

Museums have long been regarded as places of public education, both formal and informal. The learning that takes place within them has been progressively reconceptualised in line with their changing social role throughout the last hundred years or so. The public museum, as opposed to the private collection, dates from the mid 18th century, aligned with the progressive emergence of a public realm. The British Museum and the Musée du Louvre in Paris were prestigious early examples. The public museum gathers strength with the modernist project, the growth of trade and the rise of the merchant classes, coming into its own with the consolidation of nation states and the colonisation processes of the 19th century. Both the anthropological and the art museum played a part in the cataloguing and documentation of cultures, and the self-assertion of an imperial world order. The museum's educational mission was to purvey a view of national progress as much for the 'civilisation' of the working classes as the self-congratulation of a newly powerful and wealthy bourgeoisie. To this end museums pursued their educative mission as a form of public address (Barrett, 2011). Bordieu (1984 [1979]) argues that despite the avowed aim of edification, they remained inaccessible to those who lacked the cultural capital to fully benefit from their store of knowledge and artistic achievement (Bordieu & Darbel, 1969 [1990]).

Well into the second half of the 20th century museum pedagogy developed in symmetry with the role of the professional curator, becoming implicated in the co-option of an authoritative view of culture into a wider project of governing (Bennett, 1995). The function of the museum educator was to maintain a flow of information and curatorial interpretation from museum to a public with whose living conditions it saw little reason to engage. While these institutions were "intended *for* the people, they were certainly not *of* the people in the sense of taking any interest in [their] lives, habits and customs" (Bennett, 1988, p. 64). Following Foucault (1977), Bennett (1995) and Hooper-Greenhill (1992) see museums as engaged in disciplinary practices, implicated in the formation of subjectivity and mediating the relation between the individual and the state. The dominant exhibition aesthetic in such institutions is effected through quiet spaces of contemplation – the cavernous gallery, reverential atmosphere and oak-framed display case – ensuring that the visitor – a viewer in an ocularcentric institution – was kept at a respectful distance. In the instructional museum – education, an activity where there is direct transaction with the public – has been largely subordinate to collection and conservation. In the UK it is staffed by a poorly paid and overwhelmingly female labour force, who until relatively recently mediated the knowledge flows in a one way direction, positioning the public as recipients and spectators. The interaction between viewer and collection as a site of inquiry, was and is at best a secondary consideration. In the didactic educational model the idea that one might be able to read the unconscious lives of cultures through museum objects is incoherent, insofar as this can only be achieved through an active and self-reflexive interpreting consciousness.

THE DE-CENTRED AND INTERACTIVE MUSEUM

The 1990's played a crucial role in helping to dislocate a largely positivist and unified view of the nature of the knowledge dispensed by museums. Foucault (1986) saw the post-disciplinary museum as a 'heterotopia' – a place of "mythic and real contestation of the space in which we live" (1986, p. 24). A 'new museology' (Hooper-Greenhill, 1992, 1994) was influenced by post-modernist and post-colonial critique in which the role of the museum is re-conceptualised as a 'contact zone' (Clifford, 1999) – a cultural meeting point of different spatial trajectories and practices where the museum object can only be rendered intelligible in conjunction with the communities who have a stake in its origins, ownership and uses. Technological developments played an important part – making literally possible Malraux's idea

(1967) of a 'musee imaginaire' which, as Barrett (2011) points out, loses meaning in the common English translation of 'Museum without walls'. "… Malraux sought to establish a conceptual space for human faculties: imagination, cognition, judgement within the museum – to make the museum more 'humanist'" (Barrett, 2011, p. 107). Hooper Greenhill (1992) lays emphasis on the museum's re-birth as a 'post-museum' where a visual culture of display gives way to one of communication, and where notions of a homogenized 'public' are increasingly replaced by stakeholder 'communities', 'audiences', or 'visitors', sometimes conceived as consumers. This is not the place to review the extensive debate about the democratic status of 'community' versus 'public' (see Barrett, 2011, for an overview of how it relates to museums). A change in terminology does not in and of itself reposition the people who use museums in relation to the institution and its educational activities. 'Community' carries positive associations of an embodied and affective relationship between people and place – and stands as a counter-point to the individualization implicit in the visitor/consumer, but this can be a romanticisation. What defines the relationship between people and museums is the nature of their interaction which may range from a participant opportunity whose parameters are largely defined by the institution, to an epistemic role whereby knowledge and learning is in some degree co-produced (Froggett et al., 2019).

The de-centering of the museum as locus of authoritative cultural knowledge was accompanied by the rise of constructivist education theory (Hooper-Greenhill, 1992, 1994). In the context of museum education constructivist pedagogy departs from an idealist epistemology (Hein, 1995) and the principle that knowledge and meaning arise in the knower. Hence, rather than conveying systematic knowledge, the role of the museum and its educators is to create the settings and opportunities for interaction with the museum collections that correspond to the specific needs of the learners in question. In interactive museum education visitor interpretation is encouraged, along with the use of technology for uploading photographs, and video – a form of user-led curating. The justification is anti-elitist, in the sense of blurring the distinctions between high and popular culture – so that the instructional model is abandoned in favour of 'discovery', and even entertainment. Alternatively, where neo-liberal conceptions of utility, value for money and impact are required to justify any public investment in culture, museums take on an ever widening array of additional functions. Hence we have seen a variety of in-house and outreach activities increasingly working with marginalised and vulnerable groups and requiring a skill set that naturally falls within the province of social work or health work, and can even border on the therapeutic (Froggett et al., 2011).

Instruction and interaction do not exhaust the educational functions of the museum and its objects. The third possibility is of an epistemic role in which the museum setting enables the self-reflexive experiencing of objects in such a way that they are related to, understood and used to bring into awareness the unthought knowns of the sensible world by linking personal and cultural life.

REFLEXIVE LEARNING AND THE EPISTEMIC MUSEUM

Different museum practices do of course co-exist in the contemporary museum. We could posit a continuum with the authoritative, systematic, instructional museum of display at one end and the placeless, heterotopic contact zone at the other – universalistic conceptions of the public are abandoned in favour of a differentiated view of who is accessing the collections or building, and for what purposes. The authoritative role of the curator declines in the interactive museum as knowledge is dispersed into various modalities of exchange between the museum and its interested communities. In theory the museum does not so much address these communities as provide the settings and circumstances of access which may be virtual or real, and which provide opportunity for a learning experience.

In the History of the World in 100 objects we see a number of these modes available simultaneously. The accounts of the objects were elegant achievements of curatorial expertise, yet in the delivery of the programme we experience a museum 'without walls', dependent on broadcasting and multi-media, where interactive possibilities range from simply listening in, to following up the online documentation, to engaging in blogs and debates, and finally to a form of audience co-curation whereby selection and decision-making about significant and evocative objects are made by members of the audience themselves. There was little doubt in this particular endeavour that the weight of authority remained with the host institution, but the democratizing direction was clear, and the choices made by the public will no doubt occupy historians and social scientists for years to come. In principle the reflexivity could have been pursued further. The teapot could have become a stimulus for a community led investigation of contemporary tea-drinking rituals within the social settings where they naturally occur, giving rise to a co-produced analysis of what they reveal of everyday sociability as it is lived (or neglected) today. Such a project (not directly connected with the radio programmes) was in fact undertaken in Blackpool in 2016. Wabi Char, took inspiration from a 16th century tea making ritual and was commissioned from artist Caroline Jupp as part of the LeftCoast Creative People and Places Programme, funded by Arts Council England to bring art to areas of cultural under-investment. It drew together a cultural exchange around everyday tea-drinking practices among different communities in the town, including people with dementia (Roy et al., 2016).

THE POLITICAL CONTEXT

Drivers of change are often external to the museum sector itself and developments and debates within museology. As a public institution the museum always stands at an intersection of a number of cultural and policy cross-currents. By way of illustrating the recent fate of museums in the UK, I return to The Harris which, since its founding, has been largely dedicated to the curation of its collections, but is now considering its future civic role as an anchor institution for the city. This widening social remit, typical of many regional museums, has gathered impetus over the last two decades and is hailed by some museum professionals as a long overdue democratisation. In the UK, it is both impelled and constrained by the economic austerity that has been imposed on the sector since the financial crisis of 2008. One of the most noticeable impacts of austerity (fully intended by successive neo-liberal governments) has been the phenomenal contraction of the local state and the decline of municipal authorities, whose funding has been cut by up to 40% in comparison with pre-2008 levels, with further reductions foreseen at the time of writing. In this situation cultural institutions have begun to step in to fill at least part of the gap – the civic deficit that results from the withdrawal of public amenities and the degradation of sites of public encounter. Regional museums have embraced this widening social remit to increase their chances of survival. Supported and part-funded as they generally are by Local Authorities, they have been particularly vulnerable since cultural facilities tend to be regarded as dispensable in harsh economic times, unless like the big national institutions, they contribute significantly to a tourist economy. Many regional museums have closed in recent years. Re-inventing themselves as service providers in priority areas like health offers some hope of continued investment.

OBJECT RELATING AND OBJECT USE IN THE MUSEUM

The expectation that museums sustain educational and civic functions, whilst justifying their funding in terms of mass appeal, new audiences and social impact has had paradoxical effects. On the one hand it has introduced principles of consumer demand and satisfaction; on the other it has led to new strategies of engagement with disadvantaged visitors or communities who lack cultural capital. Some of this work has been very challenging and it has not been universally welcomed among museum professionals – why would one train in conservation and curating in order to work with mental health problems or addictions? In a study of such initiatives in North West England, Froggett et al. (2011) found that the strains entailed were stretching some staff well beyond their comfort zones. However, the effect has been to re-position curating and education as relational and reflexive practices, enmeshed in the tensions produced by the institution's changing social role. This stretches the curatorial mind-set. In a workshop with post-graduate student curators at the University of New South Wales, in 2016, it became clear that one of the qualities most valued and exhibited was empathy. An interesting outcome of this shift of focus towards human relations has been to cast into relief the object relational potential of museum collections and exhibitions, though this has so far been little investigated (see Froggett & Trustram, 2014, for an exception).

The following example is taken from research into a programme that operated across six of the UK's North West regional museums, and specifically from work undertaken in The Harris.[7] Although individual projects supported by this programme were largely led by museum educators the overall objective was to develop health and well-being initiatives targeted at specific communities who would not normally access museum services. In most cases there were no clearly prescribed health outcomes, the aim was to see how museum practice could be extended to become more inclusive, and how learning to make use of the collections could benefit participants who had chronic and enduring ill-health, and sometimes severe disabilities. Work was group based and ranged from people with mental health, alcohol and substance misuse problems, to dementia and disabling or life-threatening physical illness. Some of the projects were delivered on museum premises, others in the institutional health or care settings where people were living. Group numbers were small (normally between six and twelve) and invariably included intensive work which involved an element of creative activity in a carefully designed containing space. In this sense most groups enjoyed something of the intimacy and security of a therapeutic setting in which they could develop skills in art or craft, or simply appreciate what the museum had to offer. Without exception projects aimed to help people gain in self-confidence, social skills and enrichment. The staff leading the groups all intuitively tried to create a space which was both of the museum and apart from it – a 'third space' (Muller et al., 2015) which is neither a space of everyday social interaction nor a didactic space, but a potential space, in the Winnicottian sense, in which cultural objects came 'alive' for the participants, who through their conscious or unconscious use of these objects forge a personal relationship to a shared culture

In The Harris the physical setting for this space apart took the form of a small room, normally used for educational purposes, which offered respite from the overwhelming architecture of the building and its cornucopia. The group in this case had been recruited with the help of a hostel for men with multiple problems related to homelessness, including unemployment, alcoholism and mental ill-health. The aim was to take them to see a temporary digital installation by Simon Faithfull, entitled 'Recent Findings', that was showing in the gallery at the time. The artwork was used as a stimulus for a group exercise in creative writing, led by performance artist, Chanje Kunde. It became clear from the outset that the promise of sandwiches and tea (this time as gift, or bribe) before the visit was actually the principal attraction, and after these had been consumed two of the recruits disappeared. At this point the omens were not auspicious – with one or two of the participants presenting as dishevelled, distracted and possibly drunk. However, they did agree to be accompanied through the galleries to view the work, which was in three sections on large digital screens.

The first part, in black and white, consisted of line drawings of urban crows created by Faithfull on his palm pilot, as he travelled the world observing how the birds take on the characteristics of the human populations among whom they live. In cities crows are scavangers, unloved, uninvited, often aggressive, and regarded as avian vermin that foul the spaces they invade. The group were distinctly unimpressed, declaring the work itself to be "crap". As researchers we could not escape the thought that crows carried unfortunate associations for people who have lived unwanted among them on the city streets. At any rate, the group moved on quickly, unwilling to give the work further consideration. In the creative writing session that followed the crows were not mentioned – it was as if 'crap' had emphatically been evacuated from the experience.

However, the next screen had quite a different effect. It showed a grainy black and white film of about 20 minutes, devoid of obvious aesthetic appeal, yet the group was intrigued and watched it through from beginning to end in rapt concentration. Its subject was the artist himself, again armed with his palm pilot, attempting to follow the meridian line, regardless of obstacles, in a trajectory that – ridiculously – took him across ditches, along river-beds, over high-wire fences and through someone's kitchen window. Later in a jointly composed poem, the group wrote

> The World didn't seem to care
> Just like Tony Blair
> Things might slow you down, keep going
> Every paragraph is worth knowing
> Doubts disappearing through a window
> Life's journey keeps on flowing through …

The poem emerged via a method whereby Chanje asked for impressions and comments in associative manner, and no particular order. The words were captured on flip chart paper and crafted into poetic form with the active participation and agreement of the whole group. The lines showed how they related the artwork to their own lives identifying with Faithfull's improbable quest and futile persistence. Sticking to a chosen path (the Meridian Line) which has no real counterpart in the material world, whilst navigating the obstacles of nature and the orderly lives of others, made existential sense to a group familiar with homelessness. They appreciated the rueful humour and pointlessness of the artist's effort, and the dogged attempt to keep going that spoke to them not only of their situation, but of the state of mind required to retain a sense of agency in 'life's journey' which keeps on 'flowing through', regardless of the world's indifference. The psychosocial reality that the participants shared as a group found expression in the cultural text they produced. It was articulated in relation to an aesthetic object which they appropriated for their own use, projecting into it their life experience. In this way it acquired a particular a resonance for them.

It is worth pausing to consider what was happening here in terms of Winnicott's depiction of transitional phenomena which he defines as

> … an intermediate area of experience, unchallenged in respect of its belonging to inner or external (shared) reality, [that] constitutes the greater part of the infant's experience and throughout life is retained in the intense experiencing that belongs to the arts and religion and to imaginative living, and to creative scientific work. (Winnicott, 1971 p. 14)

Here Winnicott was concerned to identify the location of cultural experience and the conditions under which it takes place in what he calls the third (intermediate) area of experiencing, characteristic of play. Affirming that the *experience* of play "… is in fact neither a matter of inner reality nor a matter of external reality" he asks "if play [as the origin of cultural experience] is neither inside nor outside, where is it?" (p. 4) and answers that it happens in the potential space between the individual and the environment, "between the subjective object and the object objectively perceived, between me-extensions and not-me" (p. 80).

There is a certain instability in the group's interaction with the film depicted above. It is initially strange to them (experienced as not-me), then it intrigues them, and then acquires a very personal resonance for them as they 'incorporate' it, so that it takes on the character of a 'me-extension'. So close do they feel to the artist's experience that they continue to relate to it as if it were their own, overlaying it with the association of an uncaring world, though there is no suggestion of this in the film itself. The potential space that would allow the work its otherness has collapsed in the process of identification. The experience becomes one of fusion with the object which means that although they enjoy it, it ceases to have an independent existence with attributes that do not equate with their own. Since cultural exclusion is one of their definitive life experiences, the process in some measure re-affirms their marginalisation. I say 'in some measure' because this moment exists in a continuum, as we shall see, but it illustrates the difficulty with strategies of learning which depart from what is perceived as primarily relevant to the subject.

Alternatively, the object 'objectively perceived', would have carried layers of signification for the group that reached beyond their situation. The film could have been understood as an exploration and critical commentary on the relation between the virtual and the real, and the seductions and perils of literalism in translating digital bearings into the material world, of confusing reality with simulation. Besides the virtues of persistence it spoke of the absurdity of obstinacy, and how defiance or disregard of objective constraint can be either an act of revolt, or consignment to an autistic mode of existence. Of course these aspects of the film could also have been related to the lives of the group but they gave no sign that such interpretations were meaningful to them. Instead their subjective appropriation was selective. They projected into the object and identified with it, and in so doing they formed a relation to it (and to the institution that delivered it to them) but they were not challenged by it and in the lines they wrote, they positioned themselves as victims. As a highly stigmatised group there was some truth in this, but it was not a route to a broader *cultural* engagement.

The third screen was produced by the artist after a trip to the Arctic Circle in the hope of seeing the auroraborealis, which, in the event, never appeared. Instead, he filmed the reflections he saw in his own eye which, hugely enlarged on the screen, produced an image that the group – to judge by their exclamations of surprise and pleasure – found ravishing. A telescope satellite dish, seen from a distance, floated in the pupil, enclosed in the subtle irridescent ring of colour that is the beauty of a human iris. It was a visual meditation on the nature of perception and the mind's eye as a filter for reality; on the different modes of looking and seeing that are available to us; and on how carrying on in the face of disappointment, rather than dogged persistence, may entail first the acceptance, then the transformation of failure. The group responded to it affectively and aesthetically and when it emerged in the poem that they produced together it was distilled into the words

Northern lights in my eyes,
A light for every time I've tried

This thought is self-reflexive rather than merely self-referential. It's emotional weighting is very different to that of overcoming obstacles in the face of an uncaring world. It acknowledges both the world beyond the self and the symbolic distillation of the Northern Lights into commemorations of personal trials and disappointments – failure is neither projected onto others, nor disavowed, instead of victimhood there is the effort to take responsibility and self-forgiveness. In Kleinian terms (Klein, 1940) this would be regarded as depressive anxiety in which one fears for one's own destructiveness, but out of love of the world, rather than its repudiation. The potential space between the individual and the environment is held open and with it the possibility of transformation. The image is neither a subjective object nor an object objectively perceived, but a transitional object (Winnicott, 1971) from an intermediate area of experience, not merely related to, but 'used' and then 'released' as a cultural object to live a life of its own.

Winnicott's distinction between object relating and object use is an important one, because it identifies the transformational potential in transitional objects, which are the first objects and proto-symbols that, as infants, we co-opt and manipulate for our own purposes, thereby unknowingly gaining access to a cultural order. In object relating the observer projects into the object or the setting, appropriating elements of it for the expression of parts of the self, so that it becomes meaningfully cathected. In object use the object is placed beyond omnipotent projection, 'surviving' as a resilient object with its intrinsic qualities intact that can then contribute back to the subject. This is why the group were able to be nourished by an aesthetic experience from the third screen and were thereby connected to a shared culture and able to partake in the sensible world of which the artwork is a part.

GENERATIVE LEARNING IN THE EPISTEMIC MUSEUM

Cultural experience arises through the finding of transitional objects throughout our lives and museums offer bountiful collections of objects for this purpose. Our group completed its process with the aesthetic transformation of a visual artwork, used as a transitional object, into linguistic form through poetry. This is a form of language replete with sensual symbolic interaction forms that arise in sensory experience of the material world. The interaction forms are irreducibly social, even though their social character may only become fully evident in language. Lorenzer and Orban (1978) take Winnicott to task for referring to 'subject' and 'object', 'inner' and 'outer' as if separable – but the 'as if' is critical and in 'The Location of Cultural Experience' (Winnicott, 1971) subject/object is a heuristic device that describes *perception* of the object and its relation to the subject rather than its ontological status. Winnicott's focus is on the nature and quality of experiencing, Lorenzer's on how that experience is formed. What they agree on is the transitional or intermediate nature of culture that delivers a sensible world to us in its spatial and temporal modalities through our interactions with it.

There is an unconscious cultural content in these interactions in the sense that they are infused by a habitual or disavowed unthought known until adequate symbolic resources are found to give it verbal expression. 'Adequacy' occurs in Lorenzer's view if the *sensuous* symbolic interaction forms embedded in language maintain its vital connection to the world – as is most likely in literature or poetry. The authoritative museum interpretation that addresses its audience is less likely to achieve this than the reflexive co-option of visitors in an experiential and interpretive process (see Froggett et al., 2019, for an example of visual matrix workshops with museum visitors). This requires the communicative conditions of the epistemic museum that honours the intermediate nature of culture through the potential spaces it creates. In these spaces socially produced unconscious material that *appears* personal to the individual becomes bound to the shared symbolic repertoires of culture where both physical artefacts and the language with which we speak them establish a *felt* relation to the social world.

The learning process in the epistemic museum is *generative* – it is a cultural production with personal emotional resonance, and it is the socially unconscious aspects of the museum experience that account for this generative nature: over time and as conditions ripen, we uncover the symbolic potentials of objects, as they disclose to us the contradictions embedded in the social relations of their production and use. Thus 'provoked' we re-interpret them to find layers of signification that were not previously available to us. This is an embodied and aesthetic process, as much as a cognitive one, in that it invokes a full range of sensory and affective capacities. At a personal level these objects activate the transitional phenomena that allow us to creatively discover for ourselves what is there to be found, allowing us to dwell among the paradoxes of the hidden and visible world and of 'inner' nature, so that the knowledge thus produced is in a continual process of dynamic emergence. The museum then becomes an institution to whose care we consign the objects that matter to us, to reflect our sensibilities back to us, so that we can locate ourselves sensuously in a time and a place. From this vantage point we apprehend our relation to other cultures, past and present, and the potentials and limitations of our own.

ACKNOWLEDGEMENTS

This study was funded by the Museum and Libraries Association under its Renaissance in the Regions Programme. The Harris Museum data on which the analysis was based was collected by Dr. Alan Farrier, University of Central Lancashire.

NOTES

1 Myna Trustram (2013) asks a version of this question prompted by the Mary Gregg collection in Manchester Museum in which many of the items are everyday, mundane and utilitarian, yet appear to resonate powerfully with many visitors.

2 http://www.britishmuseum.org/explore/a_history_of_the_world.aspx

3 Although much of Lorenzer's oeuvre is concerned with the symbolization of social interaction in language – Leithäuser (2013, p. 58) draws attention to his account of way in which these forms, deriving from originary moulding actions of maternal care, themselves culturally inscribed by social practices, are transformed and elaborated in moulding actions of work processes whereby raw materials are converted into commodities.

4 Potential space supports creative illusion insofar as it allows a suspension of distinctions between fantasy and reality, and hence transitional phenomena. We do not enquire therefore "did you conceive of this or was it presented to you from without? … No decision on this point is expected. The question is not to be formulated" (Winnicott, 1971, p. 12).

5 The generic containment function intrinsic to museum experience is discussed in Froggett and Trustram (2014), while Bartlett and Muller (2017) address the anxieties provoked by a digital exhibition in terms of Wilfred Bion's conception of the container-contained relationship.

6 For an English language discussion of this concept central to Alfred Lorenzer's work see Salling Olesen (2012), Salling Olesen and Weber (2012), also in the same volume, examples of the depth hermeneutic method through which scenic experience can be interpreted; also Hollway and Froggett (2012) who bring the Lorenzerian and object relations traditions into dialogue through an empirical case study.

7 Who Cares? Museums, Health and Well-being was a two year investigation of innovations in museum based learning among six North West regional museums directed understanding the conditions under which vulnerable groups could be engaged and with what effects. It was funded by the then Museums and Libraries Association, now subsumed under Arts Council England.

REFERENCES

Adorno, T. (2002). *Aesthetic theory* (R. Hullot-Kentor, Trans.). London: Continuum.

Barrett, J. (2011). *Museums and the public sphere*. Oxford: Blackwell.

Bartlett, V., & Muller, L. (2017). Curating/Containing: Exhibiting digital art about mental health. In *Bio-creation and peace: Proceedings of the 23rd International Symposium on Electronic Art* (pp. 279–288). Retrieved from http://festivaldelaimagen.com/wp-content/uploads/2017/06/Proceedings_ISEA2017_16_Festival_Internacional_de_la_Imagen.pdf

Bennett, T. (1988). Museums and 'the people'. In R. Lumley (Ed.), *The museum time machine: Putting cultures on display* (pp. 63–85). London: Commedia & Routledge.

Bennett, T. (1995). *The birth of the museum: History, theory, politics*. London: Routledge.

Bollas, C. (1987). *The shadow of the object: Psychoanalysis of the unthought known*. London: Routledge.

Bollas, C. (2009). *The evocative object world*. London: Routledge.

Bordieu, P. (1984). *Distinction: A social critique of the judgment of taste* (R. Nice, Trans.). Cambridge, MA: Harvard University Press.

Bordieu, P., Darbel, A., & Schnapper, D. (1990 [1969]). *The love of art, European arts museums and their public* (C. Beattie & N. Merriman, Trans.). Stanford, CA: Stanford University Press.

Born, G., & Barry, A. (2010). Art-science. *Journal of Cultural Economy, 3*(1), 103–119.

Clifford, J. (1999). Museums as contact zones. In D. Boswell & J. Evans (Eds.), *Representing the nation: A reader: Histories, heritage and museums*. London & New York, NY: Routledge.

Foucault, M. (1977). *Discipline and punish: Birth of the prison* (A. Sheridan, Trans.). New York, NY: Pantheon.

Foucault, M. (1986). Of other spaces. *Diacritics, 16*(Spring), 22–27.

Froggett, L., Farrier, A., Poursanidou, D., & Hacking, S. (2011). *Who cares? Museums and social engagement*. Psychosocial Research Unit: University of Central Lancashire.

Froggett, L., Manley, J., & Roy, A. (2015). The visual matrix method: Imagery and affect in a group-based research setting. *Forum Qualitative Sozialforschung*. Retrieved from http://www.qualitative-research.net/index.php/fqs

Froggett, L., & Trustram, M. (2014). Object relations in the museum: A psychosocial perspective. *Museum Management and Curatorship, 29*, 482–497.

Froggett, L., Muller, L., & Bennett, J. (2019). *The work of the audience: Visual matrix methodology in museums, Cultural Trends, 28*(2–3), 162–176. doi: 10.1080/09548963.2019.1617939

Hein, G. E. (1995). The constructivist museum. *Journal of Education in Museums, 16*, 21–23.

Hollway, W., & Froggett, L. (2012). Researching in-between subjective experience and reality. In H. Salling Olesen (Ed.), *Cultural analysis and in-depth hermeneutics – Psycho-societal analysis of everyday life, culture, interaction and learning. Forum for Qualitative Social Research, 13*(3). (Reprinted in *Historical Social Research, 2*(38), 139–157)

Hooper-Greenhill, E. (1992). *Museums and the shaping of knowledge*. London: Routledge.

Hooper-Greenhill, E. (1994). *The educational function of the museum*. London: Routledge.

Klein, M. (1940). Mourning and its relation to manic depressive states. *International Journal of Psychoanalysis, 2*, 280–293.

Leithäuser, T. (2012). Psychoanalysis, socialisation and society – The psychoanalytical thought and interpretation of Alfred Lorenzer. In H. Salling Olesen (Ed.), *Cultural analysis and in-depth hermeneutics – Psycho-societal analysis of everyday life, culture, interaction and learning. Forum for Qualitative Social Research, 13*(3). (Reprinted in *Historical Social Research, 2*(38), 56–70)

Lorenzer, A. (1972). *Zur Begründung einer Materialistischen Sozialisationtheorie*. Frankfurt/M: Suhrkamp.

Lorenzer, A. (1986). Tiefenhermeneutische Kulturanalyse. In A. Lorenzer (Ed.), *Kultur-Analysen: Psychoanalytische Studien zur Kultur* [The analysis of culture: Psychoanalytic studies of culture] (pp. 11–98). Frankfurt/M: Fischer.

Lorenzer, A., & Orban, P. (1978). Transitional objects and phenomena: Socialization and symbolisation. In S. Grolnick, L. Barkin, & W. Münsterberger (Eds.), *Between reality and fantasy* (pp. 471–482). New York, NY: Jason Aronson.

Mack, J. (2003). *The museum of the mind: Art and memory in world cultures*. London: The British Museum.

Malraux, A. (1967). *Museum without walls* (S. Gilbert & F. Price, Trans.). London: Secker an Warburg.

Miettinen, R., & Virkkunen, J. (2005). Epistemic objects, artefacts and organisational change. *Organisation, 12*, 437–456.

Muller, L., Bennett, J., Froggett, L., & Bartlett, V. (2015, August 14–18). Understanding third space: Evaluating art-science collaboration. In *Proceedings of 21st international symposium of electronic art*, Vancouver, Canada.

Muller, L., & Edmonds, E. A. (2006). Living laboratories for interactive art. *CoDesign, 2*(4), 195–207.

Newman, A., & Fiona, M. (2006). The impact of museums upon identity. *International Journal of Heritage Studies, 12*(1), 49–68.

Ranciére, J. (2004). *The politics of aesthetics* (G. Rockhill, Trans.). London: Continuum.

Roy, A., Manley, J., & Froggett, L. (2016). *Left coast creative people and places report*. University of Central Lancashire.

Salling Olesen, H. (2012). Introduction. In H. Salling Olesen (Ed.), *Cultural analysis and in-depth hermeneutics – Psycho-societal analysis of everyday life, culture, interaction and learning. Forum for Qualitative Social Research, 13*(3). (Reprinted in *Historical Social Research, 2*(38), 8–25)

Salling Olesen, H., & Weber, K. (2012). Socialisation, language and scenic understanding: Alfred Lorenzer's contribution to psycho-societal methodology. In H. Salling Olesen (Ed.), *Cultural analysis and in-depth hermeneutics – Psycho-societal analysis of everyday life, culture, interaction and learning. Forum for Qualitative Social Research, 13*(3). (Reprinted in *Historical Social Research, 2*(38), 26–55)

Trustram, M. (2013). The little madnesses of museums. In A. Kuhn (Ed.), *Little madnesses: Winnicott, transitional phenomena and cultural experience*. London: Tauris.

Weber, K. (2012). Learning, work and language games. In H. Salling Olesen (Ed.), *Cultural analysis and in-depth hermeneutics – Psycho-societal analysis of everyday life, culture, interaction and learning. Forum for Qualitative Social Research, 13*(3). (Reprinted in *Historical Social Research, 2*(38), 26–55)

Winnicott, D. W. (1965). *The maturational process and the facilitating environment: Studies in the theory of emotional development.* London: Hogarth Press and the Institute of Psychoanalysis.

Winnicott, D. W. (1971). *Playing and reality*. London: Routledge.

PART 4

UNDERSTANDING SUBJECTIVE DIMENSIONS OF POLITICAL PROCESSES: IDENTITY AND POLITICS

LINDEN WEST

10. PSYCHOANALYSIS, FUNDAMENTALISM, CRITICAL THEORY AND THE UNCONSCIOUS

Adult Education, Islamic Fundamentalism and the Subjectivity of Omniscience

INTRODUCTION

In this chapter, I explore the quality of our relationship to knowledge and to the other, and otherness, through a psychosocial and psychoanalytic lens. I suggest fundamentalism is a defensive orientation to experience, finding diverse expression in our contemporary world, although its various forms have much in common. Whether in the defensiveness of some academic thought, or Islamic fundamentalism, market/neo-classical or Marxism, it can be a defence against the anxiety of not knowing or being unable rationally to find complete answers. The defensiveness works at a primitive, or early, pre-intellectual and largely unconscious level. I draw on auto/biographical narrative research into Islamist groups, and the history of workers' education to illuminate the conflict between fundamentalism and a democratic education. The latter attempts to keep dialogue going, with diverse others, developmentally, despite various attacks on the process. The former to close dialogue and learning down. I draw on critical theory and notions of self/other recognition to explain this. Note is made that critical theory itself was concerned with certain fundamentalisms that stalked positivistic social science as well as strands of Marxism. Herein lie epistemological questions behind claims to exclusive truth, in contrast to perspectives emphasising knowing as a relational, uncertain dynamic, shaped in part by our internal world. The dynamic encompasses unconscious anxiety around not knowing and relying on others. The capacity to live in doubt and uncertainty and to recognise how much in fact we need others for self-knowledge, are crucial for richer epistemological experience, as well as for a democratic education and building social solidarities.

INTERROGATING ISLAMIC FUNDAMENTALISM AND WORKERS' EDUCATION THROUGH A PSYCHOSOCIAL LENS

I have drawn on 'psychosocial' understandings, combining psychoanalysis and critical theory, as well as the work of John Dewey, to interrogate Islamic fundamentalist groups, and, comparatively, the history of workers' education in one particular city.

DOI: 10.1163/9789004420274_011

This to explore the struggles surrounding democratic education in diverse places and spaces, including in the academy itself. I examine processes of self-other recognition in contrast to paranoid-schizoid modes of functioning, in which unwanted parts of self, culture and thinking are split off and projected on to the other in largely unconscious ways. The world gets divided into good and bad, pure and impure, self and other, truth and apostasy. There is also the tendency towards omniscience, that we as individuals or whole groups have the truth and nothing but the truth and that our stories are sovereign. John Dewey (1969) makes a crucial distinction between such dynamics and processes of democratic education, in which, in the best of practice, there is openness to the other and the other of different ways of seeing. Experience in some groups, however, like those of racists or Islamic fundamentalism, is of closure towards otherness, and ultimately to the self and experience of those involved. It is further suggested that fundamentalism is quite ordinary, in that each of us, at times, when we feel out of our depth, can grab at ideas promising truth and nothing but the truth. Fundamentalism has found expression in social critique, including Marxism, in its claims to be able to fully penetrate reality and its compulsion to construct unified systems of knowledge. Psychoanalysis, alongside the work of critical theorists like Theodor Adorno and Axel Honneth, helps us move beyond fantasises of total knowledge into new and diverse subjective, intersubjective and symbolic democratic learning possibilities.

I use auto/biographical narrative enquiry and an interdisciplinary psychosocial imagination, to interrogate manifestations of fundamentalism in lives, as well as, contrarywise, to illuminate the spirit of more open forms of enquiry, as in the best of adult education. The former may represent, in its closure, the antithesis of democratic learning. To examine these processes, I draw on research into the rise of racism and fundamentalism, as well as the historical role of adult education, in what is now a post-industrial city in England (West, 2016, 2017a). I take the city as emblematic of wider processes in many similar communities across Europe and North America. Adult education once generated ‘resources of hope’, in Raymond Williams’ compelling phrase, for democratic experiment and self/other recognition, a social movement that is now much weakened (Williams, 1989; West, 2016).

The theoretical sweep of the chapter encompasses the interplay of culture and psyche, drawing on the work of Donald Winnicott as well as Honneth, and Adorno. John Dewey helps us consider the prerequisites for a radical, far-reaching understanding of ‘a cooperative contribution to social reproduction’, and what inhibits this. Honneth argues that the mature Dewey provides ‘an alternative in the end of work society’ where we can ‘no longer assume the form of a normatively inspired restructuring of the capitalist labour market’ (Honneth, 2007, p. 236). Honneth seeks to establish the role of self/other recognition in building social cooperation in a reframing of critical theory itself, beyond left Hegelianism and the illusion of a revolutionary proletariat. This is set alongside the pervasive and powerful dynamics of disrespect and, I add, unconscious defences against our anxiety in the face of the other. I include, drawing on Melanie Klein’s work (1975), collective as well as individual defences of splitting and projection on to the other what we most dislike in ourselves. Splitting involves paranoid/schizoid modes of functioning: of self-idealisation while aspects of ourselves we most dislike, such as greed, neediness, laziness, misogyny, and the capacity for violence can be ejected into others. Maybe our cultures are also idealised while the culture of the other is demonised. But the demons most properly belong to us. I suggest that intimate biographical vulnerabilities, alongside social disrespect and exclusion, combine to create the powerful attraction of the Islamist group (or the racist gang) and of totalising ideas. We get seduced by narratives of certainty that seemingly offer compelling, omniscient fantasies. We can also feel recognised in a gang of our own where we have somewhere to call home, with superior stories to explain in, and against, a frightening world.

The best of adult education, on the other hand, was grounded in an ethic of equality, respect, trust, dialogue as well as intellectual diversity and openness to diverse ways of knowing. It generated processes of reflexive self-other recognition, including towards bigotry as well as awareness of the complexities of knowledge and a sensitivity towards difference. Although there were fundamentalist tendencies in workers' education too: some, if by no means all, of the autodidacts in the history of British popular education could be rigid and uncompromising in their views, fuelled by dissenting 'religious' beliefs. Their adoption of versions of Marxism was driven, as we will observe, by an intolerant defensiveness towards those who thought differently (West, 2017a). In recent writing, I focused on the history of workers' education in the city where I was born, in the light of growing racism and Islamic fundamentalism now. I suggest similar processes of dialogical, democratic education are urgently needed in struggling multicultural contexts (West, 2016, 2017a). I conclude the chapter by challenging the idea that rationality and conceptual knowledge can fully penetrate and comprehend the reality of the world. And, in the spirit of Adorno, that such omnipotent fantasy really requires time on a metaphorical psychoanalytic couch (West, 2017c).

Distress in the City

In 2008, I was very troubled by the rise of racism and fundamentalism in the 'post-industrial' city of my birth, Stoke-on-Trent, in the English Midlands. In 2008/9 the racist British National Party (BNP) was strengthening its presence in parts of the city and a mosque was pipe-bombed. It seemed that racists would form the majority on the Municipal Council by 2010 (West, 2016). There were incidents of racial violence and outbursts of Islamophobia. The economic base of the city had long since unravelled and its politics were in chronic crisis, with low levels of engagement in voting. The traditional employment base of the city – coal mining, iron and steel production and pottery – had either disappeared altogether or drastically declined. Long-term structural unemployment was endemic (West, 2016). The financial crisis, from 2008 onwards, and consequent austerity, including cuts in local government funding, added to the feelings of distress and neglect. Moreover, workers and adult education, once important in the city, was marginalised, although a body like the

Workers Educational Association (WEA) continued to do important things, albeit from a fragile resource base (West, 2016).

Historical geographer Matthew Rice (2010) has written that 'maybe Stoke-on-Trent', England's twelfth biggest city, 'is just one industrial city too many' (p. 17). Yet this city was once home to vibrant pottery, mining, and iron and steel industries. Hundreds of thousands of plates, cups and saucers, all packed safely with straw in barrels or wooden baskets, were sent to food markets in India, Ceylon (now Sri Lanka), Canada, Australia, New Zealand and America. In 1925, 100,000 workers were employed in the pottery industry. By 2009 the figure was about 9000. Rice notes that wages were never high in Stoke, but cheap labour came to the area from places like Kashmir and the Punjab in Southern Asia in the 1960s. Low wages in Stoke equated of course to relatively high sources of income for migrant families. But when outsourcing gathered pace, many of the descendants of those whose grandparents had migrated were left in a jobless limbo. Having a job matters for cultural as well as economic reasons, particularly for young Asian men: to be the head of the family and support its members is a strong cultural as well as economic imperative. I use Stoke as a representative case study of tendencies across many other similar post-industrial communities in Europe, and in the rust belt towns of the United States. The distress, anger and bewilderment of many of those who live there can get translated into racist politics, and the call for saviours, or "strong" men, to put matters right, such as Donald Trump; in Britain, or especially England, this found expression in the 'Brexit' process, fuelled by fear of the other, whether the immigrant or the bureaucrats of Brussels. It was a rage against neglect, disrespect and even abandonment (with its primitive or early psychological connotations), with calls for a Trump-like father figure to put England first (West, 2017b).

Auto/Biographical Narrative Interviewing in a Clinical Style

I should explain the nature and purposes of my auto/biographical narrative research and the historical analysis. I interviewed over 50 diverse people, from white working class and Muslim communities, working in what I call a clinical style, informed by psychoanalysis. The stories people tell are always a reconstruction of events, afterthoughts, rather than the events themselves, while the powerful discourses of a culture and unconscious processes of wanting to please or appease circulate in stories. These may be seen by some academic commentators as of little relevance to any bigger picture of, for instance, democracy in crisis or the rise of fundamentalism – 'fine meaningless detail', as one historian graphically framed it (Fieldhouse, 1996). Yet, I suggest, we better understand the nuances of people being attracted to the BNP, or radicalized, or even the attractions of fundamentalist versions of Marxism, when viewed through the lens of auto/biographical narrative and historical enquiry. This is its especial power.

For one thing, the general – or bigger – picture is always there in the particular, in the narrative resources people draw on to tell their stories. We are storied as well as storytellers. Stories can constrain as well as liberate, as a bigger picture – of neo-liberal assumptions, say, or of the actions of the Western world – grip accounts. People can also internalize the negativities about 'people like us', whether emanating from the mouths and projections of politicians, policymakers or the mass media. Those targeted may be single parents struggling on minimal welfare benefits, as chronicled in my earlier work in other marginalized locations (Merrill & West, 2009). People can feel themselves to be the objects of society's disdain, caught in the gaze of the judgemental other and constantly needing to justify themselves. Those on the margins easily internalize negative projections, or feelings that they are inadequate and personally to blame (West, 2007, 2009). There is evidence within wider cultural dynamics, as organised working-class power has waned, of shifts in the representation of working class life; from the begrudging respect of Alan Sillitoe's classic film, *Saturday Night and Sunday morning,* to the television pornography of *Benefit Street,* where working class people are represented as morally feckless, narcissistic and downright lazy (West, 2017b). Those on the edge, living in marginalised communities, have also to learn to deal with many and varied authority figures day by day: the social worker, the job centre assessor, the head teacher, the health visitor and of course researchers. They can have well-rehearsed stories to tell, while 'professionals' like social workers, lawyers, and teachers can be the targets of especial disdain and even hatred. They can be experienced as agents of oppressive forces in the world, of hard, neo-liberal economics and the neglect of many communities (West, 2009, 2017b).

I suggest too that people are not simply aggregates of certain sociological, cultural or economic variables; or products of what we might call the social unconscious. They, we, are living beings with our own stories to tell of our lives, and of what it feels like to exist in specific conditions, or to experience disrespect on the street in particular ways. While much socio-cultural experience is similar, and overall patterns discernible, not everyone experiences the world 'out-there' in identical ways. Society, culture and economies are mediated through relationship, in families and communities. We are not all, as British cultural theorist Raymond Williams taught, to be reduced to a mass. In his writing on 'culture as ordinary' (Williams, 1989), Williams observed how the advertising men and women held the same essential, dehumanising view of the masses as the authoritarian left. Expensively educated people were 'now in the service of the most brazen money-grabbing exploitation of the inexperience of ordinary people' (Williams, 1989, p. 6). 'The old cheapjack is still there in the market … he thinks of his victims as a slow ignorant crowd. The new cheapjack is in offices with contemporary *décor*, using scraps of linguistics, psychology, and sociology to influence what he thinks of as the mass mind' (Williams, 1989, p. 7). But Williams' scorn was not confined to the marketing men and women. He was angry with those of his friends who talked about ignorant masses … 'one kind of Communist has always talked like this, and has got his answer … at Budapest' (in the 1956 Hungarian uprising). He insisted that Marxist interpretation of culture is not acceptable while it insists that people should think in prescribed ways. 'It is stupid and arrogant to suppose that any of these meanings (within cultures) can in any way be prescribed: they are made by living people, made and remade, in ways that we cannot know in advance'. The Marxist interpretation of culture, he argued, could never be accepted so long as it retained a directive element. This is the insistence that if you desire socialism, you must learn to write, think and learn in a prescribed way (Williams, 1989, p. 8). Williams' idea of the purpose of adult education was to create a culture of shared meanings, open to the influence of all, in relationship. The purpose of auto/biographical narrative enquiry is to create space to explore and think about the meanings people give to experience, and the emotional and unconscious dynamics involved, drawing on psychoanalytic insights as well as critical theory.

I suggest that the meanings embodied in narratives also have validity in their own terms, however difficult and distasteful these might be. The racist and fundamentalist requires our understanding, as a fellow, struggling, defended human subject. Understanding lives from the inside requires time and the cooperation of those involved, and some appreciation by them of the relevance of research. The point of enquiry is to illuminate the complexity of the choices people make, and the meanings they attach to them. Interpretation requires an interdisciplinary psychosocial, historical and educational imagination: of people as psychosocial agents, if often unconsciously, rather than marionettes on a predetermined sociological or for that matter psychoanalytic stage. People make, as well as are made by history, however distasteful the outcome might seem.

My research sought to illuminate some of the seductions and insecurities fuelling racism and fundamentalism on a white working-class estate, the place where I was born, and in areas of the city where Muslim people live. The 50 or so participants in the study were in the main 'ordinary' people: some were community activists and or ministers of religion. The sample in technical terms was opportunistic as well as purposeful – I asked officers of the City Council for names of people that might be helpful to my work and they in turn facilitated contact with others. As the research developed, the sampling became more theoretical, as I interviewed specific individuals who were attracted, say, to Islamism or racist gangs.

Winnicott, Honneth and Dewey helped me make sense of the many stories. Axel Honneth (2009) refers to Freud's anthropological idea of how we are born prematurely in comparison with other mammals and depend absolutely on the other for survival and well-being; and on feelings of being loved as a basis for human flourishing (Honneth, 2009; Winnicott, 1971). Honneth writes of Freud's great anthropological insight in recognising the psycho-biological fact that humans are carried by the mother for much less time than other mammals. From this experience of 'premature birth', the human is heavily dependent on a protective environment from the beginning. Anticipating Winnicott, Freud (1953/1974, p. 278) speaks of the young child's need for the other; for love, in short, a term Freud rarely employed. Anxiety and fear of abandonment and associated vulnerability are laid down in memory in feeling, which can be re-evoked in later stages of a life when seemingly alone, vulnerable or despairing about the condition of self, families and communities.

Axel Honneth (1995, 2007, 2009) also interrogates the role of groups in generating a second category of recognition, which he calls self-respect. This is when people feel accepted and that they belong, with rights and responsibilities, as in the good adult education group. Self-esteem provides Honneth's third category of recognition. It happens when individuals feel recognized because they are seen to contribute to a group's wider well-being and development (Honneth, 2007, 2009). But processes of recognition can be aborted, as the other is experienced, consciously and unconsciously, as a problem to be expunged in processes of psychic splitting, idealisation and paranoia. The anxieties evoked, in Kleinian terms, induce paranoid/schizoid modes of functioning, which, to repeat, are self-protective strategies in which destructive feelings are projected onto the external world and the other. The world and the other become in turn invested with persecutory powers. Splitting, after all, is an attempt to protect the self or group from difficult feelings and thoughts, by expelling them (Klein, 1975; Frosh, 1991).

Islamic Fundamentalism in the City

The people of South Asian origin who settled in Stoke came from places like Kashmir, Pakistan and Bangladesh. They make up about 50 per cent of the city's ethnic minority population and in 2011 numbered just over 9000 (Burnett, 2011). Some of these people talked about constant experiences of disrespect and everyday experiences of Islamophobia: among taxi drivers, for instance, told frequently to 'fuck off home' by white clients. The sense of everyday disrespect was amplified by stories of actual physical violence: an Asian man was killed, and others injured as well as mosques damaged. Such experiences of disrespect evoke insecurity, vulnerability and defensiveness – paranoia even – and may reinforce the tendency for people to congregate among their own in particular areas. Disrespect also ignites the feeling that other people's behaviour is wrong, grounded in some normative ideal of justice violated.

Islamic fundamentalism has attracted young people in specific mosques. Small numbers, but they exist. The Islamist and would-be Jihadist groups offer the three types of self-recognition, described above: self-confidence, respect and esteem, but this is followed by scapegoating narratives, and splitting and the stereotyping of difference. The perception of others becomes a self-motivated distortion and idealization of self and one's culture: the pursuit of material wealth or pleasure, for instance, or the sexualisation of women and a capacity for racism and violence are projected onto the other of the white working-class estate.

Culturally, in Muslim areas of the city, it quickly became clear that relationships between the generations have suffered, as male initiation rituals between fathers and sons, in the workplace, are lost. Some imams in specific mosques were recruited from the villages from which people had migrated in the last century, as a way of staying in touch with lost communities. The trouble was that these imams could be poorly educated, barely able to speak English with any fluency. Second, third and fourth generation Muslims, educated in English schools, could treat them with contempt, not least for a lack of Islamic scholarship. Narratives of the 'Christian' neglect of white Muslims in the Bosnian conflict, in contrast to the 'Christian' (that is Russian Orthodox) support for the 'Christian' Serbs, were relatively compelling, filling some of the existential as well as intergenerational vacuum. In the 1990s actions by the West, standing back as Muslims were slaughtered, as at Srebrenica, were essentially seen to be anti-Islamic acts rather than racist, given that these Muslims were white. Certain young people inwardly digested stories of Muslim humiliation, and of older generations failing to speak out, and of collective trauma, and the need to fight back in ways parents and grandparents had failed to. The political became deeply personal, as well as cultural, fuelled by the toxicity of Islamophobia as well as intergenerational and familial fracture.

A community leader I call Aasif, (the names used are pseudonyms) talked about these issues:

> … you had groups like Hizb ut-Tahrir taking advantage of the situation in Bosnia … with what's happening with the Muslims … arms not being allowed to get to the Muslims to defend themselves where Russia is providing the Christian Serbs; it was a them-against-us kind of debate with groups like Hizb ut-Tahrir … talking about the male Muslim section of Muslim community at that time; the youth, low education achievement, low aspiration … no job opportunity … perfect audience … you can recruit easy … It's nothing to do with the colour of your skin; this is not racism; this is a target on the Muslim community because these Muslims are white … I can remember some of these Hizb ut-Tahrir members who in the early '90s, pulling the youth away from the parents as well.

From this perspective, Bosnia was a trauma, in which scales fell from collective eyes: it led to increased politicization and provided a mythic rationale for fundamentalism (Varvin, 2012). Groups like Hizb ut-Tahrir (or Liberation Party) – التحرير حزب, in the Arabic – exploited these feelings. Hizb ut-Tahrir is an international pan-Islamic political organization commonly associated with the goal of all Muslim countries unifying into one Islamic caliphate, ruled by sharia law. Hizb ut-Tahrir was founded in 1952 as part of a movement to create a new elite among Muslim youth. The writings of the group's founder, Shaikh Taqi al-Dine al-Nabahani, lay down detailed descriptions for a restored caliphate (Ruthven, 2012). A young person like Raafe, for example, schooled in England, and radicalised in prison, ridiculed some of the established authorities in the Mosques and embraced Hizb ut-Tahrir.

Raafe

Another community leader, Aatif, told me about the weaknesses of mosque management and of imams and how Raafe and others exploited this. I was told that

Raafe was an individual 'who had a very troubled upbringing' and had been sent to prison:

> Raafe didn't have a very good relationship with his father ended up in crime was sent down to prison … Came out of prison and he was within a few weeks, he was, he had transformed into somebody who was a practising Muslim now to hear him … later on when we realized he was part of Hizb ut-Tahrir, but at that point to see somebody change so dramatically was wow, he made a real positive change … you couldn't explain to your parents why you wanted to … your parents who came in the early '60s … came when they were young … so very little … religious … education … so they didn't have … opportunity to question the imams and learn something; so they couldn't pass that religious knowledge on to the youth, to their children; so the parents relied upon the mosques to offer that … so that's where the communication barrier helped groups like Hizb ut-Tahrir. We can offer you Islamic information in your language, that's what attracted a lot of people in Stoke-on-Trent on topical issues.

Radicalization transformed the lives of some individuals, providing meaning, purpose and self-recognition. The portrait of Raafe, I should mention, derives from several narratives pieced together, rather than directly from the person concerned. But there were patterns in the various stories to help piece together a biographical account. Raafe's transformation almost certainly depended on feeling understood, listened to and respected by radical groups in prison. Recognition was at the heart of this, combined with a radical purpose: 'we understand how you feel, we feel the same way; we have thoughts to help you'. Various people told me that Raafe was an active member of a radical group when he left prison. He ran youth discussion groups in certain mosques. Self-recognition works at an imaginal and narrative as well as interpersonal and group level; by imaginative projective identification with heroes and causes from the past, that speak to present needs, however perversely. Narratives that offer meaning and divine purpose in lives, in the company of past as well as present Islamic martyrs.

The pedagogy of radicalization exploits the vacuums and meaninglessness in specific lives, giving people a potential place in history. It involves stories and appeals to action, rather than textual hermeneutics. Narratives of twelfth-century victories supported a call for jihad now, one requiring toughness and heroism. Jihad, or struggle, becomes constructed as a heavy responsibility that requires brutality to demoralise a more powerful opponent. The victory of the Muslim armies, against the Crusaders, led by the King of Jerusalem, Guy of Lusignan, in the twelfth century's Battle of Hattin, is interpreted as the outcome of a protracted process of small-scale, hard hitting attacks in various locations. Past struggles are reinterpreted in the light of the present in the struggle against the new and powerful crusaders of the West and its client states. Heroism and martyrdom are called for in what is a very different pedagogical process from rational, textual analysis of the Qur'an. Muslim clerics may speak in the language of theory, the jihadi groups act through stories and doing (Hassan & Weiss, 2015; West, 2016).

Thus, Islamophobia and everyday disrespect, when mixed with national politics, foreign policy adventures and intergenerational fracture within Muslim communities, draws individuals towards Islamism. Powerful forms of recognition are provided, which operate at a primitive emotional, as well as group and narrative level. Individuals feel understood and find purpose, meaning and legitimacy in the world. Recognition gives meaning to fractured lives. But in the closed fundamentalist group, the process is impregnated with misrecognition, and with dialogical and narrative closure. Ironically, there is alienation from self and experience too. The capacity to engage openly and reflexivity with experience, in all its messiness, is frozen: debate, dialogue, enquiry and self/other recognition, on which wider social solidarities and cooperation depend, are stifled.

Workers' Education: Building Dialogue across Difference

Workers' education once thrived in the city and provides a model of how self/other dynamics can strengthen rather than fracture across difference. The first ever workers' university tutorial class took place in Stoke in 1908, when 30 or so worker students met each Friday evening, over a period of years, with their tutor, R.H. Tawney, a subsequently distinguished economic historian, representing the University of Oxford. The classes were free from prescribed curricula, and its members could explore issues in their working lives from the perspectives of history, politics, economics and literature. Fortnightly essays were required, and the standard of some of these was high, although by no means all (West, 1972; Goldman, 1995). There were no formal examinations or qualifications due to a desire to eliminate competition and vocationalism from the classroom (West, 1972; Rose, 2010).

Interestingly, the Marxist Social Democratic Federation formed the nucleus of the first group of students, who were potters, miners, clerks, shop assistants and school teachers. Many came from non-conformist religious backgrounds: from families, in short, that could encourage them to think for themselves. The Social Democratic Federation was formed in 1884 under the leadership of Henry Hyndman who was the son of a businessman and became a journalist as well as political agitator. The Federation was strongly opposed to the British Liberal Party of the time, and its programme was progressive, calling for a 48-hour working week, the abolition of child labour, compulsory free secular education, equality for women and the nationalization of the means of production, distribution and exchange by a democratic state. But some members of the SDF, according to historian Stuart Macintyre (1980) held an extremely 'mechanical version of the materialist conception of history' in which the whole of human life 'was controlled by economic forces independent of human volition' (p. 17). Education, politics and consciousness were mere epiphenomena of the techniques and relations of production. The students could become very rigid in their economic doctrines (ibid.). That rigidity played out, on occasions, in the tutorial classes (West, 2017a). We can interpret this as another manifestation of fundamentalism – of having the truth and nothing but the truth, forged in a community of true believers. Psychoanalytically, once again, this can be regarded as a defense against complexity and the anxiety of not knowing. Tawney himself was aware that the same spirit of non-conformity that drove some of the worker students could narrow viewpoints and bring a tendency to over-proselytize that made it difficult to dialogue and take on board different perspectives (Goldman, 1995).

Jonathan Rose's historical work has rescued Tawney and workers' education from what had become the great condescension of posterity (Rose, 2010; West, 2017a). Rose has drawn on diverse forms of life writing to chronicle the importance of relationship and recognition in workers' education: between tutors and students, among students, but also in relation to the symbolic world in challenging bigotry and fascism. Such education offered working-class people avenues into leadership roles in local and national politics and served to radicalize and motivate them in personal as well as political ways. Surveys of students showed that most were taking part in trade union activity, cooperative societies, local authorities, religious and political bodies. They were building both a workers' education as well as a broader social democratic movement.

The classes themselves created space to question and challenge racism and other forms of bigotry. In one telling account, Nancy Dobrin, born in 1914, wrote that the study of literature had revolutionary consequences for her. She grew up in a home where learning was not valued, where there was either 'a row or an order'. She read little but later joined a WEA class and read avidly, although she admitted that she went to the class partly in search of a man. Nancy became a writer herself. She described working for a German Jew during the Second World War, wondering what on earth he was doing there and why couldn't people like him go home. Later, in another class, she met her future husband, a German Jewish refugee who described himself as a Christian Communist. This was a relationship formed in the spaces of workers' education, where literature – from Lawrence, Tolstoy and James Joyce – enabled her to question her own bigotry. Such experiences shaped in turn her relationships with her children and family and impelled her to question aspects of their schooling. Agency can take many forms: in the everyday, in families and on the wider democratic stage (Dobrin, 1980).

In certain respects, Nancy's story resembles those of later adult students, such as Brenda, in my own research among non-traditional adult students at university in the 1990s (West, 1996). Brenda found recognition of self and experience in relationship with certain tutors and students as well as in literature. Brenda could relate to fictional characters, such as an abused but resilient woman in a novel by Maupassant. The character, so to speak, became part of Brenda's internal object relational world through processes of projective identification – finding aspects of self in the fictional or actual other – and imaginatively experiencing their lives and internalizing some of their strength and resilience. These dynamics can be incorporated into a more developed and nuanced theory of recognition, embracing the imaginal and the symbolic, actively engaging emotion as well as mind. Like Nancy, Brenda learned to play with ideas and feel valued for it. Nancy learned, like many other adult students, a more democratic sensibility in the tutorial classes and later, which they describe in their own words (West, 1996; Dobrin, 1980; Rose, 2010, pp. 274–275).

Dogmatism and Its Roots

But dogmatism existed in the tutorial classes. It is interesting that some worker students admired tutors like Tawney, who remained steadfast as well as respectful even when harangued by a fundamentalist student. Leftist fundamentalists sometimes from the Social Democratic Federation and later the Communist Party, though not exclusively so, would quote texts like *Das Capital* with religious fervour. The other students admired how Tawney remained respectful in the face of agitation. One recalled a particular Marxist – the SDF could dominate the first tutorial classes – challenging point after point by reference to classic Marxist texts. Tawney took it in his stride but insisted that there were other points of view. The student accused the tutor of hopping around from twig to twig, like a bird, and a sense of bad temper pervaded the room. Tawney insisted that everyone, including his challenger, take tea together afterwards and tell stories, read poetry and sing songs. This enabled the group to re-establish some shared humanity and fraternity (Rose, 2010, p. 266). The local secretary of the SDF became so alarmed at the effect of the classes that he instructed his members to leave for fear of ideological contamination. They refused, because they were excited at being able to interrogate ideas in a liberal way, from different standpoints (Goldman, 2013).

Interestingly, there is a contemporary re-evaluation of Tawney's contribution to theorizing the role and practice of inclusive university education and in building a more effective political democracy and social solidarities (Holford, 2015; Goldman, 2013; West, 2017a). Tawney emphasized the moral and spiritual in human betterment, which could be embodied in the tutorial classes in ways inspiring ideas of fellowship and service. The aim of the tutorial classes was to make university education available to all people in their own localities: quite different to today's assumptions about the purpose of higher education for individual social mobility. Tawney was committed to a liberal and humane view of education for everyone, where citizens could acquire civic virtues and understanding in the struggle to create forms of social cooperation and mutual understanding. Holford (2015) suggests that Tawney offers a localist critique of the current emphasis on developing global skills and mobility. Communities should not be privileged or discounted because of their wealth or poverty and universities can be active agents in communities via, for instance, adult education. Moreover, Tawney represents a more constructivist view of knowledge: the classes were classes, not lectures, and ideas were explored and developed in discussion. The processes of education were democratic – students engaged in research and discovery by using original source material like historical documents, rather than being the passive recipients of received wisdom. I suggest too that Tawney was especially good at containing the many anxieties of worker students, by keeping the dialogue going, despite assaults made upon it and by recognising, in authentic ways, diverse contributions. This of course mirrors the containing functions of the psychoanalytic process itself: creating good enough space where it is possible to digest difficult ideas. Containment is not confined to psychoanalysis but can be part of educational experiences, as people negotiate who they are, have been and might be, always and inevitably accompanied by anxiety, in the transitional space of an adult class (West, 1996).

We can better appreciate the dynamics of classes like these, derived from the testimonies of the worker/students themselves, and drawing on a developed theory of recognition. We can build nuanced understanding of the importance of dialogue, of play, and of self/other recognition and of subjectification processes encompassing the interplay of inner and outer worlds. Nancy and Brenda projected and then introjected aspects of self and experience into their imaginative life, that enabled them to better recognise and engage with others. They learned more of what we can call a democratic sensibility, or cosmopolitan 'subjectification', which they describe in their own words (West, 1996; Dobrin, 1980; Rose, 2010, pp. 274–275; Bainbridge & West, 2012). The reality of these 'object relations' dynamics in adult education cannot be proved in an absolute sense: but their utility in illuminating change processes is convincing. Workers' education, I suggest, once afforded forms of recognition for ordinary people, in which they felt accepted, listened to, respected as well as treated as equals with the right to be heard and fully participate. This creates mature and capable people with stories to tell and ideas to offer, and a capacity for reciprocity.

Conclusion, Fundamentalism Recognition and the Psychosocial

Fundamentalism or the fundamentalist instinct, I suggest, takes many forms, and is really quite ordinary, which includes absolutist conceptual thinking within leftist modes of thought. Critical theorists such as Adorno (1973) challenged progressives to consider the failure of left Hegelian philosophical thought and its false predictions of inevitable proletarian revolution. Adorno thought the failure – including the resilience of capitalism and the rise of Nazism – posed a philosophical and epistemological crisis for them and for a positivist social science, including Marxism, that ignored the subjectivity of the observer. Adorno insisted that the crisis, in the spirit of psychoanalysis, de-centred the rational subject in relation to her objects of enquiry and the dynamics between them. Defensive, unconscious drives and pre-intellectual dynamics impregnated our subjectivity and relationships and thus our philosophical engagement with the world. Conceptual knowledge, as psychoanalysis has taught, is insufficient when building insight into self/object dynamics. We must examine our desires and potential illusions in and beyond our supposed rationality: the origins of perception lie in part in early or pre-intellectual experience, including the potential defences of grandiosity and omniscience, forged in early dependence on others. Adorno, drawing on Freud and Nietzsche, recognised a tendency to invest in certain kinds of thinking in order to repress other thoughts, in early experience and in childhood cathexes, with their panoply of fears, longings and loss. Interestingly Adorno thought the subject's loss of omniscience and the illusion that reality could be fully and rationally penetrated, rendered the search for unified systems of conceptual knowledge impossible. But this could then liberate the subject to engage with subjective feelings and the senses, leading to enhanced sensitivity towards what is non-identical, to diverse ways of seeing, and the domain of the other. There is considerable democratic as well as inter-subjective potential as well as relief in challenging the grandiose, omniscient rationalist fantasy that we and our philosophical schemas can and must fully represent reality.

In a different vein, the research into radicalisation processes and workers' education enables us to refine Honneth's normative concept of recognition. It encompasses, as Honneth suggests, self-recognition at an intimate emotional, relational, group but also, we can add, at a narrative, unconscious and imaginal level too. These processes take us beyond words or discursive understanding. Primitive, emotional forms of communication, in a tutor's warm response or encouragement, enable people to feel understood, cared for, loved even as well as legitimate; or their opposites, when dismissed and disparaged. Embodied, memory in feeling, as Klein (1975) called it, 'speaks' louder than words in these moments. Raafe felt cared for in prison, his struggles and troubles were understood and new narrative resources, or myths, were available to make sense of a whole. All of which enabled him, however delusionally, to work with other alienated young Muslims, to care for them in a way that he was cared for and to offer an all-encompassing narrative truth. Those young people no doubt felt recognised in turn by someone they admired, because he spoke to their concerns (and with an authority, it should be noted, grounded in actual visits to the Middle East). Raafe built narrative connections, over time, between their anxieties and those of Muslims in the past. Such narratives explained the suffering of Islam and the need for heroic struggle against crusaders, then and now. The dynamics, however perverted, provide existential meaning and the promise, for some, of entry into Paradise. Fundamentalist dynamics like these, I suggest, are not 'other'. When we feel out of our depth, vulnerable, exposed and or excluded, we can grab at stories that apparently offer total solutions, an answer to everything, including our deepest anxieties. This applies in academic life as much as formal religion, in, for instance, the continuing adherence to neo-classical economic theories in many university economics departments, despite their failure to explain how and why people acted as they did in the 2008 financial crash. The omnipotent fantasy has been that rational, mainly mathematical theories explained everything of how economies worked, grounded in a myth of the rational, calculating homo economic subject. People can continue to cling to such Zombie economics, as a largely unacknowledged defence against their anxieties, doubts and fears that they do not really know or that others might know better (West, 2017c).

John Dewey (1969) especially enables us to differentiate between the narrative and self/other closure of the Islamist group and the openness of democratic adult education. Dewey observed that the good citizen requires democratic association to realize what she might be: she finds herself by participating in family life, the economy and various artistic, cultural and political activities, in which there is free give and take with diverse others. This fosters feelings of being understood and creates meaning and purpose in the company of others. Dewey suggests that good and intelligent solutions for society, and diverse groups, depend on relatively open, inclusive and democratic types of association. In scientific research, for instance, the more scientists freely introduce their own hypotheses, beliefs and intuitions, the better the eventual outcome. Dewey applied these ideas to social learning: intelligent solutions are the result of the degree to which all those involved participate fully without constraint and with equal rights. It is only when openly publicly debating issues, in inclusive (and I might add self-reflexive) ways, that societies really thrive (Honneth, 2007, pp. 218–239). Honneth concludes that Dewey's normative idea of healthy dialogical democratic society was grounded in a psychosocial ideal of cooperation, rather than politics or communicative competence; in an openness to complex experience which challenges how we think, feel and act. Dewey offers the case of a 'robber band' as one example of closure to otherness and ultimately to truth. Honneth uses the example of a Nazi band of brothers to make the same point. The process involves collective as well as individual defence mechanisms while it is difficult to prize apart the socio-cultural from the personal unconscious. We should grasp the importance of both, in dynamic relationship, when considering the normative qualities of good enough education.

We are left with a problem of how to live in doubt and uncertainty, beyond rationalist illusion, whether as critical theorists, historians, biographers, economists, or adult students. Maybe we need to cultivate subjective negative capability, echoing the poet John Keats and Adorno's framing of his project as negative dialectics. Some tutorial class students learned negative capability rather well. Keats thought that negative capability was the quality at work when a person can live in uncertainties, or mysteries and doubts, without any irritable reaching after fact and reason. The language is not immediately clear, it is more suggestive and idiosyncratic. Obviously, the word 'negative' is not being used pejoratively but to communicate a notion that a person's potential can be defined via recognition of what he or she does not possess. Essential to literary achievement, Keats argues, is a certain passivity, a willingness to let what is mysterious or doubtful remain just that (Hebron, 2017). It might be better to break off from a relentless search for knowledge or complete conceptual truths and contemplate instead 'a fine verisimilitude' or the spirit of truth seeking; open to what we do not know, and our doubts, in the company of others. The fundamentalist seeks to annihilate these under the banner of certainty. We should recognise our uncertainties and the anxieties these bring; and our need for diverse others, including someone like Tawney, for cultivating better, more reflexive and inclusive knowledge of self and the world. Psychoanalysis, combined with critical theory, foregrounds the quality of our relationship to knowledge and experience: how in every one of us, as learners, academics or analysts, there remains the perpetual struggle between grabbing at the allusions of certainty – conceptual or otherwise – or recognizing a shared fallibility and need for others in the personal, relational and epistemological experiment called democratic adult education.

REFERENCES

Adorno, T. (1973). *Negative dialectics* (E. B. Ashton, Trans.). London: Routledge.

Auestad, L. (Ed.). (2012). *Psychoanalysis and politics: Exclusion and the politics of representation.* London: Karnac.

Austed, L. (2014). *Nationalism and the body politic.* London: Karnac.

Bainbridge, A., & West, L. (2012). *Psychoanalysis and education.* London: Karnac.

Burnett, J. (2011). *The new geographies of racism: Stoke-on-Trent.* London: Institute of Race Relations.

Dewey, J. (1969). The ethics of democracy. In J. A. Boydston (Ed.), *The early years of john Dewey.* Carbondale, IL: Southern Illinois University Press.

Fieldhouse, R. (1996a). Mythmaking and mortmain: A response. *Studies in the Education of Adults, 28*,(1), 117–120.

Freud, S. (1953/1974). *The standard edition of the complete works of Sigmund Freud* (Trans. J. Strachey, Trans. Ed. with A. Freud). London: Hogarth and the Institute of Psychoanalysis.

Frosh, S. (1991). *Identity crisis: Modernity, psychoanalysis and the self.* London: Macmillan.

Goldman, L. (1995). *Dons and workers: Oxford and adult education since 1850.* Oxford: Clarendon Press.

Goldman, L. (2013). *The life of R.H. Tawney: Socialism and history.* London: Bloomsbury Academic.

Hassan, H., & Weiss, M. (2015). *ISIS: Inside the army of terror*. New York, NY: Regan Arts.

Hebron, S. (2017). *John Keats and 'negative capability'*. Retrieved June 5, 2018, from https://www.bl.uk/romantics-and-victorians/articles/john-keats-and-negative-capability#sthash.dpuf

Holford, J. (2015, July 7–9). *Adult and higher education in the early work of R. H. Tawney*. Paper presented at Standing Conference of University Teachers and Researchers in the Education of Adults (SCUTREA) It's all Adult Education, University of Leeds, Leeds.

Honneth, A. (1995). *The struggle for recognition: The moral grammar of social conflicts.* Cambridge: Polity Press.

Honneth, A. (2007). *Disrespect: The normative foundations of critical theory*. Cambridge: Polity Press.

Honneth, A. (2009). *Pathologies of reason: On the legacy of critical theory.* New York, NY: Columbia University Press.

Klein, M. (1975). *Envy and gratitude and other works.* New York, NY: Delta.

Macintyre, S. (1980). *A proletarian science: Marxism in Britain, 1917–1933.* Cambridge: Cambridge University Press.

Merrill B., & West, L. (2009). *Using biographical methods in social research*. London: Sage Publications.

Rice, M. (2010). *The lost city of Stoke-on-Trent.* London: Frances Lincoln.

Ruthven, M. (2012). *Islam: A very short introduction.* Oxford: Oxford University Press.

Varvin, S. (2012). Islamism and xenophobia. In L. Auestad (Ed.), *Psychoanalysis and politics, exclusion and the politics of representation* (pp. 155–168). London: Karnac.

West, L. (2016). *Distress in the city; racism, fundamentalism and a democratic education.* London: Trentham & UCL Books.

West, L. (2017a). Resisting the enormous condescension of history: Richard Henry Tawney, Raymond Williams and the long struggle for a democratic education. *International Journal of Lifelong Education, 36*(1–2), 129–144.

West, L. (2017b, March 31–April 2). *The case of Brexit and forces of fear, a psychosocial perspective.* Paper presented at the Psychoanalysis and Politics Symposium, Paris.
West, L. (2017c). Re-enchanting the academy: Popular Education and the #search for Soul in the Modern Academy. In A. Voss & S. Wilson (Eds.), *Re-enchanting the Academy.* Auckland: Rubedo Press.
Williams, R. (1989). *Resources of hope. Culture, democracy and socialism.* London: Verso.
Winnicott, D. (1971). *Playing and reality.* London: Routledge.

HENNING SALLING OLESEN

11. CULTURAL IDENTITY, LEARNING AND SOCIAL PREJUDICE

The Politicization of Subjectivity in Former Yugoslavia

INTRODUCTION

Since 1999 The International Research Group for Psychosocietal Analysis has worked regularly at annual workshops in Dubrovnik, gradually developing a practice of deep-hermeneutic interpretation. The main ambition of the methodology is to track the societally unconscious subjective dynamics in different areas of everyday life by means of psychodynamic analysis applied on everyday life interaction. However, for work in this location, the experience of the war that followed in the wake of Yugoslavia's dissolution formed an overwhelmingly strong and an inevitable challenge for understanding the social psychology of those relatively abstract national and religious identities and differences that are the drivers in identity-based politics. So for this case the research group has departed from its usual terrain working to interpret the dynamics of the conflicts several times. Unlike the rest of our activity we have worked on the basis of secondary accounts and reports, which are however also abundant. This chapter will present some of the reflections on this work.

At the time, around the millennium, the extreme events in the conflict seemed predominantly pathological in the sense that they seemed entirely disconnected from people´s previous everyday lives, socialization and identities. Without comparing directly, similar questions arose to those following the Second World War: How could extremism and endless cruelty happen in a modern civilized part of Europe? It became in itself a challenge to our interdisciplinary group of people from social and humanistic sciences to be able to understand the connections between ordinary people's everyday life and their readiness to take part in a civil war in the name of national (ethnic) and religious identity, and in many cases be direct actors in atrocities against former neighbours and members of the local community.

The interesting question was how the social, cultural, and political orientations are mediated through the (individual) subjective process of socialization, consciousness building and action. We wanted not only to understand which mechanisms empowered political leaders and were utilized by them in the deliberate attempts to politicize subjectivity, but also their 'background' processes of societal change and cultural development. We wished to investigate how subjective processes are part of social interaction, being the object of historical circumstances, while they

© KONINKLIJKE BRILL NV, LEIDEN, 2020 | DOI: 10.1163/9789004420274_012

themselves provide fuel for political processes in one direction or another – which is a matter of political psychology.

SUBJECTIVITY BETWEEN LEARNING AND DEFENCE

We did also find interesting theoretical inspiration in psychoanalytically informed research of cultural identities that addressed these types of issues, and our aim was to situate these 'mechanisms' in a historical context of societal development and cultural encounters. One of the first central inspirations was V. Volkan's concept of "large group identity". His concept seems to address precisely the theme in question, where large groups constitute themselves through individuals′ affiliation to the group, and people act individually on behalf of the large group. While distancing himself from an individual psychological explanation of the significance of the group, e.g. in the form of a father figure or a motherly agency for caring, Volkan especially focuses on the significance of the large group identity for social relations within the group and for the engagement of group members in conflicts with other groups (Volkan, 2001, 2009). Volkan himself has a life history association with a nationality conflict, being born in the Turkish minority in Cyprus. He is now a prominent psychiatrist in the US, and has engaged in a number of initiatives for conflict resolution and dialogue between implacable groups around the world. His theory is in general that the belonging to a particular group, e.g. a nation, will remain a lifelong constitutive element in individual identity, while other elements of identity are added during the life course. He understands the constitution and significance of this group identity within the thinking of object relations theory. Within this conceptual framework, conflict behaviour of large groups is described as a reaction which defends group members or the group as such against humiliations or threats. This conflict behaviour is reparative, it is about defending the very identity, including its recognizable separation from other group identities. Volkan connects conflict behaviour with the psychodynamic level via the theory of socialization: while the child gradually develops tolerance of ambivalence, it will integrate some of the externalizations, or splittings, that characterize early childhood, but this integration will never be complete. The incompletely integrated elements then remain in the individual psyche as potential material for defensive reactions, and Volkan argues that group identification is psychodynamically based on these elements. Violations of the identity of the group or mere threats against it activate unconscious dynamics which shape particular current perceptions and reactions in a way which can only be understood as feelings of a general threat and a defence of the identity as such.

This context of understanding identity and culture has interesting implications for theoretical discussion, e.g. in sociological theory, and for 'contemporary diagnosis': What are the specifics of our contemporary society, where are we heading? In this discussion, the increasing significance of subjective orientations seems to be one of the few consensual aspects. Such a 'holistic' theoretical approach to the links between subjectivity and social action cuts across research topics such as peace and conflict, political reorientations in a post-nation state setting, lifelong learning, migration and cultural integration, change processes in communities and organizations, which are all also interrelated fields. However, this approach is important for understanding identity as an emotional dynamics which organizes feelings, relations and consciousness; it may encompass aspects of learning as well as defensive rejections of certain insights and experiences, i.e. an ongoing process of identification(s).

In my own research, this concept of identity is empirically grounded in studies of the subjective aspects of wage labour and (un)employment and the subjective handling of changes in working life, which reveal crucial identity processes in everyday life (Salling Olesen, 2001, 2007; Salling Olesen & Weber, 2001). Work identity and professional identities inform and reflect the subjective meaning of work and of specific professional roles and practices. The study of identification processes offers fundamental contributions to the theory of learning. In this context, I also see the opposite possibility: a theory of learning (and resistance to learning) may help us to understand how the processing of the "raw materials of subjectivity" may enable the politicization of identity. Although different contexts and domains obviously have a different subjective status, I think this indicates the sense in connecting (comparing) the examination of those challenges to everyday life practice, which may or may not elicit epistemic processes and social experiences to form the basis of identity building and sudden strong new identifications – in extreme cases leading to hostility to others and violence.

In my learning theory framework identity appears as a product of and also an active element in the subjective process of experience building (Salling Olesen, 1989), or alternatively, the lifelong learning process of the individual, acquiring the social and cultural context through everyday life practices (1989). Rather than a stable coherence of self and social practices, once and for all established through socialization, and inscribed in a stable cultural framework, 'identity' refers to a temporary relationship between individual experience and social practices in which the individual is engaging, while learning is an intended or unintended and unrecognized dimension of this experiential process. At any one time, this relationship may provide a more or less contradictory framework for dealing with new challenges and knowledge and relating new practices to habitual ones. This identity is generally a dynamic and contradictory relationship because conditions are contradictory, as are the subjective driving forces.

Intercultural relations and cultural exchanges always challenge identity. In the best case, this implies learning and development for each party involved. But not necessarily. A fundamental point of departure is that everyday life experience is located in a field of tension between potentials for learning and the inclination towards defence. Intercultural relations occurring in this everyday life are interpreted within the consciousness building rooted in everyday life, and very often this means integrating them in patterns of recognition and routine which do not affect the consciousness of everyday life, which in itself is an active form of defence. The notion of 'Altagsbewusstsein' (Leithäuser, 1976) illuminates the subjectively active production of a stereotypical consciousness as a (collective) defensive reaction to handle overwhelming demands as well as life historical anxieties in everyday life. Automatic assumptions about unknown phenomena to which one relates by coincidence or through external circumstances occur all the time in everyday life. However, sometimes they engage more emotional energy and become a cognitively defined idea, a fixed orientation in relation to strangers and unknown realities. When it results in inability to recognize people or phenomena in a differentiated and realistic way, and to learn about them we call it a "social prejudice".

The psychodynamic theory may help to understand the origins of social prejudice. The production and emotional charging and strengthening of specific cognitive patterns and ideas may be interpreted as a collective defensive action in order to handle the fragility and emotional burden of social life. The conception of the large group identity as a combination of a strong identification with one's own group and the application of specific attributes and intentions to a hostile picture of another group makes it understandable that this identification may solve problematic and challenging aspects in one's own identity process. The need for such a defence may have many reasons, combining social ruptures and contradictions and life historical subjective experiences. But focusing on the active nature of this mechanism also points out that there is an alternative way of handling these experiences and conditions which depends on alternative identifications – and the claim here is that this is the social psychology core of the political process. In this way of conceiving identity and identification, the fundamental alternative is between learning, i.e. understanding not only social reality but also your own subjectivity, and meeting challenges through the production of social prejudice.

THE POLITICS OF IDENTITY IN FORMER YUGOSLAVIA

The power of identity politics depends on the ability to mobilize socially and collectively irritations and unresolved conflicts on different levels within an identification and possible social practice. A critical study of the subjectivity of cultural conflicts should examine the interrelations between experiences and conflicts between a level of individual life history and emotionality, a level of everyday social practice and moral orientation, and a societal/political level, Only by uncovering the channels of dislocating energies between these levels can we seek to distinguish between the manipulative use of identity politics and legitimate claims of recognition (Fukuyama, 2018).

The dissolution of former Yugoslavia and the very complex and rapid development of violent conflicts and hostilities is a thought-provoking exposition of the new relevance of the theme of interculturality. In a short span of time, we experienced dramatic (re)construction of cultural and political identities, largely defining themselves in opposition to each other. This did not happen spontaneously. There is hardly any doubt that this process was driven forward and the contradictions deliberately nurtured by some of the political forces in the region, and a political science analysis might stop at examining these political forces and the interests behind them. This aspect involves important international geo-politics which I will leave aside here, and also socio-structural factors that I will partly return to. But the focus here will be on understanding the social and cultural circumstances and the level of everyday life which produced and enabled this political process and also developed a new political reality. Here we are not only interested in the identifications which seemed to reinterpret peoples′ everyday lives, anxieties and life experiences. The atrocities committed in the name of cultural identity (ethnicity, religion), the killing of neighbours and ethnic cleansings, call strongly for all possible attempts to understand the psychological processes that fuel and create such simplistic, unique orientations out of complex life experiences. This seems to be an important adjustment to the ways of understanding and evaluating the process which appear in national(ist) history writing (itself one of the collective identity productions) as well as to the rationalistic manner of the 'international community' which finally condemns but basically does not care to understand the dynamics. We want to understand the conflicts in endogenous concepts, as a complex of historical rationalities and emotions that have been dislocated, partly deliberately, partly by the difficulty of most actors in understanding themselves and their own feelings. Democracy, tolerance and humanity depend on a better understanding of what happened: a practical piece of reconciliation, of 'never again …'.

The political history of the Balkans is complicated but a broad overview of the cultural and social elements involved is necessary for understanding the identity politics. Yugoslavia was rather artificially constructed as a unified kingdom after World War I, composed of bits and pieces from the Austro-Hungarian Empire (Croatia, Slovenia and parts of Bosnia-Hercegovina) and the existing kingdoms of Serbia and Montenegro. These kingdoms were not very old but had been under Ottoman rule, Bosnia as a genuine part and the others paying tribute. In spite of the absence or fragility of nation states, these affiliations have had some implications. The Austro-Hungarian parts seem to have been influenced by industrialization and modern infrastructure from the late 19th century. Religious affiliations differed: Austro-Hungarian parts were influenced by the Roman Catholic Church, Serbia and Montenegro were orthodox, whereas Bosnia was Muslim. The population was ethnically heterogeneous and there were various mixed regions. Beside Muslims, there were both Serbs and Croats in Bosnia, Slavonia around the Danube was a total mix of Serbs and Croats, Vojvodina was mainly inhabited by Hungarians, and Krajina in Croatia was inhabited by Serbian peasants who had been given a piece of land as a reward for their participation in the war against the Ottomans.

World War II activated many of the differences and contradictions in this patchwork country. But the successful resistance to the Nazi-German invasion established a new political leadership centred on the communist partisan movement. Right-wing nationalist movements in Croatia (Ustaša) discredited themselves by allying with the Axis powers. The base of the partisan movement went across ethnic, religious and other divides, and after the war a federal republic was established with the intent of eradicating the many divisions by merging and bridging between the nations and religions, while also recognizing the problems involved, as can be seen from the many formal institutional arrangements to create and guarantee equality. A new Yugoslav national ideology emerged, later called Titoism because it projected this intention on the former partisan leader, later president, Marshall Tito. With the successful rejection of Stalinist domination from 1953, a leading role in the group of non-aligned countries, and an industrial development attempting to create a self-sufficient economy from military equipment to consumer goods, 'Jugoslavija' grew into a powerful unifying symbol both domestically and internationally. The economy was originally a typical state-directed command economy, but after the break with the Soviet Union a model combining market economy and socialist self-management was launched and formalized in a party decision in 1964. This gave a new momentum for the idea of Yugoslavia as a third way in the environment of cold war and systems competition, and both the economic and cultural modernization distinguished the country from the rest of the socialist world. During the process of modernization, free migration took place; the mixing of peoples accelerated and ethnic differences seemed to lose their importance. In Bosnia, which had the most mixed population, 25% of all marriages in the 80s were of mixed ethnicity. The public culture was generally secular. People were not very religious, neither in terms of beliefs nor practice. International influence on communications, culture and consumption was very strong. One never heard any significant reference to ethnicity, except as a historical element of regional origin within the nation state. Serbo-Croat was, until the late 80s, seen as *one* language, though written in two alphabets. However, the country also remained very heterogeneous, with strong regional differences in development, and as the authority of the partisan movement from the war faded away, it became more difficult for the communist party to maintain control. In everyday life there was an ambivalent relationship to the communist party and to centralism, which also included the usual resignation in socialist countries regarding hidden usurpation by the elite and the party. After a period of increasing wealth stimulated by loans, foreign debt was a heavy burden, and the ability of the regime to recover after Tito's death was low (Potts, 1996). In spite of ambitious attempts to create a new model of socialist self-management, the traditional party-controlled power structure also remained dominant. Nationalism was repressed, especially assumed remnants of the historical Ustaša fascism in Croatia and Serbian Chetnik royalism, but also ordinary democratic criticism was added to potential enemies of the new nation state. In the meantime modernized, quite international identities were developing, whereas Titoism with its patriotic, quite martial but also more fragile identification increasingly seemed to be 'the old system' and 'the identity of the former generation', de-legitimizing the regime and the federal state.

It seems clear that the unity of Yugoslavia was already being discussed in Croatia and Slovenia, by e.g. liberals, reform-oriented communists, technocrats of the well-developed industry, and of course by the right-wing nationalists. In 1970/1971 there was an uprising in Croatia which played out as a national resistance against Serbian dominance. It was silenced by traditional repression. A dramatic shift took place in the late 80s. After Tito's death, critical voices seemed to be heard more openly, while at the same time the economy was worsening, inflation was accelerating, and the wish to leave Yugoslavia was growing in Slovenia and Croatia. A convergence between demands for democracy, liberation of the most competitive parts of business, and Croatian nationalism was challenging the regime and also the unity of the state. Nationalism started to flourish openly. The demand for democratization and modernization was converted into a demand for national independence in Slovenia and Croatia. In this situation Milošević 'played the nationalist card' in his great speech in 1989 in Kosovo Polje, which he declared to be core homeland of the Serbs. He shifted the focus of identification of the regime from its socialist history from partisans to modernized self-management, over to a Serbian leadership with a history dating back to the battle against the Ottomans. This was the trigger for the emerging nationalist will to dissolve Yugoslavia to come out into the open.

Before that, the regime had already met Albanian demands for minority rights by the inclusion of the province of Kosovo in the Serbian state, violating the constitution (the Albanians and Hungarians, unlike other nationalities, were not granted equal national rights in the institutional arrangement, but a specific regional autonomy). The repression of Kosovo, and especially Milošević' pointing out the special role of the Serbs in the defence of the Slavs against the Ottomans indicated the end of Titoist intercultural integration (or at least institutional multiculturalism). Milošević hit the nationalist key to justify Serbian rule in Kosovo, but he triggered off a nationalist wave in both Serbia and Croatia. The right wing in Croatia openly harassed people of Serbian origin in the republic of Croatia, and also campaigned against the 'left wing'. A new paramilitary republican police force in Croatia soon started to develop into an army parallel to the federal army, with weapons imported with the financial support of Croatian diaspora. In Serbia paramilitary militias were established, partly on the basis of Chetnik groups, partly by nationalist political leaders who recruited (often former) criminals in paramilitary gangs (Šešelj, Arkan). A circular mechanism of harassment, anxiety, preventive violence, and later ethnic cleansing started to work on local levels in the minority communities in Krajina and Slavonia, later in Bosnia-Hercegovina and Kosovo – but probably never really in the country as a whole (see e.g. Liversage, 1996; Vulliamy, 1994). People who had been friendly neighbours lived in fear of attack or even killed each other in the name of ethnicity and religion.

The political mechanism rests on the combination of strong identification (Croats seem today to be very Catholic, they go to church and confess) and the construction of complementary social prejudices about the other nations ('The Serbs are lazy warriors', 'The Croats are Ustašas', 'The Bosnians want to create an Islamic state'). These prejudices were justified by historical legacy: all the hatred was allegedly there from ancient times, and was never really reconciled. All the nationalist forces and mutual prejudices had been controlled by Tito and when he passed away they surfaced again. Suddenly everybody seemed to assume that the modernization of the country had taken place without really influencing fundamental identities and without any 'civilizing' effect.

This historical explanation seems to be a reduction, which is itself part of the construction of prejudices. On the one hand, it makes sense to describe the political process and warfare in terms of a regression to conflicts and identities from before World War II, and also to describe Titoism in terms of a temporary, idealized construction which was bound to fade one day. But it seems unlikely that the intermediate process which relativized the ethnic and religious differences did not leave any effects. Besides the identity construction emerging from a collective war heroism, Yugoslavia, unlike the east European communist countries, went through a social and cultural modernization process which was similar to the rest of (southern) Europe. In spite of the authoritarian political structures, there was a demand within the communist party which urged for democratization of the political system during the 70s and 80s, more or less in line with liberal critics of the regime outside the party. There was the attempt to design a new version of socialism with worker self-management and market economy, and experiments with direct democracy in public affairs ("samodoprinos"), hardly comparable to later experiments in Porto Alegre and elsewhere, but still important. Yet the nationalist forces prevailed. Later in the conflict, external European policy obviously accepted the nationalist agenda of division; Germany promised recognition of Croatian independence without minority guarantees, followed by the EU, and a coalition of the regime and more or less criminal interests took over and accelerated the process, and as the conflicts developed it was a self-fuelling mechanism (war psychology). In general the identity politics, defining identity by ethnic, religious and national adherence, legitimized violence and built up social prejudices in an environment which was by and large in a modernization process, but also in a very fragile social situation. The challenging question is how and why the mass mobilization of nationalism and identity policies in the first place became the dynamics of the process: What are the emotional sources of social prejudice and identity politics? Could it possibly have developed differently? Such questions are in the focus of interest of the psychosocietal approach.

A PSYCHODYNAMIC INTERPRETATION OF IDENTITY POLITICS

In the mutual escalation of the Yugoslavian conflict in the second half of the 1980s, nationalist discourses played an increasing role, especially in Croatia and Serbia. In Croatia, this had been a political factor in the post-war period. In the late 1960s and early 1970s, there was a strong call for independence in Croatia, which included left-wing criticism of the communist regime, democratic voices looking to the west and downright nationalist right-wing forces. Without neglecting this, it seems particularly interesting to investigate the Serbian identity dynamics in the 1980s. Volkan has contributed an incisive analysis of this (Volkan, 2001). In the following, I will discuss this analysis with the twofold interest of developing some aspects of it, and of elaborating on the relation between psychodynamic and societal/historical perspectives.

Volkan has analysed the development of the Yugoslavian conflict and particularly Serbian nationalism, within his framework of large group identity (Volkan, 2001). Large group identity is activated when the group as such or group members are exposed to a violation or a threat; this situation is likely to produce a collective defensive reaction similar to splitting, in the form of prejudiced imaginations about other large groups and a reinforced identification with one's own group. Volkan applies this analysis to Serbian references to the famous battle of Kosovo Polje on 28 June 1389. The real history was that Serbs (and several other people from Bosnia, Romania and Bulgaria) were heroically fighting the Ottomans, the Serbs were defeated, but they were able to delay the consecutive surrender of Serbian kingdoms to the Ottomans. This battle is a myth in Serbian history, and the date of the battle (28 June) has been the occasion of the staging of significant later events: a secret treaty in 1876 with the Austro-Hungarian Empire about fighting the Ottomans, and more spectacularly, the assassination of Prince Ferdinand in Sarajevo in 1914. Volkan argues that this myth in fact rearranges historical facts; the real battle and the heroic deeds which are celebrated were separated from the real surrender of Serbia under the Ottomans by some forty years. However, precisely the fact that they have been integrated into the construction of the myth colours our understanding of the social function of the myth: it epitomizes a Serbian self-understanding of being the real defenders of Christianity against Muslims and also the identity of being the heroic victims. Volkan names the story told in the myth a "chosen trauma" (Volkan, 2001). He argues that this trauma has been celebrated and told and trans-generationally reproduced over centuries, strengthening the large group identification of Serbs.

In the recent conflict it was deliberately used in the nurturing of Serbian nationalism. The central example is Milošević's speech on the 600-year anniversary of the nominated date of this battle, 28.06.1989. At this time the dissolution of Yugoslavia was lurking, and the federal leadership had already, contrary to the constitution, included Vojvodina and Kosovo in the federal state of Serbia. In Kosovo the conflict was between the majority of ethnic Albanians and a Serbian minority, and Milosevic's message was clear: he pronounced Kosovo the heartland of Serbia with reference to the battle 600 years ago, and he spoke (for the first time I think) of using armed force to maintain the unity of Yugoslavia. This speech was highly relevant to the development of the conflict. In Croatia and Slovenia, it was perceived as a direct claim for the leadership in the name of Serbian nationalism rather than the communist party, the partisan movement, etc., as institutionalized in the federal state, and it pushed the desire for independence/separation forwards in a spiral: Milošević arguing in nationalist terms also justified Croatian nationalism.

The nationalist agenda was not entirely new, and there could of course be rational arguments and partial interests which questioned the sustainability of the federal republic. Yugoslavia was in deep economic crisis, the legitimacy of the communist party was declining, and the unity of the federal state had been questioned from several sides. But the decisive dynamics that aroused the defensive strength of the "large group identity" was, according to Volkan's analysis, the systematic communication of a connection between Muslim Bosnians and Turks/Muslims which recalled the historical colonization of the Slavic peoples by the Ottoman Empire. This narrative was being spread in many forms, feeding anxiety and aggression, suggesting but not stating explicitly (and thus open to debate) that a new contemporary conflict was approaching. In Volkan's analysis, the main way of appealing to Serbian large group identity was the reference to the historical war against the Ottomans and the battle of Kosovo Polje. The propaganda followed the scheme of Roland Barthes' theory of mythology on a semantic level (Barthes, 1957), in this case obviously activating unconscious identifications and projections.

Volkan places a strong emphasis on Milošević's adoption of the Serbian national trauma. He refers to a psychological shift in Milošević's appearance at a particular party conference in Kosovo in 1987, where the conflict between the Albanian majority and the Serbian minority had come to a head, describing his reaction as a kind of revelation: "Milosevic apparently came out of this experience a transformed person, clad in the '*armor'* of Serbian nationalism" (Volkan, 2009). Suddenly overnight Milošević identified with the Serbian "chosen trauma" and drew the consequences in the form of a nationalist policy. This can be seen in line with Volkan's more general analysis of the dialectic between the identification of members with the large group and the constraints it places on the leadership. Volkan has a long record of assisting in difficult arbitrations in fixed conflicts around the world, and he sees how the psychological carriage castle lays constraints on leaders who are forced to or are seeking to reach a liveable handling of hostile relations between two different large groups (Volkan, 2009). One might say that he implicitly applies a perspective of political leadership that may seek to mobilize the large group identity as a political tool, but may also come under pressure from it in the "diplomatic conflict resolution". In the Serbian case, he sees Milošević as the leader igniting the identification.

As a consequence, Volkan assigns great importance to the individual psychodynamic process of Milošević. This analysis seems paradoxically confined to the individual psychological level. The analysis of Milošević's individual psyche on the background of being a child of a dysfunctional family may well be correct, but it seems reasonable to interpret Milošević also as a bearer of a societal dynamics in the situation. He is a very skilled politician who, when (perhaps suddenly) in a quite dire situation, senses the power of the myth, and thereby the chance to shift his political base into Serbian nationalism. By activating the myth of the trauma from 1389 he ignites a fire, but the fuel for this fire is contemporary and societal.

If we see the trauma not as *caused by* the historical events and simply historically *remembered*, but as a reproduction of meaning in identity processes over centuries, we must seek to understand not only the psychodynamic mechanism of defensive identification which explains its effectiveness, but also the "needs" of "ordinary people" that were fulfilled by adopting it. We must analyse the shifting circumstances that have been subjectively mediated in it at any time in this transmission, including the contemporary context. There is no doubt that Serbian nationalism also existed as an undercurrent in Serbian society in the days of Titoism, and this could be understood as an identification of limited groups in Serbia. Milošević gave it a new political range, and so far his individual conviction is important. But from a psychosocietal approach, the most interesting aspect of Milošević's individual conscious and unconscious motives is his role as the "medium" of a societal damburst, where national and religious identification could become all-pervasive. What were the societal circumstances that enabled the shift? And especially: What were the subjective experiences of these societal factors in the broad masses of the people to which he gave a political direction? And of course at the end of the day: Could they have been interpreted differently, leading to more a peaceful handling of the societal difficulties and the divisions in the population?

Why is the understanding of the subjective dynamics of ordinary people important? Because, on the one hand, it provides an understanding of the conditions for the social prejudices that the manipulative leader can work with. But also because the potential for alternatives to the development of social prejudices must reside in the same subjective experience.

MODERNIZATION, MASCULINITY AND DEFENSIVE IDENTITY BUILDING

I shall attempt a modest approach to some of the historical circumstances that may have been involved in some of the most emotional and extreme aspects of the identity politics, related with gender and sexuality.

The history of the western Balkans in the 19th and 20th centuries is, like that of many other European regions, a history of people tossed around by empires and attempts to construct or reconstruct states on the battlefield. The conglomerate state of the southern Slavs was born to accommodate many historical identities and it may seem plausible that the history of Yugoslavia is about the success and failure of this construction. The dissolution of Yugoslavia was implemented as a (re)construction of national and religious identities that allegedly had a background in history. Similarly to the Serbian identification with the chosen trauma, Croatian national history is claimed with reference to a short period of the Middle Ages when the area was an autonomous state or principality under Josip Jelaćić, after whom the central square in Zagreb and many streets across the country have been renamed, and whose coat of arms is now part of the national flag. And this identification does not even have the same continuity as the Serbian one.

But the history of Yugoslavia is also a history of uneven European modernization. In spite of being a divided periphery and tossed around by the empires which contributed large numbers of poverty migrants worldwide, these countries also fostered early scientific contributions: Rudjer Bosković, now a Croatian national icon, was a precursor in atomic theory at a time when Croatia did not exist as a nation state, and Nicola Tesla, who competed with Edison concerning the electricity system in the USA (and won: AC became the dominant form of power network), was born in the Serbian community under Austrian rule in the region that became later a controversial Serbian minority in Croatia. It seems that the Slavic part of the Austro-Hungarian Empire has to some extent been the experimental scene for early industrialization, whereas those regions that were under Ottoman rule until the Balkan wars in the early 20th century were left in peace as long as they paid tribute to the Sultan, and hence remained less affected by modernization.

The socialist republic established after World War II was part of the Eastern bloc in the first phase, but broke the bonds with Stalin even before the cold war divisions became all-pervasive. It was created on the basis of the communist partisan movement across all the divisions of ethnicity and religion, and the multicultural heterogeneity was carefully balanced in the institutional structure, respecting most ethnicities, religions, nationalities and languages. The historical remnants of the different past within the two empires left a certain difference between the northern and southern parts of the country, but the federal republic secured financing from the more wealthy parts of the country in the form of investments in the southern regions. Especially after the break with the Soviet Union, the new Yugoslavia underwent a modernization process, based on industrialization, a liberal market economy and western cultural influence. The ethnic and religious differences seemed to fade and were overshadowed by differences between industrialized urban and rural agricultural communities. This rapid modernization was similar to elsewhere in Europe and the communist power monopoly was hardly more totalitarian than the regimes in several southern European countries. Nevertheless, when confidence in a progressive unified Yugoslav state crumbled, it elicited national (and religious) identifications. We have seen similar situations where identifications with more or less real historical past events have become drivers of political processes, and this fits well with the theory of large group identity presented by V. Volkan: in crises, belonging to a large group produces stronger identification and reinforced delimitation and hostility with regard to others. The obvious political translation of this collective defence mechanism is the idea of ethnic cleansing and separation of people based on which large group they belong to. This mechanism remains active even at a relatively low level of conflict; recently attempts to finally settle the separation of Kosovo from Serbia are taking place as a negotiation about exchanging two regions so that each nation can get its nationals inside its own state, i.e. negotiated ethnic cleansing. There is probably an automatic vicious circle in a conflict: much of the mutual and accelerating ethnic violence can be seen as reactions to actual experiences of violence once the theme has been played out, or based in more or less rational anxieties which require self-defence. But it seems that the Yugoslav civil war was driven by a particular aggression, especially in Bosnia, an aspect of specific cruelty which pursued the annihilation of the other population, cf. the massacre in Srebrenica. Obviously it was rooted in very fundamental feelings, such as anxiety and a feeling of potential annihilation if action is not taken.

But which contemporary experiences make these events comprehensible? It seems that a focus on gender can be a key to understanding some of the emotional dimensions of the forms of conflict. Especially in Bosnia, but also in the rest of the conflict, there were many sexual violations, including sexual humiliation of both women and men of the other side, systematic rape, and a deliberate aim at 'ethnic warfare' by making women pregnant. These phenomena go far beyond the level of all 'ordinary' war psychology phenomena of drunken and undisciplined soldiers in a civil, undeclared and lawless war, which is of course the general context. According to Volkan's analysis of the use of the "chosen trauma" for nurturing the ethnical conflict, there was a direct reference in Serbian propaganda to the reproductive capacity of the Bosnian Muslims – a rhetoric known from campaigns preceding genocide elsewhere but also from the general demonization of immigrant groups today.

To understand these phenomena it is especially interesting to bring in a historical context of masculine identity. On the one hand, some of the ideas of national and ethnic identity are closely related with masculine forms of identity building even in times of peace, most obviously in the Serbian nationalism of Chetniks, who identified themselves as soldiers or fighters. These groups formed and probably dominated the Serbian militias. But one might also see a masculinity identity of an agrarian society in the territorial forms of domination inherited in ethnic cleansing.

On the other hand, some of the forms of conflict have very clear sexual aspects of domination (in extreme cases, in systematic rapes and ideas about bio-warfare). It seems obvious to see these phenomena as indicators of a threatened masculinity which was not only reserved for subcultural social outcasts, and not only a particularly backward and under-civilized people. Rather it could be interpreted as a more durable and still maintained feeling as a consequence of the modernization process which undermines such traditional male roles.

With modernization, masculine identities go through a fundamental change. The detachment from means of production and the location (the land), internalization of the abstraction of time and instrumental action, wage labour as the form of social reproduction, etc. have to be learned, and have been learned with capitalist modernization (Vester, 1974; Willis, 1977). This process also took place in Yugoslavia, in a rapid development, but in different contexts – in some regions, especially in the south, the development was extremely uneven between industrial plants and cities, and backward agriculture. New gender relations also evolved, such as women entering the labour market, and the cultural gender relations rapidly modernizing, which was extremely different from e.g. Russia. In general, male identity is healed by adopting the role as breadwinner and wage labour – but when economic decline more broadly deprives people of this vision of a future, then it hits back. In this sense the modernization process may have paved the way for the regressive reaction to the economic and social decline. National identification and the accompanying social prejudices render legitimacy to a regressive masculinity, and maybe to a restauration of masculine identity as a 'solution' to many other identity problems, which had not been well accommodated in the previous years.

Many young men migrated to Germany, Scandinavia and elsewhere, and those who stayed were vulnerable. It seems as if the social base for Serbian militant nationalism is an extremely regressive masculine culture, which found pride in the old Chetnik warrior traditions. This type of potentially violent masculinity was activated and legitimized, first in supporting their fellow Serbs in Krajina, then intervening in/creating a civil war in Slavonia and finally in escalating the violence in Bosnia (and later also in Kosovo). In a division of labour which the Federal Army – also dominated by Serbian officers, but for some time defending the federal state and maybe also faithful to the Titoist constitution – the militias performed the illegal and aggressive work that the army would not (openly) take. The militias, which were nothing but criminal gangs and frustrated but armed young men, played a significant role in creating anxiety and defining conflicts as nationalist conflicts.

Serbian nationalism has a certain mix of this archaic warrior culture and a peasant culture, which had a strong tradition of self-defence in relation to the Ottoman Empire, fostering a warrior ideology, which in its core is a territorial defensive ideology. But in this situation it became the spark that ignited the flames. I believe that the ethnic Serbs in Krajina were from the beginning just anxious about their situation in a possibly independent Croatia, because they already saw the nationalist nature of this new state. At the time of detaching Krajina within Croatia, all within the Federal Republic of Yugoslavia, harassment and repression by nationalists in Croatia was strong and visible. In this situation the Serbs regressed into territorial self-defence, easily recognized as peasants defending their land. But they then received more aggressive support from Serbian militia groups. The mechanism of large group identification explains how self-defence is converted into more active and aggressive agency by people who had previously been peaceful citizens.

I consider that the right wing in Croatia could, though a little more subtly, also be seen as a specific regression in gender relations: the restauration of authoritarianism went hand in hand with the strong confessional turn to Catholicism and the diaspora building national armed forces. I think the fuel of these cultural shifts could also be understood in the context of a blocked development of the wage labour masculinity; an economic crisis and unemployment found a satisfactory explanation in the idea that the (lazy and backward) southerners were receiving all the money with the help of a rotten regime in Belgrade, which had already even declared the Serbs to be the leading force of the country. Croatian mainstream nationalism contains a superior self-understanding in relation to Serbs and other Balkan peoples.

Troubled masculinity is not the only societal potential for the strong development of a large group identity in Volkan's sense, but it is clearly one of those vulnerabilities that can be reinterpreted by splitting and social prejudice, and it became also an automotive dynamics in accelerating the cruelty of the warfare.

CONCLUSION

My intention is not to 'explain' the dynamics of a cultural conflict through the masculinity issue. But it provides an interesting 'window' into the link between psychodynamic processes and societal circumstances. Masculinity seems to illustrate the crossroads of a historical learning process and those temporary subjective processes of dealing with one's own life that form the ground for politicization of subjectivity. The actual history was the activation of a particular psychodynamics in a specific historical situation. But had there not been a heritage of obsolete masculinity – out of phase with a modern, intercultural reality – that could be ignited as a power strategy, the crisis in Yugoslav society might have taken another turn. We can compare with e.g. Portugal, where the army with a hope for a democratic future overturned the dictatorship in 1974.

In the wider context of how to understand identity politics, it seems that Volkan's theory of collective defence mechanisms and the dynamics of large group identification in combination with an analysis of contemporary societal conditions and people's subjective handling of critical conditions may enable deeper understanding of a phenomenon which seems hardly understandable. The analysis that horrible identity politics have their background in changing gender relations and threatened masculinity as a consequence of modernization does not justify these politics. But it gives us an insight into the psychosocietal processes whereby ideas and practices that used to be limited to very marginal groups under certain circumstances can become mainstream identifications. It is also related to much less spectacular forms of defence: families are divided, and public rhetoric and consciousness become explicitly revanchist. The politicization of subjectivity is in no way bound to be such a murderous regression; understanding its dynamic genesis is however the first condition for reflecting on and integrating feelings that might otherwise become destructive.

REFERENCES:

Barthes, R. (1957). *Mythologies. Books abroad.* https://doi.org/10.2307/40099594

Fukuyama, F. (2018). *Identity—The demand for dignity and the politics of resentment.* New York, NY: Farrar, Straus and Giroux.

Leithäuser, T. (1976). *Formen des Alltagsbewusstseins.* Frankfurt/Main & New York, NY: Campus-Verlag.

Liversage, T. (1996). *Den jugoslaviske tragedie: om krig, nationalisme og fred?* Copenhagen: Lindhardt & Ringhof.

Potts, G. (1996). *The development of the system of representation in Yugoslavia with special reference to the period since 1974.* Lanham &, New York, NY & London: University Press of America.

Salling Olesen, H. (1989). *Adult education and everyday life.* Roskilde: Adult Education Research Group, Roskilde University.

Salling Olesen, H. (1996). Experience, life history and biography. In H. Salling Olesen & P. Rasmussen (Eds.), *Theoretical issues in adult education: Danish research and experiences.* Frederiksberg: Roskilde University Press.

Salling Olesen, H. (2001). Professional identity as learning processes in life histories. *Journal of Workplace Learning, 13*(7–8), 290–298.

Salling Olesen, H. (2007). Experience and learning – A psycho-societal approach. *Studies in the Education of Adults, 1.*

Salling Olesen, H., & Weber, K. (2001). *Space for experience and learning. Theorizing the subjective side of work.* Frederiksberg: Roskilde University Press.

Vester, M. (1974). *Die Entstehung der Arbeiterklasse als Lernprozess.* Frankfurt: EVA.

Volkan, V. D. (2001). Transgenerational transmissions and chosen traumas: An aspect of large-group identity. *Group Analysis, 34*, 79–97. https://doi.org/10.1177/05333160122077730
Volkan, V. D. (2009). Large-group identity, international relations and psychoanalysis. *International Forum of Psychoanalysis, 18*, 206–213. https://doi.org/10.1080/08037060902727795
Vulliamy, E. (1994). *Seasons in hell. Understanding Bosnia's War*. London: Simon & Schuster.
Willis, P. (1977). *Learning to labour*. Stanley Aronowitz Books.

PART 5

A PSYCHOSOCIAL MATERIALISM

HENNING SALLING OLESEN AND KIRSTEN WEBER

12. SOCIALIZATION, LANGUAGE, AND SCENIC UNDERSTANDING

Alfred Lorenzer's Contribution to a Psychosocietal Methodology

INTRODUCTION

The chapter is a guided tour to Alfred Lorenzer's proposal for an 'in-depth hermeneutic' cultural analysis methodology which was launched in an environment with an almost complete split between social sciences and psychology/psychoanalysis. It presents the background in his materialist socialization theory, which combines a social reinterpretation of the core insights in classical psychoanalysis – the unconscious, the drives – with a theory of language acquisition. His methodology is based on a transformation of the 'scenic understanding' from a clinical to a text interpretation, which seeks to understand collective unconscious meaning in text, and is presented with an illustration of the interpretation procedure from social research. Then follows a brief systematic account of key concepts and ideas – interaction forms, engrams, experience, symbolization, language game, utopian imagination – with an outlook to the social theory connections to the Frankfurt School. The practical interpretation procedure in a Lorenzer-based psychosocietal research is briefly summarized, emphasizing the role of the researcher subjects in discovering socially unconscious meaning in social interaction. Finally an outlook to contemporary epistemological issues. Lorenzer's approach to theorize and research the subject as a socially produced entity appears as a psychosocietal alternative to mainstream social constructivism.

THE LANDSCAPE BEFORE AND AROUND LORENZER

In their important and influential book *The Social Construction of Reality*, Berger and Luckmann (1966) seek to create a holistic social theory, which recognizes the social significance of human agency and consciousness by synthesizing the macro-societal perspective of knowledge sociology with G. H. Mead's micro-perspective of meaningful agency and social psychology. In an interesting note they quite strongly ban recent attempts to synthesize Marxism and psychoanalysis:

> There is a considerable irony in the fact that, of late, neo-Marxist theoreticians have been seeking a liaison with Freudian psychology (which is fundamentally

> incompatible with the anthropological presuppositions of Marxism), completely oblivious of the existence of a Meadian theory of the dialectic between society and the individual that would be immeasurably more congenial to their own approach. For a recent example of this ironic phenomenon, cf. Georges Lapassade, L'entrée dans la Vie (Paris, Eds. de Minuit, 1963). (Berger & Luckmann, 1966, p. 218, note 25)

Symbolic interactionism, inspired from phenomenology, and action sociology primarily sees society as conscious and meaningful agency in the life world and Berger and Luckmann (1966) argue that knowledge sociology provides the understanding of how agency makes up the foundation for societal structure through a process of sedimentation and/or reification. Obviously they see Mead's social psychology as the concept best theorizing the subjectivity of agency. Their account of socialization is almost exclusively about the societal imprint on the individual agent – cf. the reference to Mead. The role of subjectivity in history (and B&L's theory is actually also a *historical* account of the emergence of society) remains largely un-theorized in its own right, and they explicitly and very quickly abstain from elaborating "a genuinely dialectic social psychology" which they admit would be the proper alternative to the alliance they despise (p. 230, note7).

They continue, in another note:

> There is a fundamental dichotomy between the conception of man as a self-producing being and conception of 'human nature'. This constitutes a decisive anthropological difference between Marx and any properly sociological perspective on the one hand (especially one that is grounded in Meadian social psychology) and Freud and most non-Freudian psychological perspectives on the other. (p. 220, note 7)

It is a bit strange, in view of Berger and Luckmann's ambitious project, to launch such theoretical demarcations in a note. I tend to see these comments as symptoms of a latent awareness of a problem – a stone in the shoe – a problem that has not been thematized before but presses itself into the horizon of Berger and Luckmann's otherwise extremely embracing and integrative work.

The point about Freud is beyond dispute, but also obsolete. Apart from the one work mentioned we may after all assume that most of the psychoanalysts that European Marxists approached in the 1960's already theorized psychodynamics socially, and were politically and theoretically committed to an emancipatory thinking in which human agency and consciousness was essential (e.g. Mitscherlich, 1963). Berger and Luckmann might also have noticed, at the opposite side of the gorge, Erikson's (1950) development of a cultural psychology as an attempt to understand the dialectic between the individual and society on a psychoanalytic ground – although in the first place limited to child socialization and kept within a developmental psychology framework. In Europe the ethno-psychoanalysts simultaneously analysed the dialectic between individual and society in the remote Dogon-culture

(Parin, Morgenthaler, & Matthéy, 1963), de facto defining personality structures as a result of cultural environment – later generalized into a revised psychodynamic theory (Parin, 1983).

These comments from 1966 remind about the fundamental challenge connected with the conception of subjectivity and the relation between individual and society in a social science landscape where the disciplinary domains separated knowledge of the individual from knowledge about society. It may also reflect an enduring prejudiced tendency to see psychoanalysis as a closed community, not recognizing the very fundamental ongoing discussions between Freudian psychoanalysts and several re-interpretations of the origins of the inner psychic structures. In this landscape it appears even more remarkable, that Alfred Lorenzer developed a theory which took the challenge to develop a social reinterpretation of Freud's basic ideas on a materialistic ground which might easily be mistaken for a biological and deterministic in the way Berger and Luckmann (1966) obviously see the psychoanalysis.

When we have focused on Lorenzer within a broad and multiple tradition of combining a Marxian analysis of society (Frankfurt School critical theory) and psychodynamic theorizing of the subject it has two interrelated reasons. One is that he has been particularly productive for the development of a methodology of empirical qualitative research. The other one is that his socialization theory by focusing on language at the same time as maintaining a clearly materialistic view on the body as well as on the socio-material structure of society has provided a key contribution to theoretical and epistemological issues of social science, that have become articulated much later. We shall come back to this at the end of this chapter.

ALFRED LORENZER'S INTELLECTUAL JOURNEY

Alfred Lorenzer (1922–2002) came from the background of being a medical psychiatrist, trained in psychoanalysis on a Freudian background. As a doctor and psychoanalyst, he took an early interest in societal critique and cultural theory, taking to task the Frankfurt School of thought and its critical theory. Understanding subjective structure as influenced by societal conditions increasingly came to dominate his theoretical thoughts. As early as 1970, he criticized the psychoanalytical concept of 'symbol' (1970a), placed it in a linguistic science context (1970b) and subsequently expanded the application of it into socialization theory (1972), epistemology (1974) and cultural analysis (1986). The red thread of his contribution is to provide a ground for a social interpretation of the basic psychodynamic forces without giving up the radical insights in Freud's theory. The first step in this chain from psychoanalysis to societal theory was an interactionist theory of socialization (1972) in which he reconceptualized these psychodynamic forces which in classical psychoanalysis since Freud were seen as biological, result of natural drives. Lorenzer established a dialectical theory according to which they were results of the social interaction, in the first place between infant and mother (caring person), and thereby also enabled an understanding of the unconscious – the most radical element in psychoanalysis – as a result of the symbolic interaction. The following works developed methodological ideas for an endogenous understanding of the subjective dimensions of social interaction and language – quite opposite to the direction Freud took in meta-psychological and cultural theory.

The point of departure in Lorenzer's relevance to current theoretical, social and political issues is the Copernican turn of the Freudian theory which had been initiated by a number of psychoanalysts: In continuation of Freud he analyses the development of the structure of personality as 'representing experiences of bodily interactions' (1972, p. 17). But whereas Freud saw their impact in the psyche, as predominantly distortion, disturbance and blocking of (biological) drives in the subject Lorenzer sees these social interactions and the bodily experiences of them as a dialectical *shaping* of the drives *into a subject*, and the resulting psychic dynamics as highly social phenomena. The individual sensual experiences of social relations and meanings in immediate interaction are connected with the wider social world in the form of symbols. The issues of psychotherapy, disturbances of the psychic development, were reinterpreted as disturbances of the possibility to symbolize individual sensual experiences in socially recognized language. Lorenzer's critical reinterpretation of the psychic disturbances are expressed in the early book titles 'Kritik des psychoanalytischen Symbolbegriffs' (Critique of the Psychoanalytic Concept of Symbol) and 'Sprachzerstörung und Rekonstruktion' (Language Destruction and Reconstruction) – both from 1970. On the one hand enabling a reinterpretation of the psychotherapeutic task, this critique on the other hand opens a new way of theorizing the psychodynamic aspects of societal relations. Symbolic/cultural meaning (for the individual) is seen as a complex mediation of social interaction and sensual experience, and has conscious as well as unconscious aspects. Later Lorenzer developed further his key concept of 'interaction forms' to understand the inner, pre-linguistic experiences of practices and relations. These interaction forms are connected with the socially recognized language to form symbolic interaction forms, and the developing of capacity for symbolic production can be seen as an integrated aspect of socialization. This understanding of the early socialization process enables Lorenzer to see language, interaction and bodily (drive) processes in their wider societal context – and we can add an epistemological perspective: In the context of a constructivist social science it enables us to see how ideas about societal relations are embodied in the individual socialization. Lorenzer's thoughts on the role of language in subject constitution build on the theorem of language games, which he took up from the works of Ludwig Wittgenstein and developed further. Language is anchored in concrete social practice in a dialectic unit of language use, everyday life practice and view of the world (Weber, 2010). Language games are thus defined as the interface at which subjective and objective structures interact. The question of the constitution of language games is, therefore, also one which addresses the constitution of the relationship between individual and society. Looked at in this way, language and awareness are inseparably linked with social practice. If the constitution of language games is seen as integral to the development of subjective structures under objective conditions, then the individual subject can be understood and deciphered using its ex ante social reference.

Lorenzer's contribution to the methodology gains a wider perspective by theorizing the genesis of the correspondence between unconscious dynamics in the subject and unconscious or unintended dimensions of societal and cultural processes. What is in the first place mainly a material theory of socialization – which unlike many other theories does not see the social shaping of the individual as assimilation to social structure – is in the second place a radical epistemology of societal dynamics. Lorenzer's theory of language games and his meta-psychological and methodological notions are closely linked with the search for opportunities for epistemic reconstruction of suppressed social relationships, which are (societally) imprinted in the (many individual) psyches and in their interaction. Lorenzer in brief draws the attention to the hermeneutic methodology of psychoanalytic understanding. The immediate inspiration is offered by an interpretation of interaction and cultural meaning in a way inspired by psychoanalytic interpretation, namely 'scenic understanding' whose further methodological foundations and methodical implementation will be taken up further in this chapter. Lorenzer separates the methodological principles of psychoanalysis – simultaneous attention, free association and the concepts of transfer and counter-transfer – from the clinical context of doctor-patient relationships, and transfers them to social and cultural scientific practice. He thus emphasizes the methodological experience as opposed to direct transfers of theoretical models since, in his view, these cannot be transferred from one field to another.

The socialization theory was Lorenzer's first distinguishing contribution. It builds the theoretical foundation for the development of a psychosocietal interpretation method with inspiration from the psychoanalytical interpretation of individuals. During the 1970's his work was widely cited and read both in Germany and abroad (notably the Scandinavian Countries) and today, his ideas continue to inform a vigorous tradition of cultural analysis and social research (Leithäuser & Volmerg, 1988; Leithäuser, 1977; Morgenroth, 1990, 2010; Bereswill 2008; Lorenzer, 1970, 1971, 1972, 1974, 1977, 1986, 2006; Prokop et al., 2009). A number of Scandinavian, especially Danish, researchers have published work directly referring to this tradition, or using the methods more or less in accord less in accordance with it, most of it published in Danish. For an overview see Weber (1996, 2007, 2009, 2010); Salling Olesen (2004, 2007a, 2007b, 2011) and Weber and Salling Olesen (2001, 2002). However, Lorenzer is little known outside German speaking communities. To the best of my knowledge, only one small example of his work has been published in English translation (Lorenzer & Orban, 1978). Recently another text has been introduced, translated and posted in the internet (Lorenzer, 1981; Schaffrik, 2002). But 'in-depth Hermeneutic analysis' remains largely unfamiliar to English-speaking audiences. When we in a joint research network explored the parallels between this tradition and pioneering work in the Anglophone psychosocial research (e.g. Hollway & Jefferson, 2000), the language based a-symmetry was obvious and it seemed imperative to provide access to some of the non-Anglophone research tradition to a wider audience.

In the following we will concentrate on the methodological impulse from cultural analysis in social research. In a late stage of his work, in the key text in 'Kulturanalysen' (1986), he coins the notion of 'Tiefenhermeneutische Kulturanalyse', which focusses on the systematic reconstruction of unconscious meaning dimensions in analysis of literary texts. This text played a significant role in the intensive multilingual discourse in our research network between Danish, German and British researchers, of which half were nonGerman-speaking, facilitated by a translation (by Mechthild Bereswill and Christine Morgenroth, unpublished). The book as a whole is a collective work with a number of case studies, mainly on literary texts, but also one (by Søren Nagbøl) extending the horizon to architecture. 'Kulturanalysen' (Cultural Analyses) summarizes the contribution of his interaction theory extensions of psychoanalysis from the 1960s and 1970s and may be read as the key text to the complex meta-theoretical ideas that have proven useful in empirical studies in many areas of social life under the general heading of 'Tiefenhermeneutik' (in-depth hermeneutic).

Lorenzer believes this is where what he calls the 'hard and provocative work' (1986, p. 16f.) in the psychoanalytical critique of society and culture enters. He sees the position of psychoanalysis between differing disciplines against whose borders it grates. The 'conflict potential' of a psychoanalytic approach traditionally arises from revealing the social constraints a subject faces, but, more importantly, how desires and past experiences may influence e.g. cultural productions like literature. Lorenzer here emphasizes the difference between a therapeutic and a social or literary discovery process: 'Where therapy is concerned, the origin [of the subject] is investigated by asking: how did the conflict arise in the case of this individual? In cultural analysis, however, the question is: what kind of conflict are we dealing with? The focus is on the conflict between unconscious desires and conscious values' (ibid., p. 67).

In fact the notion of conflict in the last sentence might be a bit misleading in translation – in Lorenzer's German text it reads 'Auseinandersetzung zwischen', which implies 'intensive interrelation' or 'interaction between' in the sense of connecting rather than a conflict between two independent opposing parties, or in philosophical terms: It is an intrinsic rather than an extrinsic relation. In Lorenzer's thinking the relation between the conscious and the unconscious levels of the subject is more complex than just being a conflict. They are both influenced by experiences in the past, and conscious and unconscious dynamics interrelate in the ongoing processing of cognitive and emotional aspects of experiences. Unconscious dynamics which refer to contradictions experienced in the past (and hence of cultural and societal nature), which may have become unconscious, while their conflictual meaning may have been transferred to another content are particularly important in the original therapeutic context. But the very existence of unconscious dynamics which are of cultural and societal nature, and that they remain in interaction with meaning making and conscious engagements in the present is the important insight for interpretation of social interaction and cultural meanings. Lorenzer and his colleagues eventually demonstrates this potential in interpretation of arts products, but the insights in societal nature of the subjective processes opens a door to interpret not only cultural products, but to interpret interviews and other qualitative material from empirical research of a wide range of more profane social practices and spheres.

IN-DEPTH HERMENEUTIC CULTURAL ANALYSIS

Alfred Lorenzer's introduction article 'Tiefenhermeneutische Kulturanalysen' in the book *Kulturanalysen* (1986) is as close as he comes to spell out a methodology. Basically he points to the hermeneutic (interpretational) nature of the form of understanding which is used in psychoanalytical therapeutic practice, generalizes it in what he calls the 'Scenic Understanding', and comments the nature of this transformation. The particular value of these thoughts mainly become evident in reflecting a research practice by means of researchers subjectively engaging in the interpretation, tracing aspects of social relations which are not immediately visible and may be not even conscious for social actors. For this reason we developed an interpretation process example of a text which had been presented in the research group. In the following this sample scene and our interpretation of it will be used for illustration linking our interpretation steps along this short sequence with central passages of Lorenzer's text. As it usually is the case the interpretation process became an illustration in itself – interpretation requires the engagement of the interpreters in an interaction with the text which transcends the obvious meaning of the text, and hence becomes part of the interpretation in itself. We took up a brief scene presented in the Dubrovnik workshops by our British colleague Joanne Whitehouse, who used qualitative methods to study a popular yet highly contested form of media product – the reality TV program Big Brother, which has sparked heated debate not just in Great Britain (Redmann & Whitehouse, 2008). We wanted to illustrate Lorenzer's methodological and meta-theoretical reflections using an empirical example from the discipline of cultural studies to show what scenic understanding might mean for empirical analysis.

We analyzed the reaction of a female viewer as portrayed in the following scene. We interpreted the scene as a representation, not as a factual account that can be read at face value, and not as a transparent subjective expression. We assumed that such representations are based on shared cultural experience and provide us with access to subjective and social dynamics, which we attempt to reveal with the aid of Lorenzer's thinking.

The structure of this type of program is a closed group who is monitored in their interaction, and the viewers are invited to vote about who should be sent home at each stage of the show, An interviewee, Lou, reported (to Joanne) that she had been watching an episode of Big Brother. One of the housemates, Jonny, offered a second housemate, Adele, a cup of coffee. Adele refused in a friendly fashion but as Jonny walked away she mouthed the words "Fuck off" to his retreating back. The interviewee, Lou, was so outraged by what she took to be Adele's two-faced behavior that she decided she would vote to have Adele evicted from the show and, moreover, that she had to do this straight away. Because her own phone was out of order she rushed from the house to use a public phone box on the corner of her street. Unfortunately, the phone box was occupied and, feeling increasingly frustrated, the interviewee started banging on the phone box door telling the person using it to hurry up. "I just wanted her (i.e. Adele) out", she explained in the interview.

At first glance the text we looked at irritates and confuses, displays a remarkable amount of emotion and contains a variety of action and interaction levels which all run together. It may also provoke normative reactions in the interpreter, not least as regards the contested TV format that attracts large numbers of viewers. The scientific and popular controversies concerning a program like Big Brother thus point to underlying issues of subject and society in the context of social change: on the one hand the age-old discussion about how much influence mass media has in guiding people's actions, on the other hand the much more interesting question about how the contents of the media engage with the subjective issues of the audiences.

The manifest meaning of the sequence is readily visible: we are witness to an emotionally loaded reaction in the context of a medially presented group player game. The structure of the constitutes a dual scene: contestants in the containers and contestants in front on the TV enter into a relationship with one another whereby the quality of their relationships is the key to further exclusion or inclusion of individual players. In other words, the publicly celebrated relationships between the inhabitants of the container give the viewers a chance to enter into a relationship which forms the basis for their decision on whether or not to vote for or against a particular contestant.

There are several simplistic interpretations of the scene which are near at hand (and the interpreting group did not evade the temptation in the first place): we could interpret it as a confirmation of a culturally pessimistic standpoint concerning the increasing degeneration of the mass media, or in a more or less psychological sense as an expression of a threatened if not damaged subjectivity which comes to light with the loss of key self-determination skills. Although different in focus they don't leave much space for understanding subjective agency. In a way they treat the social agent as a patient and diagnose his/her vulnerability for social conditions. Alfred Lorenzer provides the theoretical arguments for avoiding such premature classifications. In Lorenzer's work, we read that apart from the manifest and latent meaning levels 'texts' house an unconscious meaning dimension which we can enter as readers, as observers or as researchers.

> The impulse in psychoanalytical therapy is to change the patient who is being analysed. In the reader-text relationship the opposite is the case. Here it is the reader/analyst who is subject to change. If the reader as an interpreter acknowledges the emotional power of the text and does not stand in awe of it,

> his consciousness will be changed – at least, this is the case if he does not abuse the text-reader relationship by simply reading into the text a pre existing and well known version of psychoanalysis. (Lorenzer, 1986, p. 28)

This distinction takes our attention in another direction. We concern ourselves with the emotional power of the text and thus with the relationships it offers to the readers. How do we as *interpreters* take up this offer? How do we react to Lou's description – normatively, amused or intrigued? This line of thinking may be easily accepted when dealing with 'fine arts' – it resonances discussions about the criteria of quality in poetry, e.g. – but here we deal with a profane narrative about profane television watching. Posing these questions to the interpreters of the short research scene led us away from commenting and classifying the actions in the actual text per se, and towards its emotional qualities and evocative power in relation to the reader. And further the question of the 'relationship between text and reader' applies to the relation between the Big Brother-show and its viewers, in this case to Lou. What is it that makes her act so impulsively? If we go by what she says, then contestant Adele's two-faced attitude is what made Lou want to vote Adele immediately off the show and head out to find a telephone. According to Lou, Adele's behavior, which she describes as two-faced and underhandedly aggressive, sparked her unbridled anger; she is openly aggressive and attacks another person within her action radius.

The theoretical distinction of Psychoanalysis is the theory of the unconscious (Freud, 1915). It is actually a more complicated theory about levels of (un) consciousness with grey zones and displacements, which in Freud's version is a precondition for the therapeutic process as well as for the interpretation of dreams. The first methodical issue is to gain access to this level, not with an individual therapeutic aim, but in order to understand its social meaning. The interpretation of texts, be they literary works, field notes or excerpts from interviews, also constitutes a multilayered scene. In the case in question, we reconstruct a dual scene in which various interaction dynamics overlay one another and create a new scene in which we as interpreters become involved relative to those dynamics. We find Lou's extreme over-reaction difficult to understand and tend to distance ourselves from it.

Lorenzer goes on to say that literary texts contain a provocation which goes beyond individual and biographically specific reception patterns and points to societal, collective motives and meaning substance:

> The provocation lies in content in the text itself. As such, its impact goes beyond the individual, it is perhaps societal-collective (gesellschaftlich-kollektiv), possibly even spread over many epochs. The unconscious in literature under consideration, is a collective unconscious, although admittedly not in Jung's sense. It consists of praxis figures (Praxisfiguren), which – as it were – demand to enter consciousness, and contains forms of life (Lebensformen), whose access to general consciousness has been barred and whose value, in consequence, has not been openly tried out. (Lorenzer, 1986, p. 28, our translation)

In interactionist (social) reinterpretations of psychoanalytical theory, including Lorenzer's theory of socialization, the unconscious level is just as much as the conscious a result of life history experience of social interaction. For the same reason the unconscious is assumed to contain a potential for social imagination which goes beyond the actual state of consciousness – either because it contains interaction experiences that have later been excluded from consciousness, or because it contains anticipating ideas of something 'emerging' which has not yet been realized in social practice. Continuing the previous quotation Lorenzer says:

> These not-yet-conscious (Noch-nicht-bewusst) praxis figures – as Bloch says – generate a utopian potential. It is the work of hermeneutics to reveal this utopian potential and, in so doing, to take a stand against petrified circumstances (versteinerte Verhältnisse). […] Why do we prefer the term in-depth hermeneutics to characterize this approach? The answer is: because the practice of in-depth hermeneutics is the distinctive feature of psychoanalytical interpretation. … The in-depth element of the hermeneutic approach is only to be found in psychoanalysis and underlines the central subject of psychoanalytical enquiry: the unconscious. (Lorenzer, 1986, p. 28)

Lorenzer's understanding of the critical and utopian potentials in the unconscious articulates an important dimension in the thinking of critical theory or Frankfurt School. The Frankfurt School generally sees theorizing and critique as a key to social imagination and utopian ideas. And since this thinking is based on materialist assumptions it means that imagination is endogenous, i.e. must be discovered and articulated from within societal reality, as it is condensed in Adorno's argument in the positivist dispute:

> But if theory is not to fall prey to the dogmatism over whose discovery scepticism – now elevated to a prohibition on thought – is always ready to rejoice, then theory may not rest here. It must transform the concepts which it brings, as it were, from outside into those which the objects has of itself, into what the object, left to itself, seeks to be, and confront it with what it is. (Adorno, 1969/1976, p. 69)

In Habermas' thinking the term of 'Ideology Critique' spells out the need to reveal endogenous potentials for societal change through a critical analysis of social realities themselves. Change does not come from above or from outside. But whereas Habermas first of all sees the key in deconstructing observation and reflection of 'petrified social relations' and the societal institutions which make up the guises of power, social inequality and reified relations Alfred Lorenzer looks for the potentials in socialized psyche, in the dynamics between the conscious and the unconscious. And this brings the argument back to the text:

> Does this imply that the unconscious is the sole aim of psychoanalytical interpretation and that every 'manifest/apparent meaning', every deliberately

> intended meaning of the text the author makes, has no significance? Indeed not, such an approach would not justify the title of a psychoanalytical literary and cultural analysis. This collection of analyses shows that the manifest meaning in no way can be seen as a 'ladder', which can be put aside in the moment you have reached the goal 'deep down there'. (Lorenzer,1986 p. 29, our translation)

Lorenzer's theoretical deliberations point to socially taboo, degenerate lifestyles and utopian moments of social practice which while being unconsciously maintained also emerge to influence [our] conscious, for example with the help of literary texts. Their provocation, according to Lorenzer, lies in the fact that they transport aspects of a collective unconscious which forces itself into the conscious. On the one hand Lou's arguments concerning Adele's two-faced behavior lines up seamlessly with the socially accepted meaning pattern of good or bad behavior. But the emotional charge 'beyond the boundaries of language' in the vehement desire to be rid of the other woman goes far beyond such socially acknowledge configuration. To have Adele thrown off the show, Lou is prepared to throw an unknown stranger out of the telephone box.

So what is it that forces itself into consciousness? The TV show (cultural meaning) elicits unconscious desires and identifications (interaction forms) which influence the agency and produces an intense ambivalence. The reconstruction of this ambivalence helps to reveal the unconscious in the text. We will address the interpretation procedure in more detail later. For the time being, however, we will stay with the relationship between manifest and latent meaning and read what Lorenzer thinks:

> … the distinguishing feature of psychoanalytical cultural analysis as an 'in-depth hermeneutic' is about the recognition of an *independent level of meaning* below the meaning generating level of language symbolism. While the manifest meaning resides in the socially recognized figures of consciousness, a level of unconscious interaction forms (Interaktionsformen) is pushed into consciousness on the level of latent meaning. It is certainly the case that this level of meaning, 'excluded by consciousness and social consensus', is one in which psychoanalysis was originally interested, and which Freud counted to parapraxes. But, at the same time, the manifest text-meaning is still important – as the counterpart to what is concealed-forbidden. Manifest- and latent-text meaning construct a contradictory pair, which psychoanalysis must seek to resolve [aufzuheben hat]. (Lorenzer, 1986, p. 29, our translation)

For cultural analysis, when unconscious interaction forms are pushed to the consciousness it means that the latent meaning of a text offers a potential access to understand collective dimensions of the unconscious. Manifest and latent meaning are dialectically related because language use point to non-verbal or pre-verbal dimensions of social interaction as Lorenzer describes in the concept of 'unconscious interaction forms'. It does not mean that we can simply identify the unconscious and the non-verbal: unconscious meanings are in the text as latent meaning or meaning potentials.

If we look at the construction of the show – and numerous other shows of the same type – as performance of interaction, and at the same time an invitation to interaction with the viewer the point is that the show invites the viewer to exert some kind of control in the limited world in the container – and in this case make a moral judgment on the behavior of the figures in the show. However, he/she can only do it in the dichotomous form of voting out or in. You are not only invited to make a regressive simplification of complex issues, you are forced to do it, if you want to participate in the interaction. So the relation between the inner logic of the show and the seemingly extreme actions of the Lou – and in the second place the evocative power of the text in relation to the interpreting researchers – might be a key to trace the unconscious meanings. Lorenzer's attempts to characterize the unconscious:

> The unconscious is a non-verbal, non-symbolic system of meaning, which is contrary to individuals' linguistic order … It is
> - 'autonomous', because it comes into existence within specific and concrete mutual exchanges and is therefore the inscription of this particular ontogenesis.
> - 'systematic', because from the first moment in a life-history, one memory trace follows another each becoming interwoven with the other (organismisch)
> - 'meaning'-full (full of meaning) because the engrams are simultaneously the sedimented forms of past social interplay and drafts for that of the future. (Lorenzer, 1986, pp. 46–47)

In this framework Lou's disturbingly excessive action that lends the scene structure can be interpreted as systematic and meaningful in the context of biographical patterns. Autonomous elements prove to be the physical action, leaving the house, the purposeful movement in space, the hammering against the door of the telephone box. The TV show seems to set a subject's past interaction experiences in motion, which defy any language based symbolization yet remain registered as a bodily experience of social interaction. The reactivation of these interaction forms happens not in the sense of simple repetition of old conflicts, but as part of a dynamic interaction between old, past and new, current interaction experiences. The unconscious meaning of the scene points to something which is unexpressed and yet symptomatic. In the first place it evaded the perception of interpreters and gave way to irritation and premature classification of the subjectivity of only one actor in the scene (Lou). This individual psychological interpretation saw impaired ego functions: reality checks and emotional control are rendered ineffective and an archaic breakthrough of revenge impulses.

But if we look at the scene in the context of its multilayered structure, a structural double bind comes to light which neither the contestant in the container nor the voting viewer (like Lou) can escape: friendly, polite and civil behavior stands in diametric opposition to the competitive nature of the game and the dilemma it entails.

Against this backdrop, Lou's rather excessive reaction can be seen to perform the role assigned to her by the TV-show. But they may also encompass anticipations of future behavior and interaction scenarios – imaginations about a transparent and preferably dominance-free communication – her reaction is a response to the unfulfilled desire for civility towards others, which Lou believes Adele is failing to demonstrate. Paradoxically she is driven to the opposite extreme and resorts to violence herself.

This interpretation of the unconscious in the text refers to experiences prior to the development of the ability to symbolize, yet they retain their effectiveness in scenic arrangements. But it does not mean simply that unconscious/conscious is the same as pre-language/linguistic – the relation is more complex:

> The term 'configuration of practice figures' (Gefüge von Praxisfiguren) refers to the following characteristic. The interplay from which memory traces (interaction-forms) emerge is nothing but the exchange of gestures, bodily movement, and socially shaped and significant body processes: it is 'practice'. Every interaction-form is part of this practice, and therefore encompasses but goes beyond language. Practice as a whole is to some extent, submitted to the rules of language, but also partly resistant and reluctant, or is part of something utopic not-yet-conscious, i.e. part of human behavior that has not become encompassed in language. (Lorenzer, 1986, p. 47, our translation)

But how do we store these non-language-related memory traces, and how can we approach them in the interpretation? The following section explains Lorenzer's theory regarding the constitution of the scene in the context of intra- and inter-subjectivity and the role played by the body and language. The following section returns to the methodological implementation in 'scenic understanding'.

ENGRAMS, INTERACTION FORMS AND THE LANGUAGE GAME

At a very early stage in his theoretical writings, Alfred Lorenzer meant that interaction experiences become embodied during the embryonic phase and the first few months of life. Thus, through the body's senso-motoric reactions, they help to shape specific and later-life experiences. Such interaction patterns which become ingrained in the body stand for an entire lifetime in a constant dialectic with the discursive demands of the social environment which are subsequently communicated through language. The start of this development in very early childhood is both a physical and a holistic process based entirely on sensory perceptions. In Lorenzer's own words, this means that:

> The 'visual', 'tactile', 'acoustic', denote modes of sensory reception, which are directed by the central nervous system from the periphery of the body and which are then stored in precisely defined 'areas of the brain' [...] The inscription of these visual, tactile and acoustic impressions happens via

> ‘engrams’. These engrams are ‘memory traces’ in Freud’s terms. Although this process is common to all infants, of course, the engrams of a single person are the memory traces of his or her experience as a particular individual. They have an individual profile. Just as Freud (1891) pointed out, in front of his time, in his book on Aphasie, that cerebral physiological functions and ‘psychological’ content cannot be separated it is obviously the experiences of the memory traces which are codified as engrams. And this means that the contents of memory (which is, of course, social) modifies the brain’s physiological structures of the nervous system. And of course the memory traces combine into ideas of objects. And like the sensual impressions – visual, tactile, acoustic – combine into an idea of object, likewise will the objects that are perceived in different situations combine to form definite and concrete scenes. But this is expressed inaccurately: Of course it is the scene which is the immediate subject of the infant’s experience. An awareness of individual objects only emerges from the scene gradually, and may later, in differing situations, combine to form well defined poles and stable figures within the scenic Gestalt. (Lorenzer, 1986, pp. 41–42, our translation)

Memory traces are non-verbal references to life practice, of experiences. These experiences are based on the efforts to achieve pleasure and avoid un-pleasure. Lorenzer emphasizes the ‘bodilyness’ of these processes. Lorenzer’s theory of the language development and the notion of scenic understanding are actually in this sense coming close to contemporary cognitive science and the new synthesis between ‘human’ and ‘biological’ understanding of the brain (Lorenzer, 2002). Looked at today, he anticipates a paradigm shift: the current overriding view of the brain as a holistic system of complex information processing processes (Peled, 2008; Leuzinger-Bohleber, 1998). In memory research, embodied cognitive science has moved away from the notion of the human brain being a kind of computer designed to process information. Memory is now understood as an active process involving the entire organism and based on senso-motoric emotion coordination processes which occur in direct relationship with constantly adapting re-categorization processes. In Lorenzer’s terms, this means that a child’s early experiences of stimulusresponse games with its mother and other close individuals are retained as memory traces, as specific interaction forms. They are a lasting, natural impression of genuine social interaction forms in the subject. This is what Lorenzer calls ‘socialized nature’.

But how do single memory traces become a configuration of many which evolve into life experiences and a complete life world? The notion of the scenic primacy poses the question the other way round. Experience is holistic, strongly shaped by sensory impressions and by satisfying (or their opposite) experiences. “The scene takes shape step by step through alternating and mutually constitutive interactions between changing and unchanging modes of experiences.”

The self-correction in the quotation is interesting – it seems that Lorenzer here moves from one way of seeing the development of consciousness – as a combination of sensual elements into images of objects – to another, more holistic, in which an undifferentiated scenic experience oriented by the subject-to-be – gradually evolves through differentiation to become more detailed and stable object images, and it seems as if the self-correction is a trace of this theory development. The new conception aligns with empirically based knowledge about infancy development (Stern, 1985).

The process described always involves bodily processes:

If we take bodily processes into account, three aspects of the scenic become apparent

1. The imprint of situational experience (Situationserfahrung) is assimilated by an internal ensemble of tactile, acoustic etc. receptors. Likewise the receptor ensemble depicts the panorama of real impressions in the internal scenic composition of the engrams.
2. Even if not from the first moment but very early these situational engrams repeatedly go beyond the inevitable dialectic that exists between bodily sensations and their counter-impulses. The memory trace (Erinnerungsspur) is more than the consequence of a simple process of stimulus-response; in itself it already has sensorimotor qualities. A simple illustration of this scenic composition of sensorimotor experience formation is to be found in the banal fact that the stimulus is sure to provoke its reaction. For example, the noise of a mouse 'results' in the cat turning its head.
3. And the foundation for all this is in, the scenic unity between the 'inside' and 'outside', between the organism and its environment .... This interplay is the foundation for everything. It remains the basic model, from which we will also later have to depart. (Lorenzer, 1986, p. 43)

The scene is thus shaped by the bodily referent inherent in it from the outset. A child's earliest perception, no doubt while still in the womb, is a holistic experience. The perceptive instruments are an ensemble of receptors which give the external world in intra-psychical space a scenic structure. The bodily processes described by Lorenzer should not, however, be seen as natural or ingrained reflexes, even if they seem quite similar. The senso-motoric process can be readily recognized in a nursing mother whose milk production is activated the moment her child cries and not when the hungry child starts to suck at her breast. The baby's interactive need, the stimulus, is perceived and understood by the mother as a holistic experience, and her body responds immediately – holistically, scenically and faster than it could ever be triggered by any conscious decision. But they are learned in social interaction.

Hence, this describes the scenic unit between the organism and its environment. The scene always encompasses both, 'internal' and supports the statement that "this interplay is the foundation for everything". Such interplay provides the basis for human experience, it remains both active and necessary one's whole life long and constitutes an ever-more discerning ability to take in new experiences.

> Let us concentrate on the original experience: the scenic interplay and its effect on human development. This interplay, whether occurring within pre-natal, post-natal or familial constellations, has two fundamental qualities: satisfying and unsatisfying/harmful. In consequence, human development occurs against the background of 'ananke', the basic human state of vulnerability. Humans in particular are dependent on a constantly flowing and satisfying exchange with their environment. This is very obvious at the outset of life, but it continues thereafter .... This state of dependency keeps this interplay going and pushes it in the direction of the satisfaction of needs. Long before this compass orientating us to the satisfaction of needs is laid down, there still exists a requirement that needs are met. The basic human state of vulnerability is the source of the drive towards exchange and interplay: the first fundamental content of this drive is directed towards satisfying interactions and the defense against unsatisfying and damaging ones. The drive is therefore the urge both to accept and seek out specific interactions fulfilling and satisfying needs. It is clear that such requirement and needs have their origin in bodily metabolism. The need for human contact evolves from this. Sexual needs bear witness to these bodily origins. (Lorenzer, 1986, p. 44)

Lorenzer defines drive as the ensemble of all efforts to achieve satisfaction. This satisfaction is only achievable in social relationships – also for the most basic biological needs. The active search for satisfying interaction with the social environment, including specific individuals with whom a relationship is formed, shapes a structure of 'specific interaction forms'. It is the memory traces of satisfying experiences which, in interplay between 'internal' and 'external', achieve their unmistakable form and subsequently become an ensemble, a formation. Lorenzer maintains the biological dimension of the drive theory by emphasizing the pleasure-unpleasure principle. At the same time he integrates the theory into a new view of early social interactions whose ongoing importance he develops in the interplay between the internal and external, between biological needs and the social forms in which they can be satisfied and are reconfigured.

This dialectic gives rise to the life-long development dynamic of the subject in interaction with other subjects and the world.

But at what point does language come into the game? The early pre-verbal, scenically stored interaction experiences, the 'specific interaction forms', gradually include verbal images which appear in the interaction. Simple (presymbolic) interaction forms and spoken words, which are in themselves holistic and situated entities of meaning, defined in social interaction, are the material for the development of a symbolic level. Alfred Lorenzer takes up this link between interaction form and verbal images, as a process of symbol-building and emphasizes that:

> Again: word and interaction together construct the language symbol. Therefore I have called this a 'language symbolic interaction form' (Sprachsymbolische

> Interaktionsform). When word and interaction are joined in this way, practice is – via language – fully at our disposal. (Lorenzer, 1986, p. 50)

The 'power of language to regulate practice' when oriented outwardly encompasses what we term 'action' or 'conscious perception'. However, the 'power of language to regulate practice' when oriented inwardly, also encompasses 'internal reflection', 'conscious emotion' etc. In relation to the task of psychoanalysis, we can now begin to see what is meant by 'language destruction and reconstruction': the separation of the unit of language and practice and conversely the therapeutic attempt at their restitution (p. 51). Only when a complex of sounds has found its appropriate place in the context of the language-sign, and the syntactic level of language links with the pragmatic and semantic nature of language, only when this is accomplished has a full language figure (Sprachfigur) that corresponds with the scenic practice figure been established (1986, p. 52).

When the interaction form in this way is symbolically expressed and thus gains access to the conscious it enables reflection on one's own behavior and provides the conditions necessary for reasoned tentative action. Only with language does this become clearer: language symbolic interaction forms integrate social practice in a more comprehensive and differentiated organization framework.

This notion leads directly to the concept of the language game Lorenzer developed after Wittgenstein. The latter defined the language game as a dialectic unit of life practice, language use and world view (1953). Wittgenstein's language game notion was in fact primarily critical to previous philosophical ideas of language and scientific statements, seeing language meaning as a result of language use and the social practices in which language use is inscribed. Lorenzer expands this notion by incorporating unconscious dimensions which were not addressed in Wittgenstein's concept. He sees the language games not as mere conventions but as dynamic result of a negotiation between language user with different experiences and practices, and hence based in these social practices. With Lorenzer's extension it means that this negotiation also involves non- and pre-verbal experiences and also harbors elements that are products of a destroyed symbolization of experience. Language as an instrument of symbol-building is not simply *based on* the pre-symbolic interaction form, but actually *contains it*. For this reason the pre-symbolic interaction form remains virulent one's whole life long, is inseparably linked to subsequent, development history-related verbal expression or, being excluded from the language symbol spectrum, seeks out other-than-verbal ways of finding expression. Today, it is not only clinicians but also social researchers who describe this form of active expression as 'enactments'. They are the unconscious, soulless repetition of interaction experiences that the subject, either in times of great need or in response to emotional pain, has tended to separate, disassociate or repress. While they cannot, therefore, be integrated into the individual processing and development process, they nonetheless shape that process.

If, as described earlier, the early interaction experience cannot be symbolized it still remains an action-driving component of the individual-subjective structures and their experience forms. How it differs from symbolized, verbal forms is seen in the subject's inability to reflect on those experience forms. The subject is not able to draw upon practice through language. At the same time, as Lorenzer repeatedly emphasizes, the non-verbal interaction form is always linked to subsequent language symbolic forms. The ability to express one self verbally and pre-verbally involves many other aspects. The language game as a concept to identify conflict dynamics in this dual perspective of social and individual is presented in one of Lorenzer's earlier works as follows:

The term 'language-game' is productive in a number of ways:

a. As a category it refers to human 'character' rather than describing human behavior. More precisely, the model of the language-game characterizes individual structures as sedimented versions of concrete interactions (as symbolic interaction forms), including the basic elements of both language and action.
b. Understanding the constitution of the basic elements of language and action renders visible the individual structure as the outcome of a specific production process called 'socialization'. This enables us to see configurations of consciousness, as well as early drafts of future action (Handlungsentwürfe) as a synthesis of nature and societal practice.
c. When integrated into a theory of individual structures, the model of the language game – embracing its constituents practice and language – provides us with a useful backdrop that renders visible what was previously opaque, namely the active making of configurations of consciousness as they emerge in practices (both being realized in concrete interactions) (Lorenzer, 1977, p. 34ff).

The term language game thus refers to three dimensions of the social: the individual structure of the subjective, the socialization process and general Social practice. In Lorenzer's work, we learned that individual structure is expression of real interaction experiences from early life onwards. Social experiences in their ongoing production process constitute behavioral patterns which can be generalized. Through conscious verbal action, these also bring a social practice to light on which they are also based. Language games can thus only be understood in their social context. They assume a common practice-based agreement on meaning and are always the result of social practice Lorenzer, 1970b). If the language game is the link between a specific interaction form and a language figure, then potential disturbances and interferences in the language game can be identified. The symbolic unit is dissolved when it is subject to repression.

> When the word is separated from the interaction engram the latter once again becomes an unconscious interaction form. The word, for its part, loses its relation to sensual practice, it becomes emotionless, an empty sign. Thus the interaction engram becomes unconscious again losing all the characteristics

> which it had gained from its relation to the word, i.e. through its introduction into the meaning system of language. In other words, what is lost is: the capacity to reflect upon behavior patterns; and the capacity to 'try things out' (and thus make meaningful interventions in stimulus-response behavior) and to judge actions in a realistic way. ... The de-symbolized language signs suffer the opposite fate. They remain in the conscious, where they can be easily manipulated because they have been freed from their relation to practice figures. In this state, they are nothing more than calculation and cold-rational behavior, no longer capable of embodying the specific quality they originally contained and that was originally experienced. (Lorenzer, 1986, p. 53)

Lorenzer describes the characterized division between words and interaction forms in previously established language games as the destruction of language. The destruction of this symbolic unit reverses symbolization, hence the term 'desymbolization', and it may occur during (subjective) conflicts later in life. This means that once achieved, the ability to symbolize (verbal expression of a subjective structure) is withdrawn in relation to a specific problem which the individual experiences as an inner conflict. The ability to express an experience or an emotional process in words is lost in connection with the issue causing the conflict. Conflict in this sense is seen as the situated clash of irreconcilable, contradictory interaction forms.

Interaction forms which are symbolized in language figures can thus be reexcluded from the language context. This happens with the aid of resistance mechanisms: by repressing them, they are excluded from the conscious relationship between language and practice. Although this turns them back into unconscious interaction forms, the very fact of this reversion allows them to retain their energetic, dynamic relevance. They act as behavior drivers, albeit in the form of blind action and reaction which is not open to conscious self-reflection. For the individual, the recurring unconscious reenactment of a scene whose structure is similar to the actual conflict, appears in the form of need for repetition.

Symbolization through language has the advantage of being brought to mind independently of the real situation and thus fulfills an important function in the regulation of emotion. In other words, it assists the subject's independence (tentative action, hesitation). By separating the language from the interaction form, the person is again made dependent from the effects of unconscious conflict. He or she rarely has the power to free themselves from the dynamics of the unconscious scenic processes. This is in worst case the type of problems in the clinical psychoanalysis from which Lorenzer starts his theorizing.

The described division of the symbolic unit in the language game is evident in the context of spoken language, in texts and in interviews. It is expressed in the structures of a text and is characterized by the fact that it excludes the interaction partner, say the interpreter of an interview transcription, from the direct understanding. The spoken word is no longer understandable for the listener or reader. The societal reference of collective meaning dimensions and a social meaning is interrupted.

So which forms of understanding might provide access to such destroyed, de-symbolized language figures? A means of access is needed that reidentifies the scenic unit, including when there is no or only an altered form of verbal expression because the unit of language symbolic and interaction form has been lost. This is where Lorenzer's idea of scenic understanding has its methodological significance.

SCENIC UNDERSTANDING

The basic methodological idea in Lorenzer's long intellectual journey, and particularly when he summarized his ideas in 1986, was the possibility to learn from the type of hermeneutic process in psychoanalysis for the analysis of cultural phenomena.

> In the psychoanalytic process, all understanding centers on and is related to the mode of 'scenic understanding'. In this mode understanding is attuned to two specific objects: the 'scenic drafts', i.e. the 'interaction forms' of the analysand. Particularly herby psychoanalysis provides us with a model example. If we want to understand the analysand's life-practice, which does not exclude his concrete social reality, we must follow the path laid down by his subjective phantasies and outlines of relations. This means we must become attuned to his scenic interaction forms as these unfold before us. (Lorenzer, 1977, p 125)

What in this quotation is described as a therapeutic approach in the analyst's consultation room can be transferred to understanding texts, language and human behavior. Immediately, the question arises as to how a mode of understanding can be practiced which explores the scenic in a non-clinical context. Lorenzer and his colleagues have demonstrated the approach in relation to literary texts and cultural phenomena (Lorenzer, 1986; Prokop, Friese, & Stach, 2009), and we have taken it a bit further into qualitative social research in a number of more profane contexts. In the following I shall discuss the methodology of scenic understanding and its practical implementation. In other words, how could qualitative social research understand unknown subjective content and processes which include the unconscious and draw attention to non-verbal messages.

Like every hermeneutic approach it is about understanding the meaning in agency and expressions, and in practical social research. Although some measures can be taken to make the data suitable scenic understanding can be applicable to almost any text or phenomenon referring to agency and subjective expression. The prototypical material is, though, a text, or can be seen as a text. More exotic ways of producing the data in the first place are videos or conversations held while observing videos (second order field observation). Very often the text is a transcript of a focus group discussion or thematic group discussion. In other cases it may be an interview – individual or collective – or it may be a field diary from an observation.

To identify the meaning structure of a text, we may distinguish different levels of interpretation:

1. The obvious referential content of the text: What is being talked about?
2. How do people talk to one another? This question on the metacommunicative content of a text takes us to the level of scenic understanding
3. Why are the characters talking in precisely this way? How can we understand it by means of theoretical knowledge combined with background factual knowledge? The first of these steps is the same as in most types of qualitative method.

The 3 step might in its form remind about an explanatory approach which seeks a causal or rule-based understanding. Since it is a hermeneutic methodology it is not, instead it is a more comprehensive multilayered interpretation enabled by step 2. The 'scenic understanding' focuses on the ongoing tense relation between the manifest and the unconscious meanings of a text which requires an imagination of the unconscious that we can imagine as a collective reservoir of culturally rejected patterns, forbidden yearnings and suppressed desires. In-depth hermeneutic interpretation thus focuses on the characters in the relationship described in the text and on the dynamics of the relationship between a text and its interpreter(s) in order to trace the subjective structure of cultural constraints.

The reference point in the scenic interpretation is the language used in the text, with particular attention being placed on how scenes in the text point to unexpressed desires and tensions, on how the text arranges 'forms of communication which makes the unspeakable' understandable, or "secures it an un-negligible position in public space" as Lorenzer says about the task of the poet (1986, p. 24). The initial reading seeks to apply the same type of freefloating awareness ('gleichschwebender Aufmerksamkeit') as is known from the clinical situation: one's own reactions and irritations are noted without coming immediately to any particular conclusions or forming theoretical definitions. Indications of such hidden conflict dynamics include gaps, inconsistencies, unusual use of language, jumps in the story or sudden changes of subject, and remarkable ways of relating to the subject or to each other (in case of group interaction texts). But also the reactions, emotional states and associations of the readers/interpreters may be indications of the dynamics we are looking for – even if you cannot immediately understand them. Practically an interpretation procedure is most often organized in a group. Some procedures go line by line, seeking to understand each unit of text, and revising the understanding gradually as the later segments are taken into consideration. Other procedures start by an open conversation conveying 'first impressions' and reactions from the members of the interpretation group. In some cases you will experience that controversies and conflicts arise within an interpretation group, evoked by the text. Using these observations and reactions as a base, particularly powerful passages are subjected to in-depth analysis in interpretation groups. What has already been described as the transference between the individual reader and the text is now transferred to a collective understanding process: the transference and counter-transference dynamics multiply. This procedure may lead very directly to 'holistic' but preliminary interpretations that are set under discussion, or it may produce several 'loose ends'. The interpretation discussion most likely includes reference to the concrete text and its manifest meaning, and it may very well also draw on theoretical frameworks and on background knowledge which in the first place may support or contradict the interpretations suggested. The discussion gradually moves into a validation discussion. In principle the validation will refer to usual criteria and procedures for validation of qualitative analysis. In the first place it will refer to the manifest text on the one side, and a theoretical reflection of the whole complex of subjective agency and expression in the text and in the relation between the text and the interpreters.

The assumption of unconscious meaning components makes the language game an instrument with which to analyze individual structures and to identify collective social processes. Language figures and language symbolic interaction forms always possess a social character which goes beyond the individual, because they assume social understanding processes within the language community. As a result, they can be analyzed for the social meaning they contain and give an insight into the social configurations and their unconscious, not-yet-conscious component. This is the methodological bridge which enables the unconscious dimensions of experience to be accessed from language.) They can also be observed from the subjective perspective of the speaker and shed light on the individual meaning contained in a specific scene. The language figure then reports on the subjective structures and the associated experiences of social life practice.

As we were reacting on the remarkable behavior of Lou in the illustration example, led into both an individual psychological reductive interpretation, and into a cultural criticism against the seductive effects of TV shows like Big Brother. We resisted those temptations because we, led by the theoretical points of Alfred Lorenzer, to develop a more comprehensive psychosocietal interpretation. An interpretation which does not exclude some regressive aspects in the TV audience, and definitely does not exclude a critique of the quality and the political dimensions of the TV shows. But we wanted to find the collective or societal unconscious mechanism that the show (re)activates in Lou as in everybody else, and we wanted to understand why this led her to act in this enraged and seemingly irrational way – and in this sense we also wanted to rehabilitate the subject in relation to her violation of good civil behavior, assuming that she was enacting something that was collective and could not be explained and reasoned. Referring to Lorenzer's development of the language game concept we would seek to trace the relation between the manifest language meanings in her account, the societal meanings that are relegated to unconscious interaction forms pushing on conscious recognition – and the wider societal practice in which the language use makes sense.

A lot of energy in the story told is condensed in Lou's sentence: "I just wanted her out" – Lou's emotional engagement seems condensed in it, and the plot of the scene seems driven by, or explained by, this sentence.

On the one hand the words seem harmless. They refer to the rules of games which are in broad use and enjoy great social acceptance. Through play, children learn that while it is good to win, being a good loser takes far more dignity and courage. It is a standard pattern in the type of TV shows to which Big Brother belongs, and has spread to be one of the standard storylines of so called interactive TV broadcasts.

On the other hand Lou's words supported by characteristic behavior which gives the spoken words an explosiveness which seems – guided by the theory of interaction forms and language – to indicate a further meaning than the immediate referential one: The scene that Lou describes (which is told as having taken place in the recent past) seems to have harbored a trigger stimulus which forced Lou to act impulsively. Her behavior seemed designed to ensure that another person be excluded and punished. On the psychological level violence replaces symbolic reflection. This behavior, within a classical psychoanalytical horizon, recalls the link between oedipal conflict issues from the childhood: the daughter wants to push the mother out to more easily gain the father's favor. The intruder is to be destroyed. Lou might have such an individual version of a standard socialization experience. Although convenient, this dramatic constellation from each childhood triangularization phase would be reductive and not lend a cultural analytic perspective to the understanding. Instead we should look for a potential correspondence between the individual subjective dynamic and societal meanings that are implicitly present in the social setting of the TV show. We are looking for the supra-individual, societal meaning of the story Lou tells, although indirectly. The analysis so far seemed to show that the TV show (cultural meaning) elicits unconscious desires and identifications (interaction forms) which influence the agency and produces an intense ambivalence. The reconstruction of this ambivalence should help reveal the unconscious in the text.

If we recall the interpretations used at the beginning of this chapter, the dynamic of inclusion and exclusion runs through all interpretations of the text sequence. The TV games are about excluding others, exclusion is an important part of the game. This is bound up with the setting of norms which sanction the exclusion of others. The mass viewer participation seems to indicate not only social acceptance but also a widespread need to be included in the game of excluding others. Lou serves as an exemplary viewer and contestant – she stands for more than just herself, in that her reaction is representative of the desired inclusion of viewers in the game. It seems justified to see Lou's actions and the key statement as part of a language game in Lorenzer's sense – combining the explicit and manifest meaning with experiences of winning inclusion by joining the exclusion of others, and a societal perspective in a neo-liberal society where separation prevails over integration. But we may also interpret her reactions so that the participation in this language game elicits ambivalent feelings. We can relate it to the moral paradox that the exclusive action is justified by the defense for the moral integrity in the community in the TV show container.

With the positive evaluation of what is generally seen as negative behavior (exclusion), a door is opened to are judgmental and stereotypical attitudes everyday life which allow the unknown and the foreign to be negated without punishment and eventually to be eliminated. The definition of foreign, unknown elements as a justification for exclusion is reminiscent of the well-known studies on the social function of prejudices (Adorno, Aron, Levinson, & Morrow, 1950), in which projective power serves in shifting everything one dislikes in oneself onto another group and then combating it in that group. The dynamic of exclusion can take the form of collective violence if it is not harnessed and is allowed to develop uncontrolled.

Thus, the sentence "I just wanted her out" becomes a battle cry in a fight against the undesirable and alien. The vehemence with which it is spouted reveals its individual emotional foundation – the exclusion of the undesirable serves the defense of the individuals own boundaries, the collective self is stabilized through projective stigmatization of the other and the subsequent exclusion of a person deemed foreign and strange. The mass reception of such TV-shows seems to point to the societal strength of a language game – a combination between language use, outlines of life practice and a world view in which the identification with one's own group is based in excluding others who are deemed 'strangers'. A collectively fascinating TV game which not only uses this projection mechanism but nurtures it under greenhouse-like conditions helps foster general acceptance of archaic, collective defensive formations. The consciousness and norms which are communicated no longer need be subjected to conscious, reflective reality checks. Through mass fascination and the social practice it is based upon, it appears adequately legitimated.

When we finally returned to the relation of the interpretation group: Do we also have a share in the exclusion game? The individual 'clinical' interpretation of the case can be recognized as a defense against the collective regression whose analysis triggered outrage among the interpreters themselves. Whereas the interpretation of an immature, oedipal conflict constellation or an unguided individual loss of control based on a simple identification appears quite harmless. Recognizing the collective nature of the unspoken interaction forms, and the ambivalence in Lous actions also makes visible that she is actually also – utopian? – longing for community and integration.

In our fellow interpreters' account (Bereswill, Morgenroth, & Redman, 2010) you can see this interpretation presented with a main emphasis on the process in the interpretation community and the interplay between the scenes in the TV-show, the scene in which Lou acts, and the scene of interpreting. This is illustrating the methodological point that the transfer/counter-transfer between interpreters and text take advantage of the scenic imagination. Here we emphasize the aspect of theoretical guidance because the theoretical framework and the psychosocietal methodological ambition – including Lorenzer's notion of the collective unconscious and the scenic – really were imperatives which helped the interpreter group to look for the traces of the extended language game in the text which did not appear easily. And we think this is an essential lesson for doing psychosocietal research.

AN EPISTEMOLOGICAL PERSPECTIVE: PSYCHOANALYSIS, LANGUAGE AND KNOWING

Alfred Lorenzer's contribution enriches the interpretational social science with a new theory and some practical inspiration for dealing empirically with the subjective aspects of social agency and interaction. This is in itself highly appreciated. Many qualitative methods tend to take their informants/narrators/sources for granted, and to neglect the involvement of the researcher subject as well. Others emphasize the need for researcher self reflection but do not provide appropriate tools for doing so. Lorenzer, among others, problematizes the subject category – both the subjects in the text and the subjects who are researching – by redefining the need for reflection into an empirical issue. But he goes one step deeper in theorizing societal framework of understanding the subjects – or rather the subjectivities. In this way it also seems as if he avoids the risk that made Berger and Luckmann (1966) warn so strongly against the alliance with psychoanalysis, the risk of reducing subjectivity to a mechanical 'natural' causality. It seems that his consequent material and endogenous notion of the unconscious enables a clearly hermeneutic stance without giving up the bodily dimensions of the human subjectivity.

Berger and Luckmann's (1966) comments are particularly interesting because their book has been assigned the honor to be the first main work of constructivism. Both Lorenzer and Berger and Luckmann anticipate the poststructuralist critique of Marxism. And we think that Lorenzer – being one of the psychoanalysts that Berger and Luckmann (1966) warned against – exactly produced an alternative answer to their ambition of unified social theory theorizing the agency-based (re)production of societal structures.

It is contested if Berger and Luckmann's book actually belongs to the tradition of social constructivism (Collin, 2002), but at least it has been possible to interpret it into that framework. It seems more appropriate to see their book as a precursor, which made visible the wider consequences for social theory of theorizing knowledge as a societal phenomenon. (North American) constructivism has developed this into an epistemology in which the role of culture/knowledge/discourse surmounts the role the subject as well as the societal object.

Lorenzer's work indicates a different possible continuation of Berger and Luckmann's story. We may see a psychosocial theory of the subject and the role of language in subjectivity as a foundation for a parallel materialistic constructivism, with the social philosophy of the Frankfurt School in several generations as a backbone (Adorno, 1976). Lorenzer also takes over the Wittgensteinian notions of language use and language games, and anchors them in the socialization and the mediation of societal culture which for the individual may take conscious as well as unconscious forms. Applying this extended notion of language use and language game to epistemological issues offers a way around the relativist excesses of some contemporary constructivism by redefining the relativity issue into an empirical one.

The conception of subjectivity still differs widely between North American traditions, in which Mead is still a both representative and distinguished figure, and a psychosocietal conception. A contemporary discussion of the relation between Mead and Lorenzer's psychoanalysis would be really interesting. Adorno's theoretical integration of psychoanalytical theory into sociology was connected with the need to understand the psychic mechanisms which enabled the political success of Nazism. Adorno in his own empirical research into the social psychology of authoritarianism provided a timely case for this interrelation (Adorno et al., 1950). In order to understand in which way the particular is mediated through, but not determined by, the societal whole you need to understand and examine empirically also the dynamics of the individual psyche – as a mediation of societal relations. Psychoanalysis was offering a theoretically developed and empirically specified research into the psyche, and the interrelations between body and (certain aspects of) consciousness – but it needed a reconceptualization in sociological context – reinterpreting psychic dynamics as mediations of societal relations – and that is to say a social psychology of culture – with implications also for (scientific) knowledge.

Lorenzer's particular contribution is first that he presents a theory of the materiality of endogenous societal alternatives. Second the development of interpretive methods building on psychoanalysis and hermeneutic text interpretation enabled an empirical study of how the dynamics of knowing on the social level could be connected with the dynamics of inner psychic experience.

ACKNOWLEDGEMENTS

This chapter is partly based on a draft paper jointly authored with Mechthild Bereswill, Christine Morgenroth, and Peter Redman, as explained in the text. Quotations from Alfred Lorenzer: 'Tiefenhermeneutische Kulturanalysen' (1986) are taken from a translation by Bereswill and Morgenroth, unless other notice is given. We would like to thank especially professor Birger Steen Nielsen, Roskilde, for comments on earlier drafts and for help in the understanding of Lorenzer.

REFERENCES

Adorno, T. W. (1967). Sociology and psychology (Part 1). *New Left Review, 46*, 67–80.

Adorno, T. W. (1969/1976). *The positivist dispute in German sociology*. London: Harper Torchbooks. (Originally published in 1969, *Der Positivismusstreit in der Deutschen Soziologie*)

Adorno, T. W., Aron, B., Levinson, M. H., & Morrow, W. (1951). *The authoritarian personality*. New York, NY: Harper and Row.

Bereswill, M. (2008). Gender and subjectivity in the interview situation: A critical discussion. *Psychoanalysis, Culture & Society, 13*, 316–324.

Bereswill, M., Morgenroth, C., & Redman, P. (2010). Alfred Lorenzer and the depth-hermeneutic method. *Psychoanalysis, Culture & Society, 15*(3), 221–250.

Berger, P., & Luckmann, T. (1966). *The social construction of reality. A treatise in the sociology of knowledge*. Harmondsworth: Penguin.

Collin, F. (2002). *Social reality*. London & New York, NY: Routledge.

Erikson, E. H. (1950). *Child and society*. New York, NY: Norton.

Freud, S. (1891/1953). *On Aphasia: A critical study*. New York, NY: International Universities Press.

Freud, S. (1915/1957). *The unconscious* (Standard Edition, 14, pp. 159–204). London: Hogarth Press.

Leithäuser, T. (1976). *Formen des Altagsbewusstseins* [Forms of everyday life consciousness]. Frankfurt/M: Campus.

Leithäuser, T., & Volmerg, B. (1988). *Psychoanalyse in der Sozialforschung* [Psychoanalysis in social science]. Opladen: Westdeutscher Verlag.

Leuzinger-Bohleber, M. (1998). Wo bleibt das Gedächtnis? Psychoanalyse und embodied cognitive science im Dialog [Where will the conscience go? Psychoanalysis and embodied cognitive science in dialogue]. In M. Koukkou & M. Leuzinger-Bohleber (Eds.), *Erinnerung von Wirklichkeiten: Psychoanalyse und Neurowissenschaften im Dialog* (pp. 517–589). Stuttgart: Verlag Internationale Psychoanalyse.

Lorenzer, A. (1970a). *Zur Kritik des psychoanalytischen Symbolbegriff* [Critique of the psychoanalytic concept of symbol]. Frankfurt/M: Suhrkamp.

Lorenzer, A. (1970b). *Sprachzerstörung und Rekonstruktion: Vorarbeiten zu einer Metatheorie der Psychoanalyse* [Language destruction and reconstruction]. Frankfurt/M: Suhrkamp.

Lorenzer, A. (1972). *Zur Begründung einer Materialistischen Sozialisationstheorie* [Foundations of a materialist theory of socialization]. Frankfurt/M: Suhrkamp.

Lorenzer, A. (1974). *Die Wahrheit der Psychoanalytischen Erkenntnis: Ein HistorischMaterialistischer Entwurf* [The truth of psychoanalytic knowledge]. Frankfurt/M: Suhrkamp.

Lorenzer, A. (1977). *Sprachspiel und Interaktionsformen: Vorträge und Aufsätze zu Psychoanalyse, Sprache und Praxis* [Language game and interaction forms]. Frankfurt/M: Suhrkamp.

Lorenzer, A. (1981/2002). *What is an unconscious phantasy?* (pp. 29–41, Tobias Schaffrik, Trans.). Retrieved April 30, 2010, from http://bidok.uibk.ac.at/library/schaffrik-lorenzer-work-e.html

Lorenzer, A. (1986). Tiefenhermeneutische Kulturanalyse. In: A. Lorenzer (Ed.), *KulturAnalysen: Psychoanalytische Studien zur Kultur* [In-depth hermeneutic cultural analysis] (pp. 11–98). Frankfurt/M: Fischer.

Lorenzer, A. (2002). *Die Sprache, der Sinn, das Unbewusste: Psychoanalytisches Grundverständnis und Neurowissenschaften* [Language, meaning, the unconscious]. Stuttgart: Klett-Cotta.

Lorenzer, A. (2006). *Szenisches Verstehen. Zur Erkenntnis des Unbewußten* [Scenic understanding. On recognition of the unconscious]. Kulturanalysen Band 1, herausgegeben von Ulrike Prokop und Bernhard Görlich. Marburg: Tectrum Verlag.

Mitscherlich, A. (1963). *Auf dem Weg zur Vaterlosen Gesellschaft* [Towards a society without fathers]. München: Piper.

Morgenroth, C. (1990). *Sprachloser Widerstand: Zur Sozialpathologie der Lebenswelt von Arbeitslosen* [Resistance without language: On the social pathology of the lifeworld of unemployed]. Frankfurt/M: Fischer.

Morgenroth, C. (2010). *Die dritte Chance: Therapie und Gesundung von jugendlichen Drogenabhängigen* [The third chance. Therapy and healing of young drug abusers]. Wiesbaden: Verlag für Sozialwissenschaften.

Parin, P., Morgentahler, F., & Parin-Mathéy, G. (1963). *Die Weissen denken zuviel* [White people think too much]. München: Kindl.

Peled, A. (2008). *Neuroanalysis: Bridging the gap between neuroscience, psychoanalysis and psychiatry.* Hove: Routledge.

Prokop, U., Friese, N., & Stach, A. (2009). Geiles Leben, falscher Glamour, Beschreibungen, Analysen, Kritiken zu ‚Germany's Next Top Model' [Exciting life, false glamour. Description, analyses and critiques of 'Germany's Next Top Model']. *Kulturanalysen, 10.*

Redman, P., & Whitehouse-Hare, J. (2008). 'I just wanted her out': Attachment, the psycho social and media texts. In P. Redman (Ed.), *Attachment: Sociology and social worlds.* Manchester: Manchester University Press/The Open University.

Salling Olesen, H. (2004). Theorising learning in life history: A psychosocietal approach. *Studies in the Education of Adults, 39*(1), 38–53.

Salling Olesen, H. (2007a). Professional identities, subjectivity and learning. In L. West et al. (Eds.), *Using biographical and life history approaches in the study of adult and lifelong learning*. Frankfurt/M: Peter Lang Verlag.

Salling Olesen, H. (2007b). Theorizing learning in life history – A psycho-societal approach. *Studies in the Education of Adults, 1*.

Salling Olesen, H. (2011). Exploraca do sujeito problematico: Historia de vide, subjetividade, experiência de vida [Researching the problematic subject: Life history, subjectivity, life experience]. *Educacao, 34*(2), 137–146.

Salling Olesen, H., & Weber, K. (2001). Space for experience and learning. Theorizing the subjective side of work. In K. Weber (Ed.), *Experience and discourse: Theorizing professions and subjectivity* (pp. 27–58). Roskilde: Roskilde University Press.

Salling Olesen, H., & Weber, K. (2002). Chasing potentials for adult learning: Lifelong learning in a life history perspective. *Zeitschrift fur Qualitative Bildungs-, Beratungs- und Sozialforschung, 2*, 283–300.

Schaffrik, T. (2002). *The work of Alfred Lorenzer: An introduction*. Retrieved April 30, 2010, from http://bidok.uibk.ac.at/library/schaffrik-lorenzer-work-e.html

Stern, D. (1985). *The interpersonal world of the infant: A view from psychoanalysis and developmental psychology.* New York, NY: Basic Books.

Weber, K. (1996). Experiencing gender: A psychodynamic approach to adult learning – And a case of masculinity and social work. In H. Salling Olesen & P. Rasmussen (Eds.), *Theoretical issues in adult education* (pp. 25–40). Roskilde: Roskilde University Press.

Weber, K. (2007). Gender between knowledge economy and everyday life: Change or reproduction? In L. R. West, P. Alheit, A. S. Andersen, & B. Merrill (Eds.), *Using biographical and life history approaches in the study of adult and lifelong learning: European perspectives*. (pp. 91–108). Frankfurt/M: Peter Lang.

Weber, K. (2009). Talking about "tacit knowledge": Critical professionalism or collective defences? In L. Thomas, M. Sylke, & S. Michael (Eds.), *Sozialpsychologisches organisationsverstehen* (pp. 227–237). Wiesbaden GWV Fachverlage GmbH.

Weber, K. (2010). Aggression, recognition and qualification: On the social psychology of adult education in everyday life. *European Journal for Research on the Education and Learning of Adults, 1*(1–2), 113–130.

Wittgenstein, L. (1953/2009). *Philosophical investigations*. London: Blackwell.

INDEX

S

T

X

www.ingramcontent.com/pod-product-compliance
Lightning Source LLC
Chambersburg PA
CBHW071433230926
51846CB00001B/219
* 9 7 8 9 0 0 4 4 2 0 2 5 0 *